CULT OF THE MOUSE

CULT OF THE MOUSE

CAN WE STOP CORPORATE GREED FROM KILLING INNOVATION IN AMERICA?

HENRY M. CAROSELLI

TEN SPEED PRESS

BERKELEY / TORONTO

Ten Speed Press
Box 7123
Berkeley, California 94707
www.tenspeed.com

Distributed in Australia by Simon and Schuster Australia, in Canada by Ten Speed Press Canada, in New Zealand by Southern Publishers Group, in South Africa by Real Books, and in the United Kingdom and Europe by Airlift Book Company.

Jacket and text design by Ed Anderson
Front cover art direction by Henry M. Caroselli
Cover photo by Henry M. Caroselli with assistance from "mouse wrangler" Daniel Caroselli. No animals were hurt or abused during the shoot; the trap was wired so it was inoperable, and the mouse in the photo was returned to the pet store where it had been purchased.

Library of Congress Cataloging-in-Publication Data
Caroselli, Henry M.
    Cult of the mouse : can we stop corporate greed from killing innovation
    in America? / Henry M. Caroselli.
       p. cm.
    Includes bibliographical references and index.
    ISBN 1-58008-633-0 (hc)
    1. New products. 2. Research, Industrial. 3. Disney Enterprises (1996–)
    I. Title.
    HF5415.153.C364 2004
    338'.064'0973—dc22   2004019547

Printed in the United States of America
First printing, 2004

1 2 3 4 5 6 7 8 9 10 — 09 08 07 06 05 04

DEDICATION

To my children, Michael, Daniel, and Anna
and to their children, and their children,
and their children . . .

ACKNOWLEDGMENTS

I owe a lot to the crew at Ten Speed Press. Specifically, to owner Phil Wood for believing in the message of this book from the get-go, to lone wolf Tom Southern for kicking everything off, and to project editor Meghan Keeffe for her exceptional attention to detail and thoughtful stewardship toward making this book something special—and to everyone I came in contact with through their fine organization (in particular, developmental editor Melissa Stein, publicist Kara Van de Water, and designer Ed Anderson).

This book wouldn't have happened without my wife Kate Baker's relentless moral support and loving understanding, and my friend Jack Foster's constant coaching (Jack, a real idea guy, was always there for me when I needed him)—and my kids, who put up with me and make me proud.

In general, I'd like to thank: Artists Girolomo Caroselli (1860–1913) and Henry J. Caroselli for the genes, Marjorie Caroselli for setting an example of rock-solid persistence, Marc Caroselli for his brotherly advice, Ed Nemetz for his life-long friendship and smarts, Tom Lippert for his fine sense of things (that is, humor), Jim Youngs for his cool and support, Rosa Bloetscher for her clarity of thought, Leonora Moylan for her ever positive demeanor, Bob and Scott Baker for their sage advice, Mary Baker for her encouragement, Sue Giles and Dene Pierce for their love of people and the written word, Jimmy Huston for his master web-mastering, Todd Gerstenberger for his calming influence, and, last but not least, Charlie Bungert who came from a generation that wasn't afraid to call things like they saw them . . . lest we forget, my daughter's cat, Cookie, a persistent pain in the neck—but also my constant companion while authoring this book.

Moreover, I'm forever thankful to have been born into the best deal ever, a person living in America today.

DISCLAIMER

This book is in not associated with, nor approved by, The Walt Disney Company (Disney Enterprises, Inc., a Delaware corporation) or any of its affiliates. The author's objective is to provide insight as to how innovation can be restored to American business using The Walt Disney Company as a framework for this purpose. The author in no way intends to harm, or undermine the success of, The Walt Disney Company; and he only hopes for its continued success.

The use of the word *cult* is not intended to intimate or convey any religious connotations, rather it refers to a group of people characterized by a secular devotion to a person, work, idea, movement, or object (as in the term *cult film*).

CONTENTS

PREFACE

So, you may be asking yourself, "Just who does this guy think he is, anyhow?" Well, I'm an idea guy with a few observations of and reflections on how fresh ideas come about, and some advocacies about what we all need to do to nurture those particular ideas that I call "the real deal" and what it requires to keep them coming.

I love the romantic notion of idea breeding, and I intimately appreciate how important ideas are in capturing the imagination—specifically how a real-deal idea can impact the human condition, causing the human spirit to soar. I've also spent enough time wearing a tie in corporate America to know that true leadership is desperately needed in (and missing from) business, and that way too many managers today are spending the best part of their day simply managing to protect their jobs, and, as a result, avoid putting forth anything new and truly risky.

Whether you're a manager-type or a creative-type—or both—it is my hope that by reading this book you can benefit from my experiences in the business world, specifically those involved with approaching the convoluted task of innovation and idea generation. From this perspective I hope to provide you with insights on how to recognize the elusive real-deal idea; what it takes to create the kind of very subtle, fragile, and anarchical (and, at times, even somewhat schizophrenic) environment that helps foster innovation; and appreciate the tribulations involved in creating something new and out of the ordinary. I want to share with you the preciousness and rarity of those ideas that truly lead to innovation.

A little bit about my background: After rising to the position of Senior Vice-President, Creative Director, at the then-largest ad agency on the West Coast (having just finished the award-winning advertising campaign for the launch of the breakthrough Mazda Miata), I was asked the classic question, "What are you going to do next?" Well, I met with Michael Eisner, in Walt Disney's old office, and accepted the cool job to head an entire division at Disneyland. But after six wild years as the head creative guy in their in-house ad agency, I was ready for a change.

I left Disney to start my own street rod business, Rodster Inc., since I had always wanted to use my talents do something less ephemeral than advertising. This particular automotive enterprise, at the entry-level of the hot rod market, has allowed me to immerse myself (for better or worse) in all aspects of a complicated entrepreneurial business. The daunting experience of creating, developing, producing, and marketing the Rodster Street Rod alone is worthy of a book.

But the initial inspiration for this book hit me when I heard a businessperson in a marketing meeting say, "Now is the time to take some *safe* risks." I groaned in disbelief. Such oxymoronic thinking will never lead to greatness and innovation. I sure hope this book helps, in even some small way, to reverse the growing trend toward risk aversion. Moreover, I'm worried that we Americans are relinquishing our leadership role in the world of idea generation. I lose sleep over the fact that corporate greed, under the guise of maximization of shareholder equity, has begun to kill creativity and deplete the fertile idea fields we, as Americans, have tilled in for centuries. The preponderance of greedy decision-making that has crept into America's business culture has led to the slaughtering of fresh ideas everywhere.

What has made America such an amazing country to live in is our freedom to take risks and express ourselves. Such a gutsy posture enables the free flowing of fresh ideas, which is central to propelling innovation. It's essential that we Americans get back to doing what we do best: coming up with real-deal ideas, in particular the ones that capture the imagination and change the human experience for the better.

Why did I choose The Walt Disney Company to pick on? Of course, there is the obvious reason that I worked there long enough to have a vested interest in their history and future. But, there is also the fact that Disney has long been held up as the crème de la crème of innovative all-American companies, and it's become quite apparent that they are losing their edge. And if innovation from a company such as Disney is in a tailspin, then what does that portend for American business in general?

Please approach this deliberately conversational book with an open mind. If you expect an authoritative, heavy-handed exposé, or a text-book-style analysis about the inner workings of The Walt Disney Company, you'll probably be disappointed. If you're ready to engage in a more free-associative approach to the search for innovation, you love the *idea* of ideas, and you revel in the organic anarchy of the creative process . . . you won't be let down.

Thank you for taking the initiative to pick up this book. It is my hope that it will provide you with inspiration toward becoming an innovator, an everyday champion of the real-deal idea. And maybe even someone out there can do something to save our old pal Mickey Mouse from becoming an overused corporate pitchman. I, for one, think he could use the rest.

Enjoy the read.

CHAPTER 1

INTRODUCING DISNEY'S NEWEST CHARACTER:

THE EIGHTH DWARF, CALLED

"GREEDY"

Good ol' corporate America is establishing new extremes in greedy practices and pursuits. The unscrupulous shenanigans of CEOs at companies like Enron, Tyco International, and WorldCom have led to the bankrupting of giant corporations, imploding of pension plans, and diminishing of IRAs. And far too many of these white-collared crooks have walked away with multimillion-dollar golden parachutes and are now off playing golf at their country clubs instead of dancing to the jailhouse rock.

It's been difficult for the average American to swallow the thought that CEOs' salaries continue to double or even triple, while the average workers' salaries are frozen (or minimally raised) and huge numbers of employees are routinely laid off. This state of affairs is especially hard to take when upper management executives then moan that yearly earnings or profits aren't what they should be and implore their employees to buck up, expecting that remaining workers will assume the workload of those who have been laid off. And then there are the almost unbelievable stories, like the one about former CEO L. Dennis Kozolowski spending over $1 million of Tyco's money on a birthday bash in Sardinia for his wife—where vodka flowed out of the penis of an ice sculpture of David. It sure sounds like a scene that might have preceded the fall of the Roman Empire, doesn't it?

These CEOs and other corporate executives are killing American business (and the average person's ability to achieve the American Dream) with their short-sighted greed. Certainly many jobs and programs are being cut in order to help pay for their fat-cat salaries. In the process, they appear to be willing to sell out America's future in favor of short-term gains, so they can make their companies look good to stockholders—and justify their high salaries. It stands to reason that these particular executives may be disproportionately attracted to offshore production to help boost short-term profitability—of course, at the expense of American jobs. But the repercussions don't stop at dollars and cents. Unfortunately, it's in the pervasive extinction of fresh ideas and the stunting of innovation where the biggest casualties lie.

HIDING BEHIND THE EXCUSE: "SORRY, BUT I'M JUST A SLAVE TO THE SHAREHOLDERS"

Innovation die-off began when corporations began focusing more on serving their stockholders (who are now reconstituted and combined in a most powerful form—fund managers holding large blocks of stocks for pension programs and institutions) than on serving their customers and responding to the needs of the marketplace. Corporate execs got behind this maximization of shareholder equity when a big chunk of their compensation became tied to stock in the form of options. The more the stock grew, the more money the exec was able to get when he or she cashed in his or her options. (How such a program works is an employee is awarded a certain number of options on his or her company's stock at a set market price, and if the stock appreciates over time, the person can then action on the options and profit on the increase, minus some transaction fees.) This form of compensation enhancement gave many execs the perfect excuse to act like a bunch of greedy bastards and do whatever it took to drive the stock price up.

On the surface, it all seemed reasonable and innocent enough. These stock options appeared to be a performance motivator, like a bonus promised to a football player for winning the Super Bowl. However, such options pushed many corporations toward focusing on making sharp quarterly gains with an emphasis on short-term profits, and not necessarily toward growing the business—a subtle, yet very profound, paradigm shift.

Soon, innovations that don't promise a quick payback are passed over. For instance, putting money toward research and development (R&D), which might grow the business in the future, is an investment that doesn't typically result in a first quarter or even first year payback. This focus on the short-term leads businesses to those initiatives that boost profits and cut costs in order to look good to Wall Street in the upcoming quarterly report. At first, the cuts are in the interest of streamlining the operation. And to be fair, the first round of 10 percent cuts probably help remove a lot of dead wood. The real trouble comes with the second, third, and fourth rounds of these *just-one-more* 10 percent cuts.

CEOs like Disney's Michael Eisner may have begun to cut real meat from their organizations in this effort to look good on quarterly reports. Eisner (working in concert with President and Chief Operating Officer Frank Wells, until his untimely death in 1994) had a very impressive run in his first ten years at Disney. Starting in 1984, Eisner and Wells steered Disney through five incredible years of growth that nearly doubled annually, then another five years of growth of around 20 percent a year. Yep, Disney had a compound annual growth from 1984 to 1995 of 28.1 percent while the S&P 500 grew only 15.4 percent. However, to maintain the continued "promise" of double-digit growth per annum, Eisner seems to have resorted to cut-to-the-bone policies over the past ten years. These cuts may now be coming home to roost, in that for the past five years things at the House of the Mouse have been trending backward. From 1995 to 2003 Disney stock has grown only 2.8 percent per year while the S&P 500 has grown an average of 8.8 percent per year.

So what's going on here? Without getting into a long explanation of the numerous factors that contribute to the worth of any company and its stock, suffice it to say that emotion can be one important factor. Disney (ticker symbol, NYSE: DIS) is a company that has a strong emotional connection with people, and it exhibits the tendency to ride with that emotion and therefore fluctuate more than other stocks because of the public's perceived connectedness with the company. On top of that, because DIS is also held in a lot of institutional accounts, it gets traded in large blocks based on market expectations. These aspects of the stock have created a profile of rather high volatility, and in combination with the large-volume purchases, have helped it grow amazingly fast; but these particular characteristics can also contribute to it crumbling quickly. Recently, it appears that in order for Eisner to counteract any negative momentum and to try to prevent a losing trend from taking hold, he has had to make more and more cuts and go with some quick-return, safe-bet projects—pretty much the kinda things he thought would help the company present a strong profit picture to Wall Street.

We Americans, and the world for that matter, look to companies like Disney for innovation, but the special environment that is so necessary for new ideas to flourish in is slowly dying. It's almost as if when a corporation places increasing value on profit and short-term gain, it then places a proportionately decreasing value on creativity. As reported in Kim Masters' *Keys to the Kingdom: The Rise of Michael Eisner and the Fall of Everybody Else*, Michael Eisner's famous "avoid the big mistake" draft of an internal memo, written while he was at Paramount Studios in 1982, included the following statement: "We have no obligation to make history. We have no obligation to make art. We have no obligation to make a statement. To make money is our only objective." After reading those chilling words, we can kinda see why our pal Mickey Mouse has been turned into a corporate shill. It's also quite apparent that Michael Eisner has a very different approach to the business than Walt Disney did. (Note: From this point on in the book, in the interest of clarity, when I refer to Walt Disney I will often refer to him by his first name only. This should in no way be misconstrued as disrespect, but simply as a way to avoid confusion between The Walt Disney Company [which most people think of when you say "Disney" these days], Roy O. Disney [his brother], and Roy E. Disney [his nephew].)

It all leads to the dilemma this book is wrestling with: if the vaunted Disney organization, known worldwide for its innovation and creativity, is now compromising its capacity and will to generate fresh ideas, then how can the rest of corporate America not follow suit?

It's crucial that we stop runaway greed from continuing to kill innovation in American business. If we don't, then the country we hand over to our future generations won't be as wonderful as the one our parents handed us. It's really that plain and simple.

4

To find a solution to this growing problem, we must first recognize the environment that's needed for innovation and ideas to thrive. We need to understand the intrepid idea person and what makes him or her tick. And in all of our businesses, we must determine the factors that hinder creativity, and then clear the path so people with ideas can champion them and actually make them come alive. It won't be (and never has been) easy, but the rewards will be immense. Just look at the amazing quality of life we enjoy today; this abundance is due, in many ways, to the pioneering efforts of those of our predecessors who championed new ideas in all aspects of life.

HOW AN UNDERDOG BECAME THE MIGHTIEST OF MICE

It's amazing to think that it's been more than seventy-five years since Walt Disney received a trademark for Mickey Mouse. But it was a circuitous series of events that led to the creation of this cornerstone of his business enterprise. As with most innovation, Walt's path to greatness was full of twists and turns. To get an understanding of what it takes to generate and execute a new idea, let's go back and look at the origin of Walter Elias Disney's plucky little mouse—to when he was struggling to get his ideas on paper and put his little character up on the silver screen.

Walt Disney and the distributor Charles Mintz, of M. J. Winkler Productions, in conjunction with Universal Pictures for distribution, had worked and partnered together for many years when Mintz asked Walt to come to New York. They were to discuss future plans and negotiate the deal for the next series of cartoons featuring Oswald the Lucky Rabbit. At their meeting on February 7, 1928, Mintz informed Walt that he was going to cut the advance on each new cartoon from $2,250 to only $1,800 (a greater than 25 percent hit), threatening that if Walt refused the terms of his new deal, he would simply hire away a few of Disney's animators and start his own animation studio (soon after this faithful meeting, Mintz hired away four of Walt's animators and started Snappy Comedies). Walt was stunned. To cap things off, Mintz then told him that Universal, and *not* Disney, held the rights to the character—even though Disney had played the major role in developing it. Mintz's slippery move had forced him to relinquish any possible rights to the Oswald character.

After the acrimonious meeting, Walt (ever the optimist) wired his business-partner brother, Roy (ever the pessimist), writing, "DON'T WORRY EVERYTHING OKAY." On the train ride back to Hollywood, Walt schemed and came up with a plan to get even. The first thing he did upon arriving back at the Walt Disney Studio in Southern California was to ask his head animator, Ub Iwerks, to come up with a new cartoon character that Disney Studios would own outright. And while Iwerks was at it, he asked, why not make the character a little easier to draw, since Oswald's straight-edged ears had caused some "line flicker" in the relatively low-tech animation and projection process?

Ub started by adapting the Oswald character, and he and Walt settled on a mouse because it had round ears, which wouldn't exacerbate the flicker. At first, Walt wanted to name their new creation Mortimer Mouse, because he seemed to favor alliteration (Donald Duck and Minnie Mouse, for example), which helps to create a "memory hook." He shared his new creation with his wife, Lillian, who persuaded him to change its name to a friendlier moniker, Mickey.

The first short starring this little mouse, *Plane Crazy,* was partially inspired by Charles Lindbergh's heroic transatlantic flight in 1927. The character of the mouse wasn't as silly as Oswald's character, but more of a little guy always struggling against odds to do his best, played out in a series of ridiculous situations. Mickey might be seen as the personification of Walt's struggle against the greedy distributor. On May 21, 1928, Walt applied for a trademark for Mickey Mouse, and it (#71266717) was awarded on September 18, 1928—touché Mr. Mintz!

By the time they were working on their third Mickey Mouse short, Walt got lucky because he was able to utilize the breakthrough synchronized soundtrack technology for moving pictures. Walt used his falsetto voice (as he reportedly did for the next ninety-nine Mickey Mouse cartoons) and the tune "Turkey in the Straw," and the Disney crew put it all together to create the first "talkie" film short, *Steamboat Willie,* which debuted to the public on November 18, 1928, at the Colony Theater in New York City. It was an instant hit. From this classic case of creative brinkmanship, Walt Disney (and his ever-worrying brother) went on to build a gigantic entertainment empire.

What can we learn from this example? Quite a bit, actually. First, it exemplifies the adage "Necessity is the mother of invention." Second, it teaches us the absolute importance of remaining confident, flexible, and responsive; be prepared to recognize an opportunity and be willing to wholeheartedly embrace a new trend or technology. Third, it shows that you have to be ready to put your idea down on paper, film, video, or other recording medium—and understand how to own and protect it. Fourth, it teaches that it's vital to solicit and take advice from others, especially people who are close to you and aren't afraid to tell you the truth; don't be afraid to surround yourself with talented experts, like Iwerks, give them a lot of leeway, and let them perform their magic. Finally, it doesn't hurt to have a person you eminently trust, like a brother, covering your back, juggling the few dollars you have, and somehow keeping "that wild and crazy creative guy" in business.

In general, Walt Disney developed a propensity for sticking his neck out, first to find fresh ideas and then sticking it out even further to get these ideas accepted by the public. He ventured into feature-length animated movies, all kinds of films, TV shows, and theme parks. His fearless pursuit of new ideas was remarkable—he was never afraid to do the necessary homework to search out the next big idea. Numerous times in his life he gambled every penny he had, and even lots of money he didn't have, to advance a new idea. Sure, he had his share of flops, but his batting average was truly amazing. Walt put it simply: "All our dreams can come true, if we have the courage to pursue them." Over the years, he carefully built his business by putting one idea on top of another in a wonderful, upward-spiraling staircase of creativity and innovation. The Walt Disney Company is still enjoying the fruits and the force of creativity that its founder, against most odds, fostered so many years ago.

WALT DISNEY UNDERSTOOD DEEP DOWN WHAT IT TOOK TO BE AN INNOVATOR

Let's take a page from what we can learn from Walt's travails. So, how many people can say that they are willing to work diligently and take the calculated risks necessary to come up with and promote a new idea? Are you willing to swap your 9-AM-to-5-PM/5-days-a-week job for the 5-AM-to-9-PM/7-days-a-week job of one who champions ideas? Are you willing to leverage every nickel you have to bankroll your idea? Are you willing to be laughed at, and probably even scorned, if your idea is ahead of its time? Are you willing to continue to gamble it all again, and again, and again? Are you willing to seriously push others to their absolute limits in order to help realize your idea? Are you willing to fight to own your ideas and hunt down and pay to secure the necessary copyrights, patents, and trade-marks? On top of doing all of the above, can you remain optimistic and flexible, and retain a sense of humor, all the while constantly repeating to yourself Walt's deceptively simple words: "I believe in being an innovator"?

Let's take a closer look at championing ideas, Walt Disney style.

1. HE UNDERSTOOD THAT THE BEST IDEAS HAVE UNIVERSAL APPEAL

What made Mickey Mouse so successful? It definitely wasn't Walt's squeaky falsetto that drew the crowds. Of course, there was the exceptional animation by Iwerks that brought Mickey to life. And sure, there was the new technology of the synchronized sound that added a new dimension to the animation—movie audiences couldn't wait to experience this exciting new medium. But the real genius behind the Mickey Mouse character was Walt's inspiration to give him an underdog persona. (I guess this is one case where even a mouse can be a dog.)

Here was the little guy, in this case a tiny, little creature, trying to put up a good fight against all the bullies out there in this cruel, cruel world. It's a universal theme that resonates deeply in the soul of every human being. Charles Lindbergh became the first media celebrity because of our human affinity for the story of a single human struggling against all odds. Disney's little mouse had, above all else, character. (On the other hand, John Hench, who for more than fifty years was Mickey Mouse's official portrait artist, once told me that a certain amount of Mickey's appeal was due to his two large round ears, which reminded people of breasts, and everyone, from infancy, is programmed by their survival instinct to be attracted to full, round breasts. Hmm. Maybe it's as simple as all that, but I doubt it.)

2. HE WAS ALWAYS CURIOUS (EMBRACING NEW TRENDS AND TECHNOLOGY)

Walt was always ready to embrace something new. I don't know if it was because he got bored easily, or because he was always looking for a new angle, but he sure had a nose for what was coming into vogue. Artists come by this naturally, as their curiosity and visual approach to life make them really *see* things. Disney evolved the black-and-white animated short all the way to the full-length Technicolor masterpiece: *Snow White and the Seven Dwarfs* (which he, ignoring the critics who called it "Disney's Folly," spent close to $1.5 million to make—at a time when the country was in the depths of the Great Depression; when released it made 8 million dollars when an adult movie ticket was 25 cents and a kid's ticket only a dime). He later blended live action and animation using breakthrough technology in *The Three Caballeros, Mary Poppins,* and *Song of the South;* he also pushed music in animated cinema to a new high with the Oscar-winning "Zip-a-Dee-Doo-Dah." Walt went on to promote his iconic mouse with a teenybopper club on television. He developed a weekly "Walt Disney Presents" TV show on the ABC network specifically to promote his new family-entertainment project called Disneyland, and he evolved that show into *The Wonderful World of Color* (later to be known as *The Wonderful World of Disney*) just when color TVs were becoming more popular. He parlayed his single theme park concept into a multi-theme-park "World" in the then-backwater town of Orlando, Florida. Disney's company, sixteen years after his death, even anticipated the computer-hacker/virtual-reality sci-fi blockbuster with the movie *TRON.*

In business, it's always good to be on the lookout for what's coming up, but not be too far ahead of the curve (like *TRON*)—just a half step in front of everyone else in capitalizing on an upcoming trend. Walt had an uncanny ability to do just that. He was even one of the first executives to utilize a corporate plane, not for reasons of prestige or for pleasure trips to exclusive ski resorts, but to maximize his very precious time.

Maybe because he was raised in the "show-me" state of Missouri, Walt could definitely see way beyond the obvious. He developed a sixth sense for seeing around the next corner. He was somewhat unique in that respect—especially from what I can see, in that most people can barely see what's sitting right in front of their nose. And many suppress any curiosity they have for life and just sit there waiting until life is processed, put on a platter, and then spoon-fed to them. As my Granny used to say, boring people are easily bored. And all the idea people I've ever met have been anything but bored with life—interesting, challenging, unreliable, a bit crazy, never satisfied, but never bored. Walt put it more succinctly: "When you're curious, you find lots of interesting things to do."

3. HE KNEW HOW TO NURTURE CREATIVITY

Walt listened hard to the experts around him, and facilitated their creativity by giving them the tools, clear direction, and freedom they needed. And because he was such an effective champion of ideas and set such a high standard, he managed to constantly push his associates to tackle new frontiers.

The brilliance of a Walt Disney is that he learned how to deal with egocentric artists and then developed an expertise in getting them to maximize their talents and to coalesce them into a group that kicked butt. In particular, Iwerks, the guy who drew Mickey Mouse, was an artistic genius who quit Disney more than once over "artistic differences." To show the lengths Walt went to keep Ub happy, at one time Walt and Roy gave Iwerks one-fifth of the company to stay on board. (As an interesting aside, a few years later, Iwerks again got emotional and demanded a buyout—he more than once regretted selling his share of Disney Studios, but artistic types typically make lousy business decisions: the designer of the Body Glove logo got something like $45, and the person who came up with the Nike logo received only $35). But what made Walt truly great was his ability to get the best out of Iwerks and the other artists at Disney Studios by treating the artists with respect. Even the buildings at his studio in Burbank were built to maximize the amount of natural light that would pour into the offices of the Disney artists. He would even cough loudly before entering an artist's office, which allowed the daydreaming (so necessary to the creative process) artist enough time to collect his or her wits. However, he didn't let the artists take over and run wild. Walt was a master at maintaining the balance between allowing artistic freedom and maintaining the requirements of doing business—an art in itself. (See chapter 8 for more on nurturing creativity.)

4. HE WOULDN'T STOP UNTIL IT WAS DONE RIGHT

Walt was known for being a perfectionist. He knew what something looked, sounded, or felt like when it was done right, and he was willing to go through the extra effort to get it as close to perfection as humanly possible. He would never settle for "good enough." In idea generating there has to be an incessant quest for excellence, which involves identifying the real problem, determining open-minded ways to approach a solution, tenaciously sticking to the essence of your vision, and searching out an ideal: the properly innovative execution. Per Grim Natwick, the animator of the heroine *Snow White,* said, "Disney had only one rule: whatever we did had to be better than anybody else could do it, even if you had to animate it nine times, as I once did." Walt Disney developed an amazing expertise for searching out, developing, and executing ideas "done right." The public would wait in gleeful anticipation to see what he was going to do next.

5. HE BET THE FARM MORE THAN A FEW TIMES

When you're trying to get a new idea off the ground, it is always a battle to get financial support, especially when all you have is just dreams on paper. Banks like tangible assets as collateral—you know the drill: "We'll lend you $1,000, if you put down $200 cash and back it up with $1,000 in collateral," whereupon they will gladly charge you double-digit annual lending rates.

During his life, Walt complained that money was consistently his biggest headache (he even suffered through a bankruptcy early on in his career). He often drove his brother, wife, and family crazy with worry over debt. So how did he crack the money conundrum? Well, he would often almost ignore it and go out on a limb—about as far as anyone could go. For instance, because of a failed recording session Walt had run out of budget and couldn't finish up *Steamboat Willie,* and his brother was struggling to scrape up some extra dough for another session. Walt finally just told Roy to go ahead and sell Walt's dashing Moon Royal Roadster (which they had just bought) to get the money they needed. The film short turned out to be their watershed, but only because Walt had rolled the dice by saying, "this may mean the making of a big organization out of our little Dump. . . . I think this is Old Man Opportunity rapping at our door. Let's don't let the jingle of a few pennies drown out his knock. . . . So slap a big mortgage on everything we got and let's go after this thing in the right manner."

Walt was constantly forced to use his considerable powers of persuasion to cajole bankrollers into partnerships with his company so he could get his hands on some decent working capital. Walt ended up establishing a rather laissez-faire arrangement with the moneylenders, partly because most of the bankers and bean counters really didn't have a clear idea of what he was up to, and secondarily because brother Roy would diligently follow up with and hold the hands of these lenders. One banker stood out: Amadeo P. Giannini, the head of Bank of America, who got behind the brothers Disney more than once, and even when the going got tough. In one instance he stepped in with a loan when Disney's first animated full-length feature, *Snow White and the Seven Dwarfs*, went $1 million *over* the original $500,000 budget—a huge sum in 1937, particularly when the United States was in the depths of the Great Depression. Of course, Bank of America made some serious money due to their association with the Disneys, but their relationship ended up being more of a partnership—different from the typically adversarial one between banker and lender. (As an appropriate side note, A. P. Giannini eschewed a large salary and gave most of his money away, since he felt riches would make him lose touch with the people he served. He once said, "Money itch is a bad thing; I never had that trouble"—a very interesting remark, especially in contrast with the money-grubbing philosophies of many of today's CEOs.)

When Disney built Disneyland, Walt was way over budget even before opening day. When they opened the park, he had not only spent every cent in the budget (even borrowing against his personal insurance) but was still many millions in the hole. How did he solve this particular problem? Well, he didn't; he chose to ignore it, and for months he just threw any new receipts in a shoebox in his desk.

It is said that one time in their business relationship Roy Disney complained to his brother that he wasn't sleeping and his hair was falling out because of his worry over their mounting multimillion dollar debt. Walt's response was that their being in such astounding debt proved that they had finally made it to the big time; why else would anyone lend them so much money?

Money is a funny thing, but in simple terms it's human effort in suspended animation. It's your time, effort, and expertise set aside in the form of currency, and as a result you can then trade it for someone else's time, effort, and expertise. It's clear that Walt understood that wealth is only truly worthwhile if you were using it to work toward advancing an idea; to hoard money advances nothing within the human condition. Walt knew that money was a means to an end, and not an end in itself. Your time is the only commodity that is precious, and the one you can't get more of. Even gazillionaire Walt Disney left every penny behind when he was buried in the crypt at Forest Lawn Cemetery in Glendale, California.

Now think about just how far you would be willing to go into debt in order to advance your idea. Would you be willing to leverage the homestead? Well, Walt put everything he had on the line something like a dozen times in his life. He did so during the Great Depression, at times when everyone was laughing at him, when his business-partner brother was so mad that he wouldn't speak to him, and even when the woman he slept with every night was burning mad because they didn't have enough money to buy a dress for their daughter. That takes some real guts and determination. You have to be pretty sure of your idea to be able to hang in there at times like those. But how do you know your idea is worth that kind of sacrifice? How do you know you're not just being stupid and blinded by your ego? We'll explore that particular subject in chapters 2 and 3.

6. HE HAD A LONGSTANDING AFFAIR WITH LADY LUCK (FACILITATED THROUGH GOOD OL' R&D)

Maybe Walt Disney's success was all due to his amazing knack for getting lucky. But he knew a lot (much more than most of us will ever know) about sticking out his neck and finding luck. One big reason for his ability to attract luck was that he wasn't afraid to do his homework. For instance, when he was determining the location of Disneyland, he had the Stanford Research Institute do a survey to predict the future population epicenter of Southern California (fifty years later, it's clear that they were right on the money). Additionally, he studied the weather patterns and average daily temperatures all over Southern California, and he looked at the prices of land. After analyzing all of this information, he bought a 182-acre orange grove in Anaheim, California (then considered the middle of nowhere) on which to build his theme park. Why not near the beach? It would be too cloudy in the mornings, due to the Pacific Ocean's marine-layer effect. Why not Burbank, and the land adjacent to his studio? It would have been convenient, but way too expensive. Why Anaheim? He chose this spot because it was affordable, but also because a new freeway (the one that now stretches all the way from San Diego, California, to Vancouver, British Columbia) went right by the property, and he clearly saw the ever-increasing and powerful impact the automobile would have on American life. Disneyland turned out to be perfectly situated to take advantage of the population boom in Southern California; it is said that more than half of Disneyland's business comes from the locals, and nothing helps a business like having a solid customer base to cover the day-to-day overhead. Boy, was Walt ever lucky! Well, actually it would be more accurate to say, "Boy, was Walt ever willing to do his homework!"

Luck is indeed a funny thing. I got my first job in the ad business by ambushing a creative director as he walked through the door returning from lunch (I had asked the receptionist to describe him and also point him out). The creative director was impressed enough with my pluck and initiative to give me five minutes; he escorted me back to his office, sat down, and hit the button on his stopwatch. I danced my dance, and I danced it fast. I found out later that as I left his office, he had tossed my resume into the circular file. I also learned that at a meeting in his office an hour later a writer had noticed my flashy resume sticking out of the trash basket, retrieved it, read it, and told the creative director about a position that was just about to open up. These events prove that luck is important, but it only happens after you first stick out your neck. The adage "Luck rewards pluck" is as true today as it will be a thousand years from now.

TOO BAD "DISNEY'S DOWNWARD SLIDE" ISN'T JUST A NAME FOR A NEW RIDE

Now let's talk about how things progressed after Walt died. First of all, if you've ever felt that no one could ever replace you at your job, forget about thinking that again. Walt dropped dead on December 15, 1966, and his company is still going, thank you very much. His namesake company was the darling of Wall Street from the mid-1980s to the mid-1990s, but, of late, serious questions are being asked about whether The Walt Disney Company is really doing all that well.

So let's review where Disney is these days to better understand the current state of the Mouse House: As mentioned before, their hero head-mouse has been reduced to a pitchman for the corporation and myriad products. The once-proud animation division seems to have lost its way, to the point where an outside company, Pixar Animation Studios, is reportedly delivering more to Disney's bottom line than their in-house studio. (In *The Associated Press* article from January 30, 2004: "During the past five years, Pixar contributed more than 50 percent of Disney's studio profits, according to Merrill Lynch analyst Jessica Reif Cohen.") And now it appears that Disney and Pixar are parting ways after their contract is fulfilled when Pixar delivers *The Incredibles* in November 2004 and *Cars* during the holiday period of 2005. All the while, Disney's animation division continues to lay off more and more of their artists (from the February 23, 2004 *Newsweek:* "the worldwide animation department has 600 bodies, down from 2,200 in 1999"), which stands to reason would contribute to some morale problems within the organization.

The once-top ABC network, now owned by Disney, is foundering at the bottom of the network primetime ratings race—usually below newcomer FOX (*TIME,* February 23, 2004: "the ABC television network, mired in fourth place in the ratings war"). Per *Forbes*, March 15, 2004: "ABC, which loses an estimated $500 million annually, has been in a deep ratings funk, broken only by the brief hit *Who Wants to Be a Millionaire*. Its prime-time ratings are down 27 percent since 1996; it has had four presidents in that time." One piece of good news is that Disney got ESPN as part of the deal when they acquired ABC, and such sports programming has grown into a sweet moneymaker—albeit in a category that could very well be hitting saturation.

It's somewhat hard to believe that the highest rated basic cable channel among kids 2 to 11 years old is Nickelodeon and not The Disney Channel—and even though it's growing in popularity and recently been nipping at Nick's heals, they can't rest; in 1998 Nickelodeon even opened their own animation studio in Burbank, California, not far from the Disney Studio. The ABC Family Channel (previously named Fox Family, for which Disney reportedly paid $5.3 billion in 2001) is, in 2004, worth $2 billion *less* than they paid for it.

The Disney Stores have been closing left and right and that whole retail division is up on the auction block and could be sold by the time you read this. And The Walt Disney Company's foray into professional sports has been unprofitable—incredibly, even when their teams win.

The Disney theme parks seem to be losing some of their charm by evolving into super-duper-maxi malls that happen to offer rides. Disney's California Adventure, a second theme park built in Disneyland's old parking lot, has not been the hit everyone expected (who asked for an ersatz California experience anyway?). Some good news is that in 2005 Disneyland celebrates its 50th anniversary—the perfect opportunity for Disneyland to introduce something truly innovative . . . beyond the requisite decorating of the castle like a frou-frou cake, rehashing their ubiquitous parade and fireworks show, and the tweaking of a few rides. Although as the economy rebounds, their theme park business is starting to "click" (picture turnstiles turning); in general the United States is "the most saturated theme park market in the world," according to Tim O'Brien, senior editor of *Amusement Business*, a trade publication.

One positive note (for Walt Disney World at least) is that Europeans apparently enjoy their fun in the Florida sun rather than on their home turf, which on the other hand has further contributed to Euro Disney SCA's less-than-roaring success (Euro Disney operates Disneyland Resort Paris, which includes Disneyland park, the Walt Disney Studio park [new in 2002], seven themed hotels, two convention centers, the Disney Village, a shopping, dining, and entertainment center, and a 27-hole golf facility). To keep itself afloat in a sea of red ink, Euro Disney has artfully rescheduled (also known as delayed) some massive royalty payments due Disney, and, of late, per *Bloomberg* on June 9, 2004, "Walt Disney Co. and three French banks agreed to bail out Euro Disney SCA for the second time in a decade in a package that prevents Europe's biggest theme park operator from defaulting on $2.9 billion of debt." (Hey, just be glad that you didn't dump your life savings into that venture—in 1992 its stock [ticker symbol, Paris: EDLP.PA] was at almost $10 [US $9.45 adjusting for splits], and for the past two years [early 2002-early 2004] it's been acting kinda like a "penny stock" [a typically high-risk, under $1 equity from a company that has a small market capitalization].) And now, as part of the above-mentioned bailout, Euro Disney may issue more stock, potentially reducing further the value of the existing stock already out in the marketplace.

Speaking of staying afloat, regarding the Disney Cruise Line: "They don't have the same competitive advantage they once did," said Andy Vladimir, associate professor emeritus of hospitality management at Florida International University in Miami and co-author of a book on the cruise industry. So, it's interesting that in 2005, Disney will temporarily move one of their two ships to the West Coast (apparently to test that market, and officially in celebration of Disneyland's 50th Anniversary). Would they be doing this if their East Coast junkets were jam-packed?

Then there's Tokyo Disneyland Resort (which includes two theme parks and two Disney-branded hotels), which as a franchise/licensing agreement must be a sweet moneymaker for The Walt Disney Company. It now has a successful second park that's different from any other of the Disney parks: DisneySea (reported to be a dusted-off-and-repackaged version of a Port Disney park concept that was once planned for Long Beach). But the resort also has the potential to siphon off business from the original Disneyland among the traditional big-spending Japanese tourists (the Japanese seem to absolutely love Disneyland, but I guess that's why they put one in Tokyo). And what about Disney's latest roll-out of Disneyland park? Some bloggers are reporting that Hong Kong Disneyland is being built on the cheap, like with no Frontierland, no Pirates of the Caribbean, no Haunted Mansion (we'll have to wait to see how that one turns out). *And on and on.*

Roy E. Disney (who recently stepped down from Disney's board after sitting on it for almost twenty years—"He fired me," were Roy's words [*Vanity Fair*, May, 2004] in reference to how Michael Eisner, the then Chairman of the Board, handled it) has a lot to say about the current state of The Walt Disney Company on his website, www.savedisney.com. For example: "Disney merchandise once was known for its quality, its fantasy, its originality . . . today it is a shell of its former self, and the Disney Stores are being phased out. The cost of a visit to a Disney park was once within reach of nearly everyone . . . today it's for the well-to-do only. The parks were once bright and shiny refuges from the world around us . . . today they suffer from cutback after cutback, while continuing to raise their prices. And how about something *new* for a change? How many Towers of Terror can they build?" Apparently Comcast shares such concerns according to an article in *Forbes*, March 15, 2004, about their recent bid for Disney: "(Roy E.) Disney and (Stanley) Gold (ex-Disney board member and business partner to Roy E.) revel in the fact that Comcast echoes their criticisms: Disney units underperform; a high-handed Eisner mistreats creative partners; the theme parks are languishing; the stock has withered."

SO WHAT THE HECK IS GOING ON AT THE HOUSE OF THE MOUSE?

The Walt Disney Company seems to be flat running out of real, big, new, fresh ideas. What? No way, you say. Yes way. First, let's take their hero mouse. I've seen his image plastered on just about everything, from rental-car-company shuttle buses, Huggies toss-away potty training pants, cereal-box give-away trinkets, and house paint displays at The Home Depot—to the wood inlay in the furniture in Michael Eisner's office. The Mickey Mouse character has almost become some kinda cult icon; it's no longer a symbol for the underdog that all of us could personally identify with. It's sad when you hear kids say that, as far as they are concerned, Mickey Mouse is simply the official corporate greeter at Disneyland (and strangely replicated on their cruise ships and at all the other Disney theme parks worldwide)—kinda like those nice people who greet you at your friendly Wal-Mart store. It's strange that, in the vernacular, the term *Mickey Mouse* has come to mean lightweight, unimportant, or poorly made. Let's hope this ignoble status doesn't ultimately carry over to his character.

It's hard to believe that they haven't protected Mickey better, and I don't just mean from a copyright/trademark perspective. Jack Lindquist, the first president of Disneyland, used to tell me that featuring Mickey Mouse in an ad for Disneyland was a sign of laziness. He felt that Mickey was not a pitchman, but a celebrity, and that he should be treated as such. His opinion was that you don't see the top movie stars acting as gratuitous pitchmen, so why should Mickey be used that way? Mickey used to symbolize hope for the little guy, but if something isn't done soon he could become an icon for corporate greed. And it's important for everyone to remember that once an image is tarnished it is almost impossible to repair.

Now let's talk about some recent Disney movies. Released in 2003, *Freaky Friday* was a remake of the 1977 Disney movie (it's kind of fun to watch them one after another and compare the sociological send-ups from the two different time periods). For the kind of film that it was, it did well and is a testament to the fact that remakes should be part of any studio's fare. In that same year there was also the very successful *Pirates of the Caribbean: The Curse of the Black Pearl.* Got to hand it to Disney—it was a clever spin (and very well done, I might add) on the whole idea of making a sequel, where a movie is inspired by a very popular theme-park attraction. Then there was the top-grossing movie of 2003, *Finding Nemo,* which was the result of the genius of Pixar Animation Studios and cleverly distributed by Disney. But a closer look at Disney's 2003 successes reveals a lot of clever spins and adaptations, and little that's entirely new and fresh. *Brother Bear,* a new creation by Walt Disney Feature Animation, received only a lukewarm response from moviegoers (though you wouldn't know it from Disney's own glowing press releases). And *Disney's The Haunted Mansion* is an example of that clever "movie-spin-off-from-a-park-ride" concept taken about as far as it can go.

A look at the Disney films in the first half of 2004 shows numerous flops— *Hidalgo, The Alamo, Home on the Range, Around the World in 80 Days,* and *King Arthur.* This is too long of a list of simply average movies that micromanager Eisner gave the "green light" (the necessary funding to go ahead and make the movie). So who's to blame? If the buck starts with Eisner, shouldn't the buck stop there too? But any way you look at it, something isn't right at Disney, because not one of these films captured the imagination of the movie-going public.

Let's take a look at Disney's recent theme-park ventures. What about the park that once seemed to be Eisner's pet project (so much so it even graced the cover of Disney's 2000 annual report), Disney's California Adventure (DCA; sometimes disrespectfully called "Misadventure" on the Internet blogs)? Well, from what I can see when I visit the park, there are but a few "big wows!" and a few little "hmm, what about that's?" but overall the park pretty much lacks soul. Only parts of DCA capture the imagination and have crowd appeal—such as the IMAX simulated flight over California (Soarin' over California), which has super-long lines because there doesn't seem to be much else to see or experience at the park, and now the "new" Tower of Terror attraction, copied from the one in Florida.

What went wrong? First, a frickin' hotel is in the frickin' park. The Grand Californian Hotel is a giant architectural component, albeit one that's "Disneyfied," that doesn't add anything to the park visitor's experience. It may be cool for the visitors who are hotel guests, but not for those who aren't. The people at Walt Disney Imagineering (WDI), the attraction builders for Disney's parks, must have forgotten the necessity of shielding park guests from outside world intrusions in order to sustain their "magical place" theme. In this case, WDI forgot (or, more likely, was confused by micromanagement) that people want to participate with the *ideas* expressed by the architecture, set, props, or ride system. It's the old "heartware" versus hardware issue.

As an interesting side note, the Knott's Berry Farm theme park was up for sale right about the same time Disney was planning DCA. A Disney purchase would have probably saved tons of money in the long run. In addition, Knott's is only five miles away from Disneyland, and in Orlando, the Disney parks are further apart than that. Plus by doing so, Disney would have eliminated a competitor right in their own backyard, avoided taking business away from that reliable money-maker Disneyland (as DCA tends to do because of its proximity), saved the tons of marketing dollars required to launch a new product, *and* given the Disney theme park aficionado a great Wild West experience (especially once they applied some good ol' Disney operational magic to the Knott's park). I heard that such an idea was presented to Eisner, but he turned it down. I guess it wouldn't have allowed him to play the creative-guy role quite as much.

Second, how could visiting a faux-California amusement park come anywhere near what it's like experiencing the real California? Could it possibly measure up to watching waves crash onto a wide sandy beach, hearing the wind blowing through a giant redwood forest, or taking in the pure blueness of Lake Tahoe? There is no way a man-made park can compete with the natural beauty of California—like what you'd see at a Yosemite National Park. All I can think is that they believed their own hype. Who knows—maybe the bean counters based the decision to build the park on the additional money they could extract from visitors staying in that in-park hotel—without acknowledging the real reason that vacationers come to California in the first place: to see the *real* California.

Third, DCA includes the kind of amusement park that Walt Disney was trying to stay away from: roller coasters without a theme, carnival-style barkers shilling games of skill, and places selling trinkets everywhere you look. Attractions like this may be fine for a local ride-'til-you-puke thrill park or hometown fair, but they're somewhat out of place in a Disney *theme* park. On top of all that, DCA has things like mini replica tortilla and sourdough bread factories. Sure, we all enjoy peeking behind the curtain and seeing the workings of a real factory, like the Kellogg's plant, in Battle Creek, Michigan, which used to offer actual factory tours. I clearly remember the wonder of walking among these gigantic huffing-and-puffing machines, the cacophony of industrial noises, and the smells of roasted corn. It somehow made the free samples they gave out at the end of the tour taste yummier. That was the real thing, but the tortilla "factory" at DCA and Kellogg's now simulated production plant diorama at their Cereal City USA visitor center are missing a key component of a unique, worthwhile experience—reality.

Kids know the genuine article when they see it. They can spot a mean person or a nasty dog a block away. So is the faux Golden Gate Bridge spanning the entrance of DCA worth anything more than a kid's casual glance? Seeing it is nowhere near as cool as seeing the real thing in San Francisco. But it's only for show, you say, and we need to look at it as a stage prop. All right, then where's the show? It's sad how little "show" DCA offers, especially in comparison with the standard set at Disneyland, only a short one-minute walk away.

Wrapping up here a bit, it seems that in the past twenty years, Disney's gone from breakthrough ideas and executions (peaking with *The Lion King*) to of late rather replicative products (Disneylands worldwide) and clever opportunities (*Pirates of the Caribbean: The Curse of the Black Pearl*) and tail-spinning down in the past few months to a bunch of relatively average stuff lacking what you've come to expect from them in the way of pure imaginative authenticity.

WHY INNOVATION AT DISNEY JUST AIN'T WHAT IT USED TO BE

1. HAS THE BOTTOM LINE BECOME JUST THE BOTTOM LINE?

"Maximization of shareholder equity" (also known as "pure greed"), when held as the primary principal of a company, means that generating profit, not creativity, becomes the most important goal. For instance, to get the most profit out of every square foot, "improvements" to Disneyland's Main Street, U.S.A. have nearly turned it into something resembling an overstuffed shopping mall, thereby almost obliterating the sleepy, albeit charming turn-of-the century small-town experience that Walt Disney so carefully crafted. When ideas are subordinated in favor of profits, ideas tend to always lose. And that looks to be what's going on at the mouse house these days. In other words, some CEOs may feel they can go around taking advantage of people (employees, partners, and customers), thinking it's justifiable as long as it contributes to the increase of the stock price (and in their defense, isn't that what CEOs are paid to do?). As is often the case in this greedy process, the firm's equity (as in the case of Mickey's image), which is typically based on the power of ideas, has the potential to become diminished. This is the kind of thing that happens when a company focuses on short-term gains and reaching lofty quarterly/yearly goals—which can often conveniently help drive the stock price up . . . and, of course, help the mucky-mucks get rich from all of the stock options they can cash in.

2. DO THEY LOATHE R&D (OR AT LEAST HOPE TO MAKE IT SOMEONE ELSE'S PROBLEM)?

Linus Pauling, a guy with two Nobel Prizes, said, "The best way to have a good idea is to have lots of ideas." Idea generation is basically research and development, and R&D is always a very messy proposition. At best, 1 percent of those ideas generated are usable or worthwhile—but without the other 99 percent, you'll never find the gems.

Much of corporate America, including Disney, has seemingly come to loathe the perceived waste of R&D. New ideas without the mess, expense, and turmoil are what they want. In the 1980s, IBM reportedly tried to cut back on their R&D and almost imploded due to the resulting lack of innovation. But just in time, they realized their error and they now spend considerable amounts of money on generating ideas. For eleven years straight, "Big Blue" (IBM's nickname) has been awarded the largest number of U.S. patents, including 3,415 in 2003—1,400 more than any other company. In contrast, recently Mercedes backed off on R&D spending (10.2 percent of its revenue versus BMW's 14.1 percent), and this spending reduction has led to a sales lag for Mercedes. Duh!

I once heard a bigwig at Disney say that they were going to reorganize and do more outsourcing so they could get just the "cream" (that is, only buy the top 1 percent). As if that's all it took. Whether inside or outsourced, if you want more ideas you need to generate more ideas to choose from. The only way to get more cream is to milk more cows.

One thing this kind of thinking leads to is rehashed off-the-shelf thinking. Why? Big corporations typically don't want to pay outside vendors to do massive amounts of R&D (thereby reaching the critical mass of ideas needed for more "cream": one hundred ideas equate to one great idea, one thousand equate to ten, and so on)—that is, they don't want to pay for ideas that are deadends. Often what the best vendors can afford to do within budget is to take what they have at hand, or what they can easily get their hands on, and slice and dice it into something that isn't necessarily a new idea but has the appearance of newness. Risk-taking is minimized or avoided because the vendor must deliver. Pixar is one obvious exception, but it is hardly a vendor, rather a partner—a partner that isn't afraid to invest in developing new technologies and spend time wrestling with big ideas in order to create their own business model, and which as a result, may come to not need Disney's distribution clout after all. Does this remind you of Walt's dealings with Mr. Mintz? Could it be that the tables have been turned?

3. DOES "NEW" NOW MEAN (RE)USING OLD IDEAS?

Today the focus at Disney seems to be the pursuit of not big *new* ideas, but small (albeit sometimes clever) executional tweaks to existing ideas, which are deliberately geared to squeeze out higher returns on assets. In a perfect example of tweaking old ideas in order to maximize profit, is how the parks, now spread all over the world, have become franchise operations: two park/resorts are partially owned by Disney (39 percent of Euro Disney and 43 percent of Hong Kong's new park), and one, Tokyo Disneyland Resort, is owned entirely by an unrelated Japanese corporation, the Oriental Land Co., Ltd.

Even after a cursory look at what Disney's been up to lately, you'll find yourself asking Where are the Disney artists? Where are the blank-piece-of-paper dreamers? Where are the new big paradigm-changing ideas, like *Snow White* was in the 1930s, coming from today? Sure, Pixar is bringing such breakthrough products to the table, but where will Disney be without them?

But, you might ask, isn't Michael Eisner a creative guy? Well, not exactly, at least in the hands-on way Walt Disney was. From everything I've seen he's at his best being an editor of ideas. Of course, a good editor knows a good idea when he or she sees one, and if that person is clever he or she will know how to properly get the most out of that good idea. In a way, Charles Mintz of the Snappy Comedies Animation Studios was another editor: he knew Walt had some great ideas, he knew full well how to get them distributed, and he did his utmost to take advantage of them. On his own, however, without Walt's ideas, Mintz lacked inspiration and his studio eventually folded. Old Chucky Mintz thought all he had to do was steal away a few "Disney" animators and he had himself a studio, but he forgot the most important component: the ideas behind the films. To state it minimally: people react to ideas, not just a bunch of words, pictures, and music. It takes more than a bunch of cute words, snappy pictures, and bouncy music to move people's souls and create a lasting impression. Eisner knows an idea when he sees one, as well as anyone who will follow in his shoes should.

The Walt Disney Company has had tremendous success mining and editing their stockpile of ideas. Just look at all the money they've made on video (and now, DVD) releases of their classic films—one specific video release generated over $800 million in gross revenues, and over $500 million to the bottom line in profit (yes, it was *Snow White*). Basically, all Disney had to do is take the film off the shelf, copy it onto a low-cost video cassette tape (or nowadays, to a potentially cheaper DVD media), art up a plastic box, slap on a sticker, do some clever marketing and promotion, and send out mass quantities to the stores. It's a great merchandising opportunity, but the release to video wouldn't have done jack if there weren't a groundbreaking film like *Snow White and the Seven Dwarfs* (specifically, one that The Academy of Motion Picture Arts and Sciences honored in 1939 as a significant screen innovation with a special Oscar, as this one was) on that piece of Mylar tape.

Disney's exploitation of existing ideas, which has the potential to get out of hand, is clearly visible in their merchandising efforts. Sure, they've come up with some great cross-promotional deals, like the ubiquitous kid's-meal toys (featuring characters from the latest Disney movie) at McDonald's, or the numerous cards that fall out of a Disney video case when you open it up, or the giant self-promotional Disney Channel, where the commercials sell more Disney stuff. However, this excessive merchandising is catching up with them, and as a result the Disney Stores are oversold and starting to implode. "They just got way too big for their own good. There are still way too many [Disney Stores]," said Marty Brochstein, executive editor of the *Licensing Letter*, a New York–based industry newsletter.

All of this merchandising shows that Disney's giant machine can rehash, sequelize, promote, market, trivialize, spin, homogenize, distribute, merchandise, and finance—but have they forgotten about good ol' R&D, which is the process that creates the innovation that everything else is built upon? An example of how things have gotten away from Disney is the fact that *Toy Story* (I and II) and *Finding Nemo* (the latter of which grossed $850 million at the box office and ranked top-selling DVD of all time with 24 million DVD/VHS units sold in North America) were both brilliant movies created by an outside company, Pixar, and only distributed, albeit very well, by Disney. And, to add support to this, it's quite telling that John Lasseter, the guru of digital-animation at Pixar, is *ex*-Disney. In Walt's day he'd most probably still be working for the mouse house. (Rumor has it that Eisner tried unsuccessfully to hire Lasseter back, but Walt Disney Feature Animation shouldn't have let him get away in the first place.) Last summer (2003) Lasseter was paid quite a compliment when he was compared with Walt: "What Pixar has that we don't have is John Lasseter," Eisner said during an investment conference. "It's like Walt in a way. He has that quirky sense of humor and understanding. John is unique."

In addition, it looks like Disney has come to believe that their job is that of some entertainment service provider, rather like a McDonald's, which serves up the same old burgers time and time again. It's almost as if Disney thinks that providing a constant stream of entertainment is akin to putting out a song that people will want to listen to over and over. The trouble is that, even with songs, after awhile people get tired of hearing the same old thing, and they stop listening and quietly turn away.

Disney has been fortunate, because so far there is constantly a fresh crop of kids who (with a little prodding by their parents) are ready to embrace the Disney family experience, so they have gotten away with more or less rehashing the same old thing again and again—but this strategy is typically successful only to a point. Key to their future success is their ability to come up with fresh, big ideas to keep feeding the world's seemingly insatiable appetite for entertainment. Disney should keep in mind that it's important to approach entertainment like a comic does, because *no* audience wants to hear the same joke again and again and again.

In order for Disney to return to the top of their game, they need to do more than rely on just the rehashing of old ideas for success—they need to reestablish the pursuit of innovation, not just the pursuit of profits, as their modus operandi.

4. IS THE EMPHASIS NOW ON "CULT" IN THEIR CORPORATE CULTURE?

The Walt Disney Company may have simply gotten way too frickin' big. Like the British Empire in the 1900s, it reaches so much of the world that the sun never sets on it. As we will explore in more detail in chapter 5, The Walt Disney Company is mimicking many of the characteristics of a cult: a charismatic leader, an iconic symbol and dogmatic belief system, a takeover mentality, and strict rules of behavior that seem to stifle individuality.

As mentioned, Disney, by all appearances, has started to believe its own hype, and the mumbo-jumbo is starting to infiltrate its belief system. As happens with any business (or, for that matter, a cult), Disney wants to carefully manage people's perception of their activities. The ardent followers are fed the company line and gleefully swallow it. But as the hype is ratcheted up, the internal corporate culture is starting to show signs of becoming as twisted as the words in their spin-and-dazzle press releases. It's weird to think that the spin and dazzle may have infiltrated the corporate culture. For instance, a Disney press release of March 22, 2004, boasted of the success of the animated film *Brother Bear* beyond its domestic box office release: "In commenting on the stellar *Brother Bear* global performance, [Chairman of The Walt Disney Studios Dick] Cook said, 'The acceptance of *Brother Bear* by the global theatrical marketplace is a tribute not only to the creative force of the Disney animation team, but also to our distribution and marketing executives worldwide as well. The appealing, classic nature of this traditional Disney property, coupled with the marketing and distribution expertise has helped propel *Brother Bear* to these levels around the world.'" Or some more spin in the press release of May 21, 2004, covering a meeting that was set up "to review specific steps the company's management is taking to build long-term shareholder value as well as steps the Board is taking in the area of governance": "'The Disney Board plans to continue to hold management accountable for performance, by measuring management's success based on its ability to execute on its strategic priorities, and to prepare for the company's future,' [Board Chairman George] Mitchell said. 'We expect this success to manifest itself in, among other things, continued growth in earnings, increased free cash flow, and increased returns on invested capital.'"

After reading these words you kinda hope this kind of PR spin isn't really what The Walt Disney Company is, down deep, all about. But looking at it for what it is, a PR piece, you kinda understand what Dick Cook (who, by the way, is a genuinely good guy) and George Mitchell are trying to say, and it all sounds kinda good, but the general question remains: Why don't the collective *they* at Disney just level with the collective *us* in America and just give us some straight talk about what's going on? And this insidious mumbo-jumbo seems to be expanding exponentially whether in business, politics, or the TV news.

As part of Disney's strategy to somehow control public perception, they schmooze the press in an effort to prevent them from ever saying anything bad about the company. No surprise here, as that's pretty much standard for any public company. But when a company, or its CEO, begins to believe its own press releases you have a problem on your hands: it can set up an insular emperor-has-no-clothes corporate ethos.

For example, when Eisner "almost" had a heart attack that resulted in emergency multiple-bypass surgery, it appeared that the Disney PR group went into super spin mode, trying to make it sound like he merely had a heart condition that was remedied through good care. Whew, Disney dodged a bullet there, since the event didn't seriously affect the price of the stock. But the real fallout is the apparent effect this particular spin had on Eisner. You'd think that surviving such an ordeal would have a sobering effect and cause him to change his lifestyle a bit. But the company-line, in combination with his type-A personality, transformed this brush with death into some sort of calling, his rebirth as the scion to the entertainment megalith of the mouse . . . the king of the castles . . . the sovereign of the Disney empire . . . who is seemingly more determined than ever to make his mark on the world.

Okay, okay, I'm going to take a lot of heat by putting the word *cult* in the same sentence as the word *Disney.* My intentions are simply to show how a cult-like mentality in a company can kill creativity and stifle innovation. Drawing parallels from Disney's cult-like behaviors helps illustrate how insular thinking can diminish the power of an idea and, in general, the generation of new ideas; *only* an open approach will allow the widespread flourishing of ideas. Great ideas and innovation come from embracing and responding to the collective craziness of the world outside. Whenever big companies start taking on a cult-like mentality and the accompanying mantle, fresh thinking starts closing down.

5. HAS MICKEY-MOUSE (IN THE NOT-SO-NICE USE OF THE TERM) MICROMANAGEMENT STIFLED THE CREATIVE PROCESS?

A new idea needs a champion and an audience. Innovation comes when people have the freedom to think outside the box and assume some risks. Yet, it looks like Disney has begun micromanaging the creative process to the point where almost no innovation can take place; at best, any "new" idea is a spin-off of stuff already in the system—leading to too much inside-the-box thinking. When I first joined Disney, in order to get something approved, I had to take the creative work of my division first to the vice president of marketing, who would pretty much bless it, next to the president of Disneyland for a cursory once-over to make sure we were on track, and finally up to Eisner for a one-on-one. A lot of outstanding work was done this way. But by the time I left Disney, I had something like seven layers of decision makers between Eisner and me. I often sat in meetings with twenty-five people trying to present commercials and the like in an attempt to get a go-ahead. Yuck. Creative work, by its nature, is very personal, and big groups tend to dilute it. These mondo groups also tend to bring out the big dog in everyone, and in these meetings I saw a lot of people trying to put their mark on whatever creative work that was being discussed, especially in front of the big boss. I also saw a lot of people, before a big meeting, trying to show how smart they were by attempting to second-guess Eisner's reaction and almost forcing their ideas to reflect what they thought he'd like. What happens in this ridiculous, counterproductive process is that the creative work often morphs into whatever's the easy sell, which is typically average at best and invisible to the consumer at worst.

· · ·

From everything I've observed, I think Eisner is an all-around clever guy, but, of late, the easy exchange of ideas at Disney just isn't a happening thing. This stagnant atmosphere was evident in one of my last meetings with him (which included the now-requisite twenty other people); I shot Eisner a friendly zinger (this particular time it was regarding his ability to always have a quick and tough opinion to put forth) as I had done so many times before in meetings. The sucked-air-through-the-teeth noise from all the minions nearly drowned out Eisner's appreciative chuckle. No one in a cult-like environment wants to tell the emperor that he has no clothes . . . but the emperor will only be stronger if someone does. Walt Disney could always trust that his brother, Roy, would help keep him from losing focus. It's too bad Frank Wells is no longer around to help keep Eisner similarly centered.

Let's talk about Frank Wells a bit, since he contributed so much to the turnaround of The Walt Disney Company's fortunes. As a young and hungry lawyer, he got his first major gig in the entertainment law business by representing James Garner in a dispute over Jack Warner's alleged breach of contract over the show *Maverick*. Wells argued successfully, and Warner was required to pay up. As Warner was walking out of the courtroom, he turned to one of his assistants and said something like "Someday I'm going to hire that guy, because anyone who can beat me should be working for me." Sure enough, Wells went to work for Warner and did very well representing the Warner Studios in business affairs, rising to president of the studio in 1973. After a full career there, he decided he had had enough and, in 1982, took a sabbatical from the business world to climb the highest peak on each of the seven continents (he got very close to accomplishing that feat—only on Mt. Everest did he come up short, due to an extreme storm that cost the life of one of his Sherpa guides). He subsequently coauthored (with Dick Bass and Rick Ridgeway) a book about his climbing experiences, called *Seven Summits*.

In 1984, Roy E. Disney and Sid Bass of the Texas Bass brothers (both major Disney shareholders at the time) brought together both Eisner (from Paramount Studios) and Wells to head up and reorganize the Disney Company, which was foundering under the misguidance of the surviving Disney family members. (It was in such bad shape that it had almost succumbed to a hostile takeover by corporate raider Saul Steinburg.)

Wells, a Rhodes scholar, wasn't interested in being the head guy; he knew where the true power lay—with the person who controlled the purse strings. In the negotiations he calmly conceded the CEO position to Eisner (who jumped at the chance), with Wells settling on the position of president and COO. Wells got right to work making things right at Disney. As described in *Co-Leaders: The Power of Great Partnerships*, "Disney CEO Michael Eisner had such a happy corporate marriage with co-leader Frank Wells before Wells' untimely death in a helicopter accident in 1994. Eisner would visit Wells' nearby office dozens of times a day, seeking his advice on virtually every decision. As Eisner told *Fortune* magazine in 1991, Wells loved to play 'devil's advocate' and, by constantly challenging Eisner, helped him achieve their common goal in running Disney—making sure the best ideas won out. But what seems to have been the glue that made Eisner and Wells such an extraordinary team was their easy camaraderie. As Wells explained, 'For Michael, I make life easier. For me, he makes life more fun.'" Fundamentally, Wells knew exactly how to do it right and properly champion ideas.

In the meetings I had with him, I always admired his laser-like view of the market situation and his input on how it would help or hinder what was being presented. Unfortunately, Wells died in a helicopter crash on his way to take "just one more run" while snow skiing in the Rockies. He was quite a risk taker. In that crash, Eisner lost a true and fearless adviser. And he sure could use one now.

WILL THEY INSTALL A BRONZE STATUE TO MICHAEL EISNER IN THE TOWN SQUARE?

The question on the table is: given the current state of affairs, how will Disney protect its legacy (and Eisner his)? Well, Michael D. Eisner, if you're reading this, you could start by backing off a bit and refocus your efforts to help create a process and environment that allow fresh ideas to percolate to the top. It's vitally important that you let the ideas (and customer) be king again, instead of you (or even the stockholders). After all, in the seminal words of Viacom's CEO and board chairman, Sumner Redstone: "Content is king" (which, in 1996, became the title of Bill Gates's famous missive about the Internet). From everything I know, people respond to fresh ideas expressed through compelling content—and that's why content rules the world. (In a 2000 speech in Los Angeles, Redstone specifically evolved his ubiquitous line to a more succinct "*Creativity* is King." He added, "Without creativity there is no content. There is—quite literally—nothing.")

American companies in general need to wake up to the fact that a lot of current business practices lead to employees' valuable ideas being shredded like yesterday's newspaper. In contrast, the ideas of their "corporate cult-leader" CEOs are then worshipped. Ideas do, and must, have a life of their own—and they're certainly not the purview of only one guy in an organization. From what I've observed, no one's that frickin' smart to have all the answers, especially when it comes to idea generation. Maybe CEOs are powerful enough to call the shots, but no way are they as smart as the collective team—or as powerful as an idea whose time has come.

If Eisner realizes all this before he retires, maybe he can get Disney on *Fortune* magazine's top-ten list of "America's Most Admired Companies." In 2003, it was: (1) Wal-Mart, (2) Berkshire Hathaway, (3) Southwest Airlines, (4) General Electric, (5) Dell Computer, (6) Microsoft, (7) Johnson and Johnson, (8) Starbucks, (9) FedEx, and (10) IBM. (To be fair, Disney ranks number one in "Entertainment" when the long list is broken down into sixty-four separate industries, and in 1998 Disney did make the top-ten overall list.) Or even better, maybe Disney can get listed in *Fortune* magazine's "The 100 Best Companies to Work For." (You would think Disney would make this long list, especially when other Dow Jones 30 companies like American Express, IBM, Intel, Merck, Microsoft, and Procter and Gamble do.) Another magazine, *Forbes*, gives Eisner an efficiency grade of "F" in their article on "Pay for Performance Rankings (2003)," which means the only way is up . . . *or out.*

It will be interesting, to put it mildly, to see how Mr. Eisner's contributions at Disney look when we examine them, let's say, forty years from now. Will his initiatives have the lasting power that Walt Disney's did? Or will he be remembered more for his *deals* than his *ideas?* It's entirely possible that his legacy will have more to do with creating (speaking metaphorically) an eighth Dwarf named "Greedy" who grabs guests by their ankles and shakes the last few dollars out of their pockets as they exit a Disney theme park. I guess only time will tell if he rates a life-size bronze "pigeon perch" in the middle of Town Square, U.S.A.

CHAPTER 2

"MOMMY, WHERE DO IDEAS COME FROM?"

Let's go back over the past 125 years or so, examine some big ideas from that time period, and see what we can learn from them about the creation of new ways of thinking. We're talking here about pure innovation and real paradigm-bending, real-deal ideas like the Wright brothers' powered/controllable flight, Jobs and Wozniak's personal computer, Fleming's antibiotic medication, and even Hershey's affordable milk chocolate.

The ideas discussed in this chapter are examples of pure innovation. Most were life changing, whether in a big way or a very small way, but they all had enough impact to change people's behavior, thinking, perceptions, and way of life. Humans responded to these ideas, and life was never the same.

I've loosely grouped the discussions about these innovators on the basis of the methods they used and the results they achieved, so that we can follow their path toward innovation and discover a few answers to the question "What's innovation and how do you get there?" (As you'll see, there is no such thing as a typical path.)

1. EMBRACE NEW TECHNOLOGY (AND BUILD ON KNOW-HOW)

THE WRIGHT BROTHERS

The Wrights' odyssey is a classic example of the life of a new idea. The Wrights didn't exactly pull an idea out of the sky, but they brilliantly tweaked existing aerodynamic thinking, applied careful scientific process, and took full advantage of an emerging and powerful technology (photographic reproduction) to help spread the word about their accomplishments. Their tenacity also served them well in their lifelong fights for the rights to their inventions. They left a remarkable legacy and died rich men.

The Wright brothers spent years slaving away in the back of their little bicycle shop in Dayton, Ohio, trying to unlock the mystery of flight. Starting in 1899, and each subsequent summer for four years, they'd drag their butts (and wagonloads of gear) over six hundred miles of rudimentary roads, to the windy sand dunes along the Atlantic shoreline near Kitty Hawk, North Carolina (which had the most consistent headwinds they could find). Another reason they preferred testing in Kitty Hawk was the place's remoteness and, hence, its lack of "lookie-loos." The Wrights built and tested many gliders, and most of these designs were based on the contemporary theory of a couple of brilliant guys named Otto Lilienthal (1894 Glider), from Germany, and Octave Chanute (1896 Glider and 1897 Powered Glider), from Chicago, Illinois. The Wrights persisted like a couple of crazed hobbyists while many naysayers were having a jolly good laugh at their expense.

When the brothers couldn't find an engine light enough, they, along with a mechanic named Charles Taylor, doggedly built their own lightweight one utilizing an aluminum block, an ultra-high-tech solution for its time. The results of their R&D on propeller shapes fundamentally established the formula for every propeller made since. They built their own miniature wind tunnel and studied hundreds of wing shapes with different aerodynamic cross-sections and aspect ratios. They incorporated a couple of vertical stabilizers to help turn their glider, and they developed a neat little elevator at the nose to control the up and down motion.

After many years of effort they finally created a high-lift wing and figured out how to warp the wings so they could actually control their powered glider. The brothers Wright had achieved balance and control along all three axes (roll, pitch, and yaw). Orville's first liftoff, into a headwind of twenty-seven miles per hour took place at 10:35 A.M. on December 17, 1903. *Yeeeeeee, they were flying!*

Their insatiable curiosity had also led to an active interest in amateur photography, and among their wagonloads of gear was a very expensive 5-by-7-inch Korona-V dry-plate camera (for which they paid $85, at a time when the average yearly salary was just over $700). On the day of their historic flight, the Wrights set up the camera and had a local named John T. Daniels snap the photo (the first photo Daniels had ever taken). Now the Wrights had irrefutable visual proof that mankind had challenged the effects of gravity in a controlled flight, if even for only a measly twelve seconds and 120 feet (although they did have other, longer flights that day—Wilbur had one as long as fifty-nine seconds and 852 feet). The photo didn't prove that they could turn their craft (a year later, they proved that by flying in a circular pattern in front of a crowd), but it did allow them to take advantage of the emerging technology of photo reproduction and expose their remarkable feat in the broadest media at the time: newspapers. Earth-bound humans the world over responded to this famous picture, and it was still several years before most people started to actually believe what they saw in the photo.

You would guess that all the Wrights had to do now was sit back and reap the rewards. But that wasn't exactly the case. Even though they were smart enough to secure a fairly broad patent, they still wound up spending a good chunk of their lives fighting infringement by others, particularly Glenn H. Curtiss, a man with strong business acumen, who had big ideas about getting the aviation industry going. Curtiss, with the backing of the esteemed Smithsonian Institution, also had ideas about how to circumvent the Wrights' patents—his ailerons, instead of the Wrights' wing warping, became the norm. Curtiss even got Henry Ford involved in starting the aviation industry because of the tremendous opportunity to sell aircraft to the government (and also maybe because Henry had successfully avoided paying any licensing fees to the guy who held the patent on the automobile, but that's another story).

Unfortunately, the incessant haggling over the patent in America allowed the French to take the lead in the development of an aviation industry. And the Wrights' rights got somewhat trampled during World War I, when protecting the skies became an overriding national priority. Orville and Wilbur Wright finally got satisfaction and full credit only later in life—and ultimately got rich when they finally merged companies with the business-smart Curtiss. The Curtiss-Wright Corporation (NYSE: CW) is still in business today.

HENRY FORD

Henry Ford tried three times to get an automobile business going—even losing one namesake company to its investors. Then he started a new company incorporating the idea of interchangeable parts, which was finding acceptance in firearm production. Ford applied this idea to a linear production line with a conveyor belt where the vehicle moved from station to station (a division of labor he had observed in Chicago's meat-packing plants) as it was being built. Up to that time, it had taken teams of highly skilled craftsmen to custom build each car. His idea of breaking the assembly process into a series of steps (where one specific step was all the worker had to be trained to do) was effective once he had established a flow of consistent interchangeable parts.

Ford's automobile production line revolutionized the manufacturing industry. But another idea of his might have been his most creative: convert those mountains of sawdust leftover from the production of the automobile's wood framework into charcoal. He had heard about a process that did just that, and with a little help from his friend Thomas Edison and one of his enterprising dealers, Edward G. Kingsford (who happened to be Ford's cousin), he built a plant to convert sawdust into little burnable charcoal cubes. Yep, I'm talking about the very same Kingsford brand charcoal briquettes you see everywhere today (even the shape of Kingsford's logo pays homage to Ford's oval logo). Ford saw profit potential where most people saw piles of waste. More than once Ford shrewdly embraced emerging technologies in one industry and then applied them to another business. He gets credit for having ideas, but he also knew more about how to put one plus one together to make them add up to more than two. Any entrepreneur will need to do exactly that, or he or she won't stay in business very long.

CLARENCE BIRDSEYE

Clarence Birdseye, a naturalist and taxidermist who enjoyed cooking, took advantage of an emerging technology and created a whole industry. When he saw freezers being added to electric refrigerators he thought they'd be useful for more than just making ice cubes for drinks. Then, while he was working in the Arctic for the government he observed that the locals quickly froze their seafood by putting it outside in the blowing cold and later thawed the fish for eating. This "flash" method kept the ice-crystals from forming within the cells, which provided for a tasty product when unfrozen. He developed and got a patent for his high-pressure flash freezing process and got busy selling Birds Eye Frosted Foods. He sold the works to the General Foods Corporation in 1929 for $22 million. So simple, so obvious, so convenient, and so right on the money. Occasionally an idea is just sitting out in the cold waiting to be discovered.

GEORGE BEAUCHAMP AND ADOLPH RICKENBACKER

In the early 1930s, George Beauchamp figured that if you could amplify a voice you should be able to amplify a guitar. Working on a kitchen table, using wire from an old motor and some small horseshoe magnets, he made some small and very sensitive electric-coil microphones and placed the strings through them. So now when you strummed the guitar, the sound was amplified.

To put his new idea into production, he got together with his buddy Adolph Rickenbacker (cousin of World War I flying ace Eddie Rickenbacker), who had a tool-and-die shop in Los Angeles. They chose to call their product a "Rickenbacker," capitalizing on the famous pilot's name. After Beauchamp died in 1940, Rickenbacker soldiered on, making the first electric guitar that didn't look like its acoustical cousin. He sold his guitar business in 1953, just before rock 'n' roll took off and took their cool little invention in a whole new direction. Rock music's blending of bluesy Mississippi River valley riffs was brought to life by those little microphones coiled around those guitar strings. One simple idea, like amplifying a guitar, will often eventually lead to another, larger idea, like rock 'n' roll. Sometimes it just takes time.

GEORGE EASTMAN

Photography was invented in France in 1839. As the technology became more widely used, it slowly evolved into a silver-nitrate emulsion on glass-plate process (typically with long exposures in a controlled studio environment). But in 1899 the giant breakthrough came when George Eastman put this "film" of silver nitrate on flexible nitrocellulose (a thin, clear plastic-like material). His "celluloid" also naturally led to the development of moving pictures, since it could be wound through cameras on sprockets.

New executions of existing ideas or technology can change the world. Just look at a skateboard, for example. Isn't it simply a board with some roller-skate wheels attached to it?

2. MAKE SOMETHING EXPENSIVE OR SCARCE INTO SOMETHING ACCESSIBLE TO THE LITTLE GUY

STEVE JOBS AND STEVE WOZNIAK

In 1976, computers were giant mainframe apparatuses that cost millions of dollars. Computers were for banks, and NASA, and the government, but not for Ma and Pa. So just think how crazy it must have seemed to people that Steve Jobs and Steve Wozniak were working in a garage trying to create a computer for the average person.

These two guys wanted to make a computer that would be as common as apples (reportedly the name for their company was a play on the word *bytes*) and would sit on a table in every small business and home. They persevered, thinking that they'd maybe sell a few to some of their friends in the surrounding California valley (which would later be nicknamed "Silicon Valley"). Their critics snickered at how rudimentary the invention was and about the fact that it gave up a big chunk of its processing power in order to be user friendly.

Jobs and Wozniak had the last laugh when their Apple II was the number one selling computer for five years in a row (1977–81). Apple Computer went public in 1980 and instantly created more millionaires than any company in history. (It's interesting to ponder if going public had anything to do with their subsequent reversal of fortunes, because by the mid-1980s the PC with Microsoft's disk operating system [MS-DOS] started to take over the market with its overall cheaper specs. The PC really took off when Gates somewhat mimicked Apple's desktop look and navigational tools [which Apple had already mimicked from the Xerox Palo Alto Research Center's Star/Alto] with his "Windows," and incorporated the Apple-introduced mouse that PC traditionalists were snickering at.)

Apple computers are now standard in the design and publishing world, and their cheerful look and user-friendly approach continue to garner loyalty among users. Even my old-school, octogenarian mother loves sending and surfing with her iMac.

It does seem that sometimes two guys in a garage can see much more clearly than a bunch of guys sitting in some office tower. So don't think your ideas aren't big just because you're toiling away in a basement somewhere.

MILTON S. HERSHEY

Milton Snavely Hershey was born to a dreamer-schemer dad and a more-practical mom. His parents separated because of their divergent views, and the young Hershey grew up with his mom and her family. She urged him to get into a business that was practical, like making food products.

Using money from his maternal aunt, Hershey tried and failed more than once in the candy business in Philadelphia, Chicago, New Orleans, *and* New York. When he finally returned home to the village of Derry Church, Pennsylvania, he was snubbed a bit by his family because of his failures. However, an old friend lent him enough money to start yet another candy business, the Lancaster Caramel Company, which did become quite successful—and which he sold for an amazing $1 million in 1900 (something like $23 million in today's dollars).

Hershey, now thirty-three, had visited the 1893 World's Columbian Exposition in Chicago and had brought back to Pennsylvania some German chocolate-making machines to start a chocolate company, which he had up and running by 1905. Using these machines, his advanced production methods, and knowledge that he had gained in his caramel business, Hershey's new enterprise came to provide milk chocolate candy for the masses, which previously had been an expensive, handmade treat available only to the wealthy. Of course, as you know, his affordable Hershey's Milk Chocolate bar was an enormous hit.

Not intending to stop there, Hershey built from scratch a model town around his factory. Critics called it a fool's dream—that is, until it became successful and was well received by his employees. In 1906, the locals chose to rename his hometown (which now incorporated his model town) after him.

Hershey kept on building: rail lines, a stadium, a museum, a department store, a bank, a hotel, and an amusement park. He and his wife, Catherine, even founded a boarding school for orphans in 1906. (After Catherine's premature death in 1915, Milton decided to donate the entire corporation to this school; this same industrial school still holds over 40 percent of the company's stock.) Through the Great Depression he kept building and hiring, and again the critics shook their heads—but his employees (always a high priority for Hershey) were ever so grateful for the work. He liked to brag that no one was laid off at Hershey during the Depression years.

Hershey developed a special nutritional ration (in the form of a chocolate bar) for the troops in World War II. Wildly popular, it became a virtual black-market currency in post-war Europe.

Believing that a product's inherent quality should speak for itself, Hershey eschewed advertising. Even after his death in 1945, Hershey Foods Corporation continued the tradition and didn't advertise until 1970 (and only because they had begun losing market share to heavy-advertiser Mars Candy).

Hershey's legacy was plain and simple goodness—which was manifest in his concern for his employees, orphaned children, and affordable chocolate. *How many CEOs today will leave such a legacy?*

SIR HENRY BESSEMER

Steel is an amazing material. Islamic armies wielding Damascus steel swords decimated the European crusaders trying to free the Holy Land. These flexible, amazingly sharp, amazingly strong Damascus steel swords cut right through armor and caused the European armies to flee the Holy Land in full retreat. With no one to stop them, these Saracen hordes marched across Africa and into Spain and were pushing into what is now southern France, until around 732 c.e., when they were met by a massive Frankish army led by the grandfather of Charlemagne, who finally turned the Saracens back at the Battle of Tours. Europe had come very close to Islamic domination because of the superiority of Damascus steel.

Today, steel is the key material that goes into railroads, automobiles, skyscrapers, and many other products we use every day. But up to about 150 years ago steel was almost impossible to produce in anything but very small batches and therefore was very rare (the processes to produce steel were highly protected and almost considered magic). At the time, the use of steel was limited to special tools, utensils, cutlery, and armaments. In the late seventeenth century, the best crucible-steel-making methods, used in Steyr, Austria, could produce barely two thousand pounds a year (about equal to the amount of steel in a large automobile today).

When Englishman Henry Bessemer (later Sir Henry) developed a unique process that turned pig iron into steel, however, the metal suddenly became almost as common as dirt. He received a patent on his process in 1855 and shopped it around, but none of the British steel producers would license it or help him improve the process to where it would be practicable on large-scale factory production. Why should they, when they were getting filthy rich making small quantities for a huge profit? So Bessemer was forced to start his own steelworks, which succeeded in breaking the monopoly that the established Sheffield steel producers had on the trade in the United Kingdom. This single development, Bessemer's low-cost steel, is credited with initiating the industrial revolution. Today, roughly one hundred million tons of steel are produced in the United States every year.

Bessemer's story illustrates that, if you come up with a great idea (like a way to remove gold from seawater, because the oceans hold in solution vast quantities of gold, but only in miniscule amounts), you just might have to start your own company, factory, or production works in order to gain any momentum for it.

CHARLES KETTERING

Kettering initiated a massive societal paradigm shift when he engineered the self-starting ignition for the automobile in 1912. Up to that time, in order to start an automobile, one had to turn a crank several times by hand, which required a fair amount of strength, so most drivers were men. Even on a nice warm day, with the motor in perfect tune, hand cranking wasn't considered an easy chore. In 20-degree weather, or with some bad gasoline in the tank, expect much cursing because starting the car was even more of a challenge. The initiative to come up with something better came about when a man was fatally injured when a hand crank hit him in the head.

By the 1920s self-starters had become the standard. As a result, car sales to women absolutely skyrocketed. This one device may have inadvertently contributed to women's liberation, since a woman no longer needed a man's help with her personal transportation.

In the 1800s, the Quakers were enlightened enough to believe that everyone was equal, regardless of race or gender, but just maybe Charles Kettering's invention was the impetus that really got the women's rights movement started. Sometimes you can't anticipate the social impact of new ideas; they have a life and a power of their own.

3. APPEAL TO UNIVERSAL THEMES AND EMOTIONS

GEORGE LUCAS

The idealistic little guy fighting the big bad guy is a pretty universal concept in movies and books—the naive cowboy riding into town to fight the established rich land barons in the Wild West, the wet-behind-the-ears detective fighting organized crime. Basically, these storylines are takeoffs on the David versus Goliath story: where the young protagonist eschews the platitudinous blather of the elders and instead chooses to develop his or her own strategy to defeat the formidable antagonist, whom he or she alone must face.

George Lucas had the idea to use some new-tech special effects to set this universal conflict in a galaxy far, far away. Up to that time sci-fi had been mostly a cult interest, but the underlying story (excellently scripted and produced) transported his movie beyond the sci-fi genre. In order to execute his vision and broaden the appeal of the film, he brought together an amazing team: Dykstra, Daniels, Ford, Fisher, Guiness, Hamill, Jones, and Williams. His dazzling, brand-new special effects alone caused a sensation in the film industry.

In 1977, when *Star Wars* was released, it was the boomers' turn to go out into the world and fight the good fight. In the film, Lucas gave the baby boomers, then in their teens and twenties, a gentle lesson: the apprentice kid turns off the targeting computer and relies on "the force" to guide his actions in the destruction of the giant death star. This David versus Goliath universal struggle drew the movie-goers back to the theater more than once, making *Star Wars Episode 4: A New Hope* the first lines-around-the-block blockbuster.

By the way, when Lucas was shopping the film around, every Hollywood studio passed on it except for 20th Century Fox. And, at that, the studio pretty much thought they were ripping him off because he wasn't asking for a ton of money—just control of the project. George Lucas had insisted he retain the right to make the final cut, 40 percent of the net box-office gross, all rights to future sequels . . . *and* ownership of all the merchandising rights (the general opinion at the time was that merchandising rights to sci-fi films were worthless). Such a deal would eventually make Lucas a billionaire. There is a lot to be learned from what went on here.

WALTER ELIAS DISNEY

Weren't there always theme parks? No, not before Walt Disney came along. So where did he get the idea? The story goes that he was sitting on a bench in Los Angeles' large Griffith Park while his daughters were enjoying a ride on the carousel. He mused to himself, why wasn't there an amusement park where a regular guy could take his whole family? Sure, there were amusement parks, like The Pike in Long Beach, California, but they all had too much grime, hucksterism, and make-you-sick thrills.

Walt was onto something big. Why not make an amusement park that takes you away from the stress of everyday life and transports you (and your family) into a make-believe world—maybe a squeaky-clean world that imagines the future, creates a sense of adventure and fantasy, or takes you to the old Western frontier, or allows you to step into a quaint, old-fashioned American town?

There's nothing wrong with a little escapism, especially when it's shared with people you love. Walt put it simply: "We believed in our idea—a family park where parents and children could have fun—together." This shared experience is the simple magic of his parks: the special moments people share there become locked in their memories. In a bizarre way, it's like experiencing a survivable car accident with someone you know and love—an event like that is indelibly etched in your psyche. And, if you look carefully, you'll see the survival theme throughout Disneyland. The park masterfully brings families closer together with each "adventure."

THOMAS MORAN

In 1871, a Civil War hero named Dr. Ferdinand Vandiveer Hayden put together an expedition to survey and chart the Yellowstone Basin. People in the East just didn't believe what was being said about this part of the uncharted wild West—who'd believe that there was really a natural geyser that shoots water two hundred feet in the air and does it every hour or so? To find out what was really going on out there, Hayden, with the financial support of the U.S. Congress, took off to Yellowstone with a bunch of geoscientists and a photographer (at the time, photography was a newfangled "visual-proof" technology). Then along came a flamboyant artist named Thomas Moran, who had never ridden a horse but nevertheless horned his way into joining the expedition, partially with the help and funding of the Northern Pacific Railroad. Hayden figured that this new guy, who appeared to be an effete city-slicker dilettante, wouldn't last long, and he worried that the artist would end up in conflict with his expedition's photographer, William Henry Jackson. However, as it turned out, Moran was hardly a dilettante and didn't falter during the arduous journey; he and Jackson became immensely supportive of each other, respecting the other's visual sense and even collaborating on how to depict certain scenics.

When they got back to Washington, D.C., it wasn't the five-hundred-page report or the visual-proof photographs of the discoveries made on the expedition that got everyone excited—it was Moran's spectacular paintings. Moran lobbied President U. S. Grant (using the artwork as his entrée) to preserve this beautiful valley for all Americans, and Ulysses signed a bill, which was approved by the Congress and the House, making the Yellowstone Basin our first national park. The majesty of Moran's paintings captured the imagination of everyone who viewed them, and did it much better than the photos, with their cold depictions of reality. Today, Thomas Moran, not Hayden or Jackson, is considered the father of our national parks. The lesson here is that *real* beauty captured by a *real* person will elicit *real* human responses.

By the way, Thomas Moran got quite rich and famous off the paintings he did in Yellowstone. Because he wasn't an official part of the congressionally funded expedition, he retained ownership of his canvases and was able to sell them for vast sums. As always, being ambitious, hard working, talented, and clever enough to recognize an opportunity is one very successful combo.

4. BE TRUE TO YOUR PASSIONS AND CONVICTIONS

GALILEO GALILEI

Galileo, an absolute genius, discovered in 1613, through careful scientific observation using the powerful telescope he had made, that the planet Venus showed phases like the moon. He concluded that therefore it must revolve around the sun, and that the earth must *also* revolve around the sun.

Since that didn't jibe with Scripture, Galileo was asked by the Roman Catholic Church to denounce his findings or face excommunication. As a scientist, he wouldn't compromise his integrity and therefore had to refuse, so he was found to be "vehemently suspected of heresy." He spent the rest of his life under house arrest in his villa north of Florence.

In 1992, exactly 350 years after his death, the church finally got around to exonerating him. I doubt that anyone today will come up with an idea as earth-shattering as Galileo's, but anyone with radically new ideas should be prepared for some ridicule and resistance. Oftentimes, the idea business can be very lonely.

REV. DR. MARTIN LUTHER KING JR.

As a preacher, Martin Luther King, Jr. obviously knew the power of an idea. On December 1, 1955, in Montgomery, Alabama, a black woman named Rosa Parks was arrested when she refused to give up her bus seat to a white man. (At the time, it was customary in the South for blacks to ride in the back of the bus and to give up their seats to whites if the bus became full.)

King figured it was time for action, and he called a meeting of the local black leaders at his church. In a surprising decision, they concluded that the best way to fight this injustice was with inaction—they called on the black community to boycott the local bus company.

For quite a while it looked like neither side would budge. After about two months, when King's house was bombed (thankfully his wife and baby girl escaped injury), a mob of angry black people gathered out in front shouting for revenge. King quelled their anger by saying, "We must learn to meet hate with love." With astonishing clarity of vision, King knew that reciprocating with violence would only hurt their cause. The boycott continued for more than a year, despite the financial hardship it caused for the bus company (since blacks were their biggest customers).

Finally, the U.S. Supreme Court intervened and declared segregation on buses to be illegal. King must have had a proud smile on his face when, on December 21, 1956, he sat in the front seat of a bus next to a white minister named Rev. Glen Smiley.

King had grabbed the moment and then held strong to his convictions. If you know your idea is right, don't give into naysayers—especially if you can say what Dr. King so eloquently said seven years later on the steps of the Lincoln Memorial: "I have a dream." *I guess that pretty much says it all.*

ANNA ELEANOR ROOSEVELT

When you hear the name Roosevelt you probably don't immediately think of Eleanor. But she had immense social impact, because she was responsible for setting a new and higher standard for the modern woman. She showed leadership and stood tall when people all around her were telling her to sit down and shut up.

For instance, on March 6, 1933, Eleanor Roosevelt became the first wife of a president to hold a press conference (she went on to hold over three hundred of them). From the beginning, she wisely restricted these confabs to women journalists, knowing full well that if news organizations wanted access to the First Lady, many would now be forced to hire their first female reporter. In another example, she made a powerful statement in 1939 when she defied segregation laws by sitting down not with the whites but with the blacks at the Southern Conference for Human Welfare in Birmingham, Alabama. On July 17, 1940, she became the first woman to give a speech at a national party convention—a speech that helped her husband, Franklin, win an unprecedented third term in office. And even after her husband died she kept right on going—in 1946 Eleanor Roosevelt was elected as head of the United Nations Human Rights Commission.

As her life shows, ideas aren't restricted to art or technology—they are initiatives that impact the human condition (and her example also teaches us that if you have connections, don't hesitate to use them). A prolific speaker and writer (and the mother of six children), Roosevelt once said, "I think, at a child's birth, if a mother could ask a fairy godmother to endow it with the most useful gift, that gift would be curiosity."

America today benefits from the engaged involvement of its entire population, thanks to the gutsy leadership of people like Eleanor Roosevelt.

5. INVEST THE EXTRA EFFORT TO PUSH YOUR VISION THROUGH

BILL GATES

How about Bill Gates's disk operating system (DOS) for computers? Talk about a guy who saw an opportunity. Gates was basically an electronics geek who wanted to get in on the development of computers. He and a guy named Paul Allen started a little company called "Micro-soft" and they had written some programming language and applications, but they really wanted to develop an operating system. Gates first approached Steve Jobs and Steve Wozniak of Apple Computer about licensing their disk operating system software (which was the current state of the art), but the two Steves were too busy developing and selling hardware (and also a bit too protective of their inventions) to fool with Gates.

In 1980, Gates approached Tim Paterson (a twenty-four-year-old local who could write code) of Seattle Computer Products, who had developed a QDOS ("quick and dirty operating system"). Paterson let him have the entire rights to it for $50,000 on a relatively informal promissory basis.

Gates somehow got IBM's attention, and they gave him the contract to deliver an operating system for IBM's new "personal computer" (the PC), a relatively small unit intended for use by businesses. Since IBM was focused more on hardware than on software, they thought it just fine to use someone else's operating system. After all, they thought, hardware had to be the best way to make money, and how many DOS products could anyone sell in a year? Gates really stuck his neck out saying he could deliver, even though he didn't yet have the system completed. Gates had to thrash for a few months to get some bugs out, and also to tailor his DOS to meet the specific needs of IBM's PC. Of course, along the way he renamed it Microsoft Disc Operating System (MS-DOS). He negotiated an unrestricted lease agreement that gave IBM unlimited use of the MS-DOS on their machines, but the true genius was that Gates was able to retain ownership of MS-DOS and then lease it to other computer companies on a per-PC basis. He has never sold his operating system outright. (Tim Paterson, who *had* sold his QDOS outright to Gates, didn't get a piece of the action. Instead, he went back to school to work on a business degree and later went to work for Microsoft.)

There is obviously plenty to be learned from Bill Gates's story. He is now one of the richest men in the world because he had a particular vision, chased it, wasn't afraid to approach the big guy, and had the guts to negotiate shrewdly.

THOMAS ALVA EDISON

Thomas Edison, famous for his electric-filament vacuum bulb, was a dreamer . . . also a bit of a schemer . . . and must have been one hell of a salesman. In 1878, he secured $30,000 of investment seed money up front (from a syndicate of leading financiers like J.P. Morgan and the Vanderbilts) to build his lab, so he could then invent his lightbulb. This is like getting someone today to give you over a half-million dollars (the amount Edison received converted for inflation) to help you develop your idea.

With the seed money, not only did he build himself this slick (but not too ostentatious) "world's first true research facility" (his words) to work in, but he also hired a staff to help him realize his ideas. I guess that's why he held a record number of patents (over one thousand) and spilled out countless ideas, like the first audio recording device (phonograph) and the moving picture camera and projector.

Interestingly, Edison didn't actually invent the lightbulb, but perfected it and, most important, developed an infrastructure of dynamos, fuses, and such that made it *practical* for home use. Edison even applied for a patent for his particular invention of the lightbulb in 1879, and it was subsequently invalidated. To give credit where credit is due, Heinrich Goebel, a German inventor, built some light-bulbs in 1854—and even though the bulbs burned for four hundred hours, he never patented them. Joseph Swan, a British inventor, obtained the first patent for a carbon-filament lightbulb in 1878. And James Woodward and Matthew Evans received a patent for a specific carbon-arc lightbulb in 1875—which Edison bought the rights to for $30K, plus royalties.

Edison set the standard for R&D, one that corporations today would be smart to emulate. Edison's think tank must have been a really exciting place to work. Henry Ford thought so too, since in 1929 he saw fit to move Edison's entire Menlo Park, New Jersey, laboratory piece by piece to his Greenfield Village Museum in Dearborn, Michigan. It's right down the street from the Wright brothers' bicycle shop, which Ford also purchased and had moved from Ohio.

What this particular case teaches us is that we mustn't be afraid to sell, sell, and sell in order to push our ideas through. We're all in marketing, whether we like it or not. And your most important product to sell is *yourself*—specifically as the champion behind your idea.

6. ESTABLISH THE REAL PROBLEM, TRY THINGS, LEARN YOUR CRAFT . . . ALL THE WHILE DOING YOUR HOMEWORK

SIR ROGER BANNISTER

How can a runner breaking the four-minute-mile barrier have anything to do with idea generation? Well, Roger Bannister didn't break it just by practicing hard. At the time, there were faster runners than Bannister, so he knew that if simply running faster were the answer, these faster runners would have already broken the barrier.

A medical student and therefore curious about the workings of the body, he began to investigate the true barriers to human speed. After some careful examination, he figured out that oxygenation was the problem. He deduced that the lungs weren't supplying enough oxygen to the blood to keep the muscles in the legs going fast enough, and long enough, to break the barrier.

So for over a year, Bannister worked on his breathing patterns and developed ways to expand his lung capacity, while also doing his general "legwork." It paid off on May 6, 1954, when he surprised the world by running a mile in 3:59.4 minutes.

Idea generation is typically linked to problem solving, so dig deep to deduce the base problem, as Roger Bannister did, and then have the guts to think outside the normal construct in search of the solution. Smart-thinking Sir Roger (knighted in 1975 for his services to neurology during his medical career) used his brain to figure out how to get more out of his lungs, so he could then get more out of his legs.

DR. JOHN HARVEY AND WILL KEITH KELLOGG

Two brothers running a sanitarium wanted to find cheap ways to provide good nutrition to their patients. One guy, a doctor, was a bit of a quack who believed that excellent nutrition reduced the desire to masturbate. *(Okaayyy. . . .)* But the other brother believed good nutrition is always a good idea, so they started experimenting with food products to create one that their patients would like.

After many trials, they had progressed as far as soaking some grain in water for a while, then boiling it, next mashing this mixture into mush, and then rolling it flat. As part of a failed experiment they let this sheet of mush sit out, and it of course dried out. They then figured they might as well try putting what they had in an oven, and amazingly it formed into these little roasted flakes (one per each kernel—kinda like the way a mud flat will dry up and crack into flakes).

Bingo! You can imagine the brothers saying things like "Let's see, something at room temperature is surely good, because then you wouldn't have to keep the food warm on a stove" and "Hmm, so it can now be easily stored dry, and moisture (like milk) can be added when it's served. Hey, maybe we're onto something here."

They applied for a patent on the process in 1884, and the brothers started to market their product as a health food. A whole breakfast food industry was started with this simple "flaky" idea. Again, like Bannister, John and Will Keith Kellogg first recognized the problem (even though John Kellogg's thinking was perhaps a wee bit unscientific), which then put them on a path to finding a solution.

In 1906, Will Keith Kellogg finally wrested control of the cereal company from his brother and then aggressively brought the cereal flakes into the mainstream. Early on, Will Keith even had the inspiration to run an advertisement that told people to please buy only one box, so that the production capacity of his Battle Creek Toasted Corn Flakes Company (later changed to Kellogg Company) could catch up to excessive demand. This was an absolutely brilliant move, since it made people only want the product even more.

Next time you pour some cereal flakes in a bowl, take a moment to appreciate the pure simplicity of what you're about to enjoy. Don't underestimate the power of a solution to a simple need.

PABLO DIEGO JOSÉ FRANCISCO DE PAULA JUAN NEPOMUCENO DE LOS REMEDIOS CRISPÍN CIPRIANO DE LA SANTÍSIMA TRINIDAD RUÍZ PICASSO

Pablo Picasso had immense talent (and a long name) and is known for his groundbreaking cubist paintings, but his early classical drawings are also simply magnificent. If you ever get to Barcelona, Spain, be sure to check out his old house that was turned into a museum. He left Spain due to his political differences with the then fascist dictator, Francisco Franco, and expatriated to Paris where the thinking was more open. But before Pablo could get his stuff out of Spain, Franco ordered the confiscation of his house and its contents (which also included most of his early works). There's a drawing of some pigeons in a park that has all the subtlety and technical excellence you'd expect from a drawing by Leonardo DaVinci. The early works of Picasso are a testament to how well he had learned his craft before he ventured off into his modern work. And boy, did he venture. Picasso's cubist work virtually rocked the art world, and even to this day his influence is seen. This tells us that it's a good idea to first diligently study and master the traditional aspects of your craft, so when you break the rules you'll do so in a more meaningful and skilled way. Picasso worked hard to achieve greatness.

Picasso is listed in the Guinness World Records as the "Most Prolific Painter" in that he is estimated to have produced about 13,500 paintings/designs; 100,000 prints or engravings; 34,000 illustrations for books; and 300 sculptures/ceramics. Prodigiously productive Pablo was also smart enough to have an excellent agent. His agent would cull through his work and release only a few choice paintings, sculptures, or lithographs at a time. This led to a higher perception of quality and produced a reasonable scarcity for his work, thus contributing to keeping the interest up (along with the prices). The "culled" work was warehoused and, after his death, is now being released for a cool profit by his heirs.

There's a good marketing lesson here regarding not flooding the market with your product. Price is always relative to availability versus scarcity (the old supply and demand curve).

7. BEG, BORROW, OR EVEN MAKE THE RIGHT TOOLS TO EXPRESS YOUR VISION

THE BEATLES

The Beatles changed popular music because they were four cute guys with a great rock 'n' roll beat, a catchy name for their band, charming English accents, and trendsetting haircuts—and on top of all that they were accomplished musicians and awesome lyricists. But what truly set their music apart was their expansive use of multi-track recording. It used to be that a recording was cut on a single track as everyone in a group performed at the same time. Audio recording took a big jump to using four tracks on the tape where the artists were now allowed to perform in multiple passes and mix the layers of voice and accompaniment to create a richer and fuller sound. But a technological paradigm shifted in 1967, partially driven by the creative demands of The Beatles' *Sergeant Pepper's Lonely Hearts Club Band* album. Ken Townsend, a sound engineer, stepped beyond the limitations that even four-track recording imposed and invented Artificial Double-Tracking (ADT), a system whereby two four-track machines could be linked together. This new eight-track sound was geometrically more intricate as each separate track could be synced, manipulated, leveled, distorted, or whatever. As the industry progressed, recording studios went on to increase the tracks to sixteen, then twenty four, and so on (and now, because of the use of computers, the tracks and combinations are virtually endless).

Sure, the Beatles had an awesome package, as mentioned above, but the creative freedom made possible by ADT multi-track technology allowed these musical geniuses to break new ground, and do it faster.

New technology scares most people, but aren't you glad the four lads from Liverpool were fearless in their pursuit of a new sound? The lesson here is to stick your neck out to find the necessary tools to express your ideas, even if these tools are new and unproven.

TABITHA BABBIT

The Shakers were master craftspeople who brought woodworking almost to the level of a religious experience. You see, the Shakers believed that you could reach perfection through hard work, and that new ideas were gifts from God to all of mankind. This work ethic and belief led the Shakers to develop the clothespin, propeller (water-screw), waterproof fabric, corn-straw "whisk" broom, cut nails, and even the "clothes-mill" washing machine. However, woodworking always remained an integral part of Shaker life (most of what survives from the Shakers is their superbly crafted, and now eminently collectible, wood furniture).

Now, before 1814, if you wanted to cut up a log into boards you had to use a straight saw. This meant that a guy at one end of the saw was in a pit underneath the log, while another guy at the other end of the saw sat perched above it on a scaffold. This was difficult, unsafe, and messy work. Then one day a Shaker named Sister Tabitha Babbit was doing some spinning on her wheel when it occurred to her that a disc with saw teeth around its circumference would make sawing boards much easier. The circular saw blade was born, making the production of wood products so much easier, speeding along the building of America's burgeoning cities. Babbit was open to this kind of visionary thinking because Shakers believed in working toward the betterment of all humankind without regard to personal gain. This selflessness was good *and* bad, as the Shakers never patented anything, and everything they did was offered to everyone, and therefore the rights instantly entered into the public domain. (Note: they also believed that celibacy was more honorable than marriage—this obviously hurt their group's propagation; and that all men and women were equal, regardless of race—pretty enlightened for the 1800s.) Unfortunately, the whole Shaker experiment caved in around the turn of the century after only 100 years; apparently from a lack of funds and new members.

Anyway, wouldn't you like to hold the patent on something like the clothespin or circular saw blade? And I guess it would be safe to say that Maytag never offered any Shaker a royalty.

Beyond telling us that an open selflessness is quite helpful in idea generation, in that it encouraged Babbit's free-association in the search for innovation, it is also a lesson that if you don't protect your ideas with patents, and then fight to protect your rights to them, you can expect them to quickly revert to the public domain.

8. SERENDIPITY MAY STRIKE AT ANY MOMENT, SO BE RECEPTIVE

SIR ALEXANDER FLEMING

Let's talk about recognizing opportunities. In 1928, a Scottish-born scientist, Alexander Fleming, in the course of his experiments to find a bacteria killer, was growing a germ in a Petri dish. When he went on vacation he left the dish uncovered on a counter. It turned out that while he was gone, a cold spell in London produced a temperature profile that was perfect for incubating his experiment. Upon his return, he noticed that a speck of dust had fallen into the dish, and that there was something different about the speck—it seemed to interrupt the growth of the germ. It turned out that the dust was an errant airborne mold spore (a rare strain named *Penicillium notatum* that had somehow drifted in from a mycology lab, which was one floor below) that caused what is now called an antibiotic reaction.

That little discovery led to the development of penicillin, the wonder drug that, since it was first injected into a human in 1941, has clearly saved more lives and reduced more misery than any single discovery in the history of humankind. Sadly, even though he won a Nobel Prize, and was knighted, few people in America remember the name of the scientist who so profoundly changed our lives.

The message here is that we should always open our minds to opportunities and ideas, even if they seem to fall from the sky.

CHARLES MENCHES

Serendipity is great, but you have to respond to it when it happens. In 1904, at the World's Fair in St. Louis, an ice cream vendor, Charles Menches, just happened to have his stand next to a vendor, Ernest A. Hamwi, who was selling *zalabis* (a Middle Eastern wafer-thin waffle with syrup on top). It was a scorcher of a day, and the ice-cream vendor ran out of throwaway dishes. Not wanting to lose business while waiting for more dishes to arrive, he asked the waffle vendor to roll some waffles into a cornucopia shape, so as to hold his ice cream. The ice cream cone was born—a simple, cheap, and edible container.

There were more than forty ice cream vendors at the fair, along with the man who held the patent on edible *cups,* Italo Marchiony, an Italian American from New York. Italo was an ice cream vendor on Wall Street who had gotten tired of people walking away with his bowls. In 1896, he made a wooden mold, took an Italian *pizzelle* (a wafer-thin, vanilla-or-anise-flavored waffle), and, just after removing it from the waffle iron (while it was still warm and pliable), draped it over the mold and let it cool. In this way, he made simple, cheap, and edible cups for serving ice cream. He patented the idea in 1903. Very possibly Menches was "inspired" by Marchiony's edible ice cream cups when he created his patent-skirting cornucopia-shaped cones. It's funny how fast ideas evolve when there's money to be made. Whatever the case, Menches had the good sense to take advantage of a serendipitous opportunity, and he changed the way we eat ice cream. *Yum.*

9. LOOK AT WHAT'S REALLY GOING ON AROUND YOU, AND ASK WHY? WHY? WHY?

THE MCDONALD BROTHERS AND RAY KROC

Dick and Mac McDonald ran a little hamburger stand in San Bernardino, California. They stored the potatoes they used for french fries in an old shed with chicken-wire bins that, along with the desert winds, caused the potatoes to cure a bit. This curing effect allowed the deep-fat fryer to do its magic better. People lined up to buy these yummy fries (and the typically accompanying burger and malt), and this incessant demand forced the brothers to figure out ways to get their food out faster and faster. However, the brothers were too busy to see what they were sitting on, so Ray Kroc, an enterprising fifty-two-year-old blender sales-man, was the person who studied their operation to deduce what was going on.

Kroc figured out what it was that contributed to making their fries so irre-sistible, and searched out a way to replicate the curing process in a large factory. He packaged it all up and took their great fries and the faster, faster, faster food idea (spawned by the demand for those delicious fries) into the world of fran-chising.

Sometimes a big idea is as close as the shed out back. And quite often the people who have a big idea really don't know what to do with it. My advice: every so often, take a few moments to get your bearings, because a real-deal idea may be right under your nose. And a good friend, especially if he or she's a smart sales-person, might help you see the idea that may be "hidden" in plain sight.

ROBERT NOYCE AND TED HOFF

So it goes that in 1968 Robert Noyce, after inventing the integrated circuit, left Fairchild Semiconductor (a company he cofounded in 1957) and joined up with fellow engineer Gordon Moore to form their own company. A Japanese customer, Busicom, presented their new company with a problem. They wanted to build a calculator that had twelve functions. At that time, the current wisdom was that each function required a custom dedicated chip, and to make twelve chips was a serious dilemma, because chips were quite expensive to develop and produce.

It was a mighty tall order for Noyce and Moore's fledgling company. Noyce sat down with Marcian E. "Ted" Hoff, an engineer, and laid out the problem. Noyce was known for having a casual work style and always gave employees a lot of latitude (but not without responsibility) to create. Hoff went to work and came up with the general idea to develop some kind of processing switch that could perform all twelve operations using only one integrated circuit. He had figured out that silicon-gated technology might make a single-chip central processing unit (CPU) feasible. He was the first person to recognize such a possibility. The concept of a chip expanded at that moment from a single-function circuit to a multitasking microprocessor "brain."

Ted, working with Fredrico Faggin and Stan Mazor, developed a slick-little microprocessor that did the trick. On November 15, 1971, they announced a four-bit microprocessor that contained the equivalent of twenty-three hundred transistors, which made sixty thousand interactions per second. Along the way, Noyce figured they were on to something big and cleverly bought back the entire rights to the chip from Busicom for $60,000. Now, the question became what else could be done with this neat, little device, so Bob showed and shopped it around. It was all about on/off . . . or Xs/Os (later known as "0/1") to the explosive future world of these new "microprocessors" (né: computers). *With apologies to Longfellow: "From that tiny chip, a mighty industry grew."*

Oh, by the way, the company he and Moore started in 1968 was called Intel. From their website: "Twenty-five years later, the microprocessor is the most complex mass-produced product ever, with more than 5.5 million transistors performing hundreds of millions of calculations each second."

Oh, as far as Busicom, they went bankrupt in 1972.

Idea generation often takes off in an unexpected direction, almost all by itself. As it is often said, life rewards action.

(And if all of the above wasn't confusing enough, Jack Kilby, of Texas Instruments, concurrently developed an integrated circuit that he put in the first handheld calculator. Kilby actually beat Robert Noyce to the patent office with his version by about five months, but years of wrangling in court led them to share the license.)

ED ISKENDERIAN

It's hard to believe that a grungy hot-rodder could have started something that changed marketing forever. But Ed Iskenderian, nicknamed the "Camfather," known for being part engineer, part magician, part artist, and all-around mechanical genius, did just that.

The scene was post-World War II California. Early hot-rodders, in search of more speed for their rod, beat a path to his shop to get one of Iskenderian's special "Isky" camshafts. His pioneering "grinds" (as the lobe pattern is called) altered the engine's valve timing and let more atomized gasoline into the cylinder, which contributed to making more power.

These hot-rodders who showed up at his shop had established, as an extension of their renegade personas, a style of dress that flouted the button-down-collared shirt establishment: white undershirts and blue dungarees (now known as T-shirts and blue jeans). In the late 1950s, with a handshake deal, Iskenderian put his company's name in big letters on the side of "Big Daddy" Don Garlits's race car, creating the first corporate sponsorship of a race operation. And, as Ed was constantly looking for ways to make his name known, he was one of the first businessmen to print a company logo on one of these hepcat-cool white undershirts everyone around him seemed to be wearing. He then had Garlits's pit crew members wear these shirts during the meets all across America. In a desire to be associated with Garlits's "world's-fastest dragster," the fans started asking to buy the shirts off the backs of the pit crew members. Of course, one thing led to another, and the logo T-shirt became an indelible part of American culture.

Hard to believe as you walk through a mall today that everyone didn't always wear T-shirts, and that there weren't always logos on them—and amazingly, there was a time when race cars weren't plastered with a plethora of sponsor's stickers.

Like Iskenderian, be on the lookout for an artful way to associate your idea with a trend, and be ready to act when the opportunity presents itself. Thanks in part to Iskenderian's pioneering efforts, Nike now gets something like $18 (at retail) for a $2 white T-shirt with its trademark "swoosh" logo on it.

INSATIABLE CURIOSITY AND A DOGGED TENACITY ARE THE REAL-DEAL IDEA'S BEST FRIENDS

So what's the take-away from all this? It comes down to the fact that developing something truly innovative isn't all that easy a task, and three things must happen for the idea to become the real deal.

First, whether in a big corporation or a ma-and-pa start-up, the "singular vision"—the initial spark—must be recognized and championed.

Second, since simply having an idea isn't the end-all and be-all, the process of idea generation usually involves some artful collaboration. And, along the way, the problem and task must be clearly delineated and not capriciously messed with by the people involved. Of course, the careful tweaking and evolution of any idea must be allowed, but the pursuit must remain clear and focused to the task and vision.

Third, if you are in search of new ideas, it is of utmost importance that you constantly watch for the idea that may capture the collective imagination and have real and lasting impact—and expect that what you're looking for will be a "1 per-center." After all, if innovation was so easy, everyone would be doing it—and as a result real-deal ideas wouldn't be so exceptionally rare.

But, by all means, never give up hope: true innovation is not all that impossible—it's just that the search is circuitous and the process complex. You, the reader, are already way ahead in the game—your curiosity is your single best resource in the search for the real-deal idea. Couple that with a healthy dose of tenacity, and you'll be flying before you know it. *Yeeeeeeee!*

CHAPTER 3

OLD HOLLYWOOD ADAGE:

"IF IT ISN'T A NEW IDEA, IT HAD BETTER BE A DAMN GOOD ONE."

Every enterprise pretty much starts with someone saying something like "I think I can build a better mouse trap" (product) or at least "I think I can offer a better way to rid the world of rodents" (service). This raises the question, How *new* does a new idea have to be in order to be the real deal, and how does the intricate process of advancing that particular innovation play out in the marketplace?

PROVING A NEW IDEA FIRST IN BUSINESS AND THEN IN THE MARKET (AND IS WHAT YOU HAVE NEW ENOUGH TO SUSTAIN GROWTH?)

A company typically starts out with an idea or dream, some fearless passion, and a rudimentary plan—and at its base a relatively egocentric perspective. The classic romantic notion is put forth. In the case of Walt Disney, he believed he could come up with a better cartoon than anything else that was in the marketplace at the time. His notion that he could beat Oswald the Lucky Rabbit and Felix the Cat (both distributed by Charles Mintz) was a lofty one. The key here is that if one applies too much logic at this early stage, the venture may falter, since pure logic may not apply to these first tottering steps into the game. In other words, if Walt had thought about it, he really didn't have the wherewithal to take on Mintz and Universal Pictures. He was dreaming. The first step is to have a clear idea and believe strongly that you can make that idea a reality. It is not all that imperative that the idea be totally new, but more that it has the potential to improve on what's been done before. If you look at a drawing of Oswald the Lucky Rabbit you can pretty much see how Disney and Iwerks evolved it into their mouse, but more important, Walt added an underdog persona . . . and serendipitously a sound track.

Wide-eyed enthusiasm will next propel the company into areas that will need to be addressed as they arise. This progresses into a trial by fire, which should lead the company to develop plans that become more formalized. Tough decisions must be made now to properly marshal resources and secure venture capital. Expect a good amount of tension at this point of the game, especially if you're wrestling with a real-deal idea; this is the point where some tough honesty must enter the picture, but not so much as to dilute the essence of the idea and reduce it to mush. Thankfully, Walt had his brother Roy picking up the pieces behind him during this stage of the game.

It will actually be quite amazing if the product actually reaches production, establishes and returns a decent margin of profit, and is able to find success in the marketplace. So many things will conspire against its success, such as distribution headaches, cost overruns, liability issues, and the exorbitant marketing costs involved in launching a new product. You can easily have a hit on your hands, with no profit left in the till. Walt's biggest ally in getting his idea through all these headaches was his astounding tenacity.

The next step is growing and then sustaining the share of the market you're in. You can never rest. For example, Walt, Ub, Roy, and company had to start cranking 'em out. Not just more Mickey Mouse cartoon shorts, but adding characters to the stable. Early on, he added a girlfriend Minnie; an ingenious hound, Pluto, as a sidekick to Mickey; a dim-witted foil, Goofy; and, a star in his own right, Donald Duck. Cranking away with breakthrough animation to the point of the full-length features *Snow White, Fantasia,* and beyond.

If you're phenomenally lucky and the business is an absolute roaring success, you may not have to make an initial public offering (IPO) of stock in order to generate enough cash flow to keep things going. (An IPO typically makes the officers of the company quite rich [at least on paper], as their wealth is locked up in shares of common stock that they can't sell for three to twenty-four months.) This is the point at which the company's innovation can easily unravel, because the focus can easily change to creating a buzz for the stock so it will appreciate, instead of working to grow the company for the future and responding to the needs of the consumer. If restraint and foresight are not applied, quick-fix short-term goals can become the focus. The long-term plans that some particular ideas may need in order to properly evolve into outstanding products or services can be compromised at this stage of the game. As we've discussed, once you're a public company the focus can change from responding to the marketplace to then responding more to the stockholders, which can compromise your new initiatives if they aren't quick profit makers.

This is also the point where the hard work of carefully developing a product or service to its potential can easily be overwhelmed by "idea killers" (see chapter 6). They take many guises, from an overt focus on cost-engineering (making the product as cheap as it can be) or operational implementation (a service as cheap as it can be), to easy-sell proposals, or the need to do things that lead to good press-release fodder (generating sound bites that sound good to Wall Street). In other words, the sincere work task becomes subordinated to that which appeals to a potential stock buyer, which will then lead to more buying pressure, which pushes up the stock price—and the wealth of everyone who holds the stock.

Unfortunately, this scenario favors the producer of high-profit-margin software or soft goods over the small-profit-margin production of hardware or hard goods. In doing so it also tends to subjugate any new initiative that may require a lot of R&D. Let's take T-shirts, for instance. To produce a high-quality cotton T-shirt, you'd need cotton-growing farms, shipping infrastructures, fabric mills, inventory control, storage, assembly and sewing production, sales, and distribution. In a worse case scenario (which isn't all the rare these days, especially when you factor in overseas competition), the producer of T-shirts could easily not have a nickel left over in profit. On the other hand, companies like Nike can buy such a shirt for less than $3, then screenprint/embroider its logo on it, and sell it for something like $10 at wholesale (which then equates to something like $18 at retail). Isn't it obvious which side of this equation you'd like to be on?

Of course, Nike has to keep up its brand's visibility by doing plenty of promotion. But it is remarkable that consumers pay extra for a shirt with a company's promotional logo on it, because as they wear it around town they actually further promote the brand, which, in turn, helps the company sell more shirts like it. To promote the brand even more, the company uses the profits from selling the shirts to pay someone like Tiger Woods tons of money to also wear a shirt with the logo on it. The consumer ends up paying much more for something that is hype (the logo) than for something that is real (the T-shirt itself).

The whole market dynamic seems to be skewed toward supporting certain quick-return ideas (like licensing) that don't necessarily add value to or advance the human condition. Ultimately this will create a situation where money instead of real innovation becomes king. Fewer and fewer investors want to put their money into hard goods like plain T-shirts, especially when the money to be made isn't close to what can be made from plastering a cool logo on them.

No business or marketplace can prosper for long on simply the quick-buck schemes. In other words, the marketplace needs more than just *more* stuff like Mickey Mouse T-shirts—it needs new, real-deal ideas. Even Nike started out with an idea to evolve the sneaker, which led to a breakthrough running shoe in response to a need in the marketplace. Like Mickey Mouse, it was a new enough idea to initiate amazing growth. So the idea doesn't have to be all-new, but for any growth to happen it must be fresh and innovative.

WHAT'S THE BIG DEAL IF SCROOGE MCDUCK TAKES OVER?

So what's going on at The Walt Disney Company these days, relative to delivering damn-good ideas (new or otherwise) to the marketplace? To start with, Walt Disney set in place an organization that has had an amazing track record of offering innovation in family entertainment. He truly understood what it meant to deliver a high-quality experience that was an all-around good value. He knew the movie-goer/guest/viewer would respond to damn-good ideas whether they were totally all-new or not. He would also humbly under-promise and over-deliver.

To see what's currently going on at Disney, let's compare *Snow White and the Seven Dwarfs* with *Toy Story*. *Snow White* was a masterpiece that has made Disney multimillions of dollars in release, re-release, and video/DVD release. Walt Disney had learned his lessons early, and so he went out of his way to own everything, right down to Dopey. Michael Eisner got immense credit and Disney made huge profits by taking an entire library of classic Disney films, like *Snow White and the Seven Dwarfs*, off the shelf and re-releasing them on video (and now, also on DVD). It isn't that tough to run off a bunch of copies, put them in a slick plastic box, all for less than a few bucks, and then retail them for $15 to $20.

On the other hand, aiming to cut overhead with the intention of increasing profits, Eisner now seems enamored with outsourcing. Why produce in-house? Why maintain those costly and difficult artistic types? Why not just use outside suppliers to deliver the high-quality animated product and then co-slap your name on it? Starting in the 1990s, Disney began a progression of laying off more and more animators, ultimately leading to Disney shuttering "Secret Lab," their in-house Computer Generated Imagery (CGI) facility in 2001. The Scrooge McDuck bean counters probably figured it was cheaper to metaphorically sell a big chunk of the farm and let someone else bear all the headaches of creating a hard product, and then Disney could concentrate on the real moneymakers of marketing, distribution, and licensing.

With this thought, Disney and Pixar teamed up to do *Toy Story*. Steve Jobs, of Pixar, negotiated a deal, somewhat lopsided in Disney's favor, because his new company needed their distribution and marketing power. Five days after *Toy Story* hit the theater screens, Pixar went public with an IPO—the biggest of 1995. I would guess that Disney was a little surprised that their little friend had suddenly grown up, although they put out some PR spin saying that everything was OK, because Disney had a contract for Pixar's next six films. But what would happen after the contract runs out? (Think about this: What if Ford Motor Company decided to stop making cars so they could just concentrate on distribution, financing, and marketing? How long would it be before they were on the ropes?)

Now, with the deal running out, Pixar probably doesn't feel they have to re-up because they don't need Disney anymore. *Now* who has the power? Disney desperately needs the breakthrough product (since their in-house feature animation studio is but a shadow of its former self), but Pixar can now leave to find a better distribution deal. It looks like The Walt Disney Company seems to have forgotten the lesson that Walt Disney learned from Oswald the Rabbit versus Mickey Mouse: the distributor can win in the short term, but the producer of the high-quality product will usually have the upper hand in the long run. Unless Disney wises up, the situation will evolve to the point where they need the Pixars of the world more than the Pixars will need Disney.

I guess this is all an outgrowth of how Disney absolutely loves partnering with companies, and they've had many fruitful collaborations, but of late it's becoming more common to hear from some of their partners how difficult Disney is to work with. I would guess that in up front negotiations they are quite good at rubbing Disney's warm and fuzzy reputation all over the discussions. But behind all the yakity-yak and hand waving of the details, the tough Disney executives pretty much expect to get a lopsided deal that will work in their favor. They may have forgotten that in order for a partnership to work, both sides must benefit, but for some reason, probably good old greed, Disney doesn't seem to be as willing these days to "play fair" in these partnering situations. It's possible that the Disney heads feel that even if they burn out one partner there will always be another waiting in the wings. This aggressive posture may work for switching around cola or ice cream suppliers, but it can get very complicated when a whole resort complex, like Disneyland Resort Paris, struggles to get healthy, partly because the deal wasn't on a healthy footing from the get go. A classic case of how difficult it is to negotiate with Disney is playing out, as of this writing, between Disney and Pixar. What was once a sweet deal for all concerned has turned into a couple of billionaire CEOs trading acrimonious barbs in the press. For instance, Eisner jabbed at Jobs in front of a group of Wall Street analysts attending a Disney conference in Orlando, Florida, saying in feigned praise, "He created the computer, or at least Windows, or whatever he created, and did a good job." Jobs has said more serious things, like "Not even Disney's marketing and brand could turn Disney's last two animated films, *Treasure Planet* and *Brother Bear,* into successes. Both bombed at the box office." He's also said, "We feel sick about Disney doing sequels because if you look at the quality of their sequels, like *The Lion King 1-1/2, Peter Pan* sequels and stuff, it is pretty embarrassing."

Even McDonald's now wants to revamp its long-standing deal with Disney. From a *Los Angeles Times* article of June 14, 2004: "They get locked into whatever Disney decides to lock them into" said Dick Adams, a consultant to five hundred McDonald's franchisees. In the same article, it said that about half of their Happy Meals are tied to a Disney film, video, TV show, or theme park, and they're getting tired of being forced to promote flops like Disney's *The Emperor's New Groove* and *Treasure Planet.*

Disney may have a problem on its hands in the future, since potential new partners could get wise to all this and simply stay away, or make increasing demands up front. The point is that if fresh ideas are to be generated, the atmosphere must be open and free and, in the case of partnerships, mutually beneficial. From what I've seen, a closed and confrontational environment will ultimately kill the good ideas and ultimately benefit no one, especially in the long term.

How did Disney get so blindsided? Bean-counter greed seems to be the only explanation for it. The state of affairs deteriorated to the point where a head bean counter went along with the deep cuts because he wanted to keep his or her job. Thereafter, the shareholders and stock option holders, like Eisner, also went along with the cuts because they increased profits, and so helped the stock price to go up, creating a nice little chain of greed.

So why didn't this happen in Walt Disney's day? First, he was pouring the profits back into the company, not taking them out in a gigantic salary with bonus. Second, Walt knew how to get the most out of his artists because he, being an artist himself, knew intimately where these creative-types were coming from. Eisner is not specifically a creative person, and as such he has had to rely on those messy creative-types to bring ideas to him, so it probably looked like a good idea to him to outsource the creative process and avoid the turmoil of it all.

Obviously, outsourcing results in layoffs—some serious ones in this case. Unfortunately, the fear of losing one's job usually results in one of two paths: if you're any good, you've probably got other options—and you leave; if not, you get into playing cover your ass (CYA) games to protect your position. In this type of atmosphere, who's going to dare to rock the boat?

Quite a few of the folks in and around Hollywood, and even some inside the organization, think creativity is being compromised at Disney. "All the great executives have been driven from the company," said Harvey Weinstein, the cochairman of Miramax Films (a studio owned by Disney since 1993). "I think there is no camaraderie anymore, no great esprit de corps that I found earlier. I think there was more risk-taking, a more fun company. I don't know why, and it's sad that it is." And if that wasn't enough, of course, disenfranchised ex-Disney Board member Roy E. Disney has something to add, "The drain of talent over the past several years from the company's feature animation department in Orlando, Burbank, Paris, and Tokyo has been absolutely gut-wrenching. People are being asked to leave because management—particularly Michael—can't figure out what to do with them."

SEQUELS, RETREADS, REMAKES, REPLICAS, AND OTHER NON-IDEAS, OR "LET'S GET LIGHTNING TO STRIKE TWICE IN THE SAME SPOT"

In the movie business, or even the advertising business, having *real* ideas that move people to spend their hard-earned money can make one very, very rich. Movie studio moguls, like Eisner, are paid ridiculous amounts of money to recognize a real-deal idea when they see one. In my meetings with him, it was clear to me that Eisner knows an idea when he sees it. When not distracted, he can be a laser-quick study with an exceptional ability to tap into his gut feelings.

The trouble is, not many fresh ideas seem to be percolating up to him (all the cuts in R&D sure haven't helped this situation). It's probably hard for him to tap into something that isn't necessarily there. Also, just like most other studio heads today, he is pretty much asking for sure bets, which means he is getting a steady stream of proposals for sequels, retreads, and remakes. But within this low-risk scenario, the best they can hope for is fewer losers, and definitely *not* more big winners—at least as far as the moviegoers/guests/viewers are concerned.

Hollywood absolutely loves, and lives for, the "lightning strike"—a block-buster hit that has money simply pouring in. Because most studios only put out a few movies a year (among all their operations [distributing through Buena Vista and Miramax], Disney puts out roughly twenty theatrical releases yearly—and they're in the process of cutting back on this quantity), they hope and pray for (and desperately need) at least one huge blockbuster movie, in order to cover their duds. Because it's so hard to predict whether a movie will be a hit or a flop, the studios have to use a hit-and-miss approach: get enough product out there and maybe get lucky with one or two per year. (Sort of like dating in a way—the proverbial kiss-a-lot-of-frogs-to-find-a-prince situation.)

A movie takes a ridiculous amount of money to produce, and typically at least double that amount to promote and market it. A studio hopes to recover at least the production and marketing costs in the domestic box office release, so that the revenue from merchandising, the overseas box office revenues, and video/DVD sales will then be pure-profit "gravy." Disney and Universal receive the added revenue from the use of their proprietary characters, themes, and music from their movies in their theme parks.

When lightning strikes with a movie, everyone in show business flocks to the source to see what they can learn from it. A movie sequel or spin-off is an obvious opportunity. It's so much easier to get a green light when you're pushing a sequel or spin-off, since studios know marketing a sequel is eminently easier because they can trade off of the equity of the original. However, they still need the frickin' original movie in order to sell the sequels. Many studios have forgotten how important it is for the sequels to be entertaining and not simply follow the for-mula of the first film (as it's said in Hollywood, the last sequel of the series is the one the movie studio shouldn't have made). Generally, the basic idea that held viewer interest in the first rendition has been run into the ground by sequel two or three.

Eisner may have established a gauntlet that almost forces the divisions to go with products that are "in the system" and therefore will be an easy sell to the multiple corporate levels. Spin-offs and rehashes like Hong Kong Disneyland, *The Lion King* on Broadway (and, soon to come, *Mary Poppins*), and 2003's *Freaky Friday* all make sense as long as you *also* have some new innovative product coming down the pipeline behind them. In order to be successful, Eisner needs to formulate the following challenge to The Walt Disney Company as a whole: "Let's first see innovation, and *then* let's talk replication."

Lawrence Kasdan, a very successful screenwriter (*Star Wars: Episode V—The Empire Strikes Back, Indiana Jones and the Raiders of the Lost Ark, The Bodyguard*, and others) and writer/director (*The Big Chill, Silverado, The Accidental Tourist*, and others), with whom I had the pleasure to be teamed with at an advertising agency early in our careers, bemoaned the fact that even though he has a track record of delivering new original hits, most studios ask him for spin-offs of his work. This is certainly a compliment to the quality of his work, but it doesn't exactly encourage new thinking.

So what's going on? By and large, any scriptwriter working nowadays is forced to think of movie number two before number one is even out of the laser printer. Plus, he or she has to factor in demographics (teens are big moviegoers), internal product placement (extra bucks to be made there), co-op marketing efforts (cuts down on marketing expenditures), merchandising (licensing deals bring in millions), and the draw power of a star (pick the star first, and then back him or her into the script). You'd think such parameters would effectively tie the writer's hands. Well, they do. Before the computer even gets turned on, the writer today can be burdened with the conditions that the movie have a plush doll, a can of Pepsi, a BMW sports car, a cool logo for a T-shirt, an action-packed teen theme (with hopes of a video-game spin off), a music soundtrack marketable enough for a CD release, a marquee-level star to help promote it, *and* the potential for at least one sequel.

But all that stuff is just fluff if it doesn't have a great idea (story line and script) behind it. That's why so many movies are made that appear to have the right stuff but formulaically only have the right *fluff*. Such a movie won't excite the audience and put butts in seats at the cineplex. We've all seen movies with painfully average scripts that had great actors, great special effects, and great photography but were still flops. When a studio's profit margin is held up as paramount, what you often get is mediocre thinking, which equates to mediocre movies. To create a fresh, original work, the creative person should begin with a blank piece of paper, not a list of items that he or she must work into the script. When the focus is on marketing opportunities, then the result is often mush, not brilliance.

A non-Hollywood example of over-replication is the franchising of the Disneyland theme park worldwide, to the detriment of the original Disneyland. If you constantly replicate something, sooner or later it's not special. It may work with fads that reach saturation quickly, like Beanie Babies and Razor push scooters, since after the fad has run its course you quickly cease production and then unload what's left in the warehouse at a deep discount. But with a real property like Disneyland Paris and the surrounding hotels, you can end up with an empty park and empty hotel rooms—and boy, do profits disappear fast, given the overhead of keeping them up.

The "suits" in the business world may talk like they're sticking their necks out, but in reality what they're typically doing is a masterful job of hedging their bets. There aren't many people these days who are willing to take risks like Walt Disney did so many times during his career. And it's too bad, because there is something about risk that helps promote a clear vision for the project. As the head of a creative department, I always looked for the clear idea in a piece of creative work, and for the person with a razor-sharp vision of how the finished piece would turn out. Taking a risk on that vision may have been a little scary, but it was usually worth it.

BIG OR SMALL, AN IDEA'S GOTTA BE THE REAL DEAL

Must every idea be as big a breakthrough as the lightbulb (now a symbol for an idea itself) or the Kitty Hawk flier (which spurred the expression "take a flier," synonymous with "take a risk")? Of course not. Ideas don't have to be gigantic or totally new to be worthwhile, but they must be innovative to have any impact. Let's take situation comedies (sitcoms). In their sitcom *I Love Lucy,* Lucille Ball and Desi Arnaz added a nice twist to the three-camera formula that had just come into vogue, initiated by the successful TV show *Truth or Consequences.* This new format consisted of running three *live-TV* (kinescope) cameras at the same time; with one camera used for close-ups, a second focused on a medium shot, and the third used for the wide shot. This method gave the technicians in the booth some options for shot selection, which obviously made for a more dynamic and visually interesting show.

Desi Arnaz took the idea one step further: his idea was to use three film cameras for shooting *I Love Lucy* and actually *record* the show on film for possible sale in other countries (Arnaz, originally from Cuba, was considering distribution in Latin America). With a live audience in attendance, they would shoot the show in sequence and get a tight, medium, and wide shot with each performance, picking the appropriate shot later in editorial. The format also allowed for more spontaneity, and it gave Ball, with her immense talent, the chance to play off of a live audience. Because of the use of film and its processing, the production costs were obviously going to be higher than for an ordinary show, but Ball and Arnaz were willing to take a pay cut in order to offset this, on the one condition that they would retain 100 percent of the rights to the recorded programs. However, they weren't able to get anybody to buy into their idea of recording the show on film; CBS and the sponsors couldn't see any advantages to this method. So the couple started a production studio of their own in order to make it happen. They had to gamble almost every nickel they had, but as mentioned, they felt it was worth it as long as their Desi-Lu Productions retained the rights to the recorded shows.

The first *I Love Lucy* show, produced by Desi-Lu, aired on CBS on October 15, 1951. After a successful first season, Lucy became pregnant and the producers were forced to run ten prerecorded episodes (starting with episode five); as a result, on October 20, 1952, the rerun was born. To Ball and Arnaz's everlasting credit, the money is still rolling in for the owners of the 179 episodes, as people the world over continue to watch the reruns today. The great idea in this example is that Ball and Arnaz took great comedic showmanship, executional technique, and negotiation skills, and combined these with brilliant forward thinking.

The sitcom genre isn't new, but many companies have since taken the format and three-camera technique and produced outstanding comedies (obviously, all now dutifully recorded). Norman Lear's *All in the Family,* Jerry Seinfeld and Larry David's *Seinfeld,* and basically all sitcoms pay homage to Ball and Arnaz's pioneering effort. The artistic success of these new sitcoms was due to the fact that the producers made their shows better than what had come before. Each show added a dimension that captured the imagination of the viewer. Take *Seinfeld*'s quirky focus on the mundane—the show was about "nothing," so just imagine the pressure such a limited subject matter put on the writers each week. It's hard work to do something fresh, but they managed to do it each week. As a testament to the success of the sitcom genre, Jerry Seinfeld has a mind-boggling vintage Porsche collection, and Norman Lear has a thirty-car parking "garage" at his house—all because they added a creative dimension to an existing genre. The idea of adding solid creativity to what has gone before is a very good one—as long as you add to it, not just replicate it.

WHAT ABOUT THE AD BIZ? ISN'T IT ALL A BUNCH OF BS?

The ad business has an important role to play in the marketplace, especially when you're selling an idea or product that isn't necessarily totally new. Without appropriate marketing, your bright idea may forever be hidden under a bushel basket.

Look at how Coca-Cola became successful, for example. At one time, there was a cola-type drink that was actually bigger than Coca-Cola. It was called Moxie, and it was so big that its brand name entered the vernacular, meaning "courage combined with inventiveness." The people in charge at Moxie decided that they could rest on their laurels, and they drastically cut back on their advertising budget. This allowed Coca-Cola to grab a giant hunk of Moxie's market share, one that Coke has aggressively protected ever since. The consumers were willing to trade one refreshing caramel-colored sweet-flavored fizzy water for another. From this we can learn that, unless an idea is truly unique (like a car that runs on tap water, or a great-tasting chocolate that causes consumers to shed weight instead of gaining it), you can expect to have to fight for your place in the market, and in the consumer's fickle heart and mind. It is wrongheaded to think "If we build it they will come" (paraphrasing a classic line from the movie *Field of Dreams*).

An effective commercial is akin to a joke well told. As a viewer, you are fed the setup, the conflict, and then the wrap-up or punch line. This doesn't mean that all commercials are funny; it's just that the creatives have a short time (usually thirty seconds—or much less, since the viewer has the option of hitting the remote) to engage the viewer's attention, establish the dilemma, and then hit the viewer with the "you gotta add this to your shopping list" resolution. As David Ogilvy, who wrote the book on advertising, said, "If it doesn't sell, it isn't creative."

In a print ad, you may have a little more time or room to get the "sell" across, but if at first you don't get the reader's attention with a visually interesting graphic, layout, or typographic treatment that delineates a clear proposition, then the reader will flip to the next page, and the opportunity will have been missed.

Let's discuss how important the core idea is in a piece of advertising. The advertisement's underlying idea must advance the inherent drama of the product, or it's all just a giant waste of (air)time. It's pretty evident that most agencies hate such a discipline, since they seem to prefer to make ads that are edgy, funny, or cute—the kinds of commercials that are fun to watch but don't create a mental association with the product, so the viewer may later remember the commercial but forget the specific product it was selling. (Agencies know that these kinds of commercials often do well at advertising award shows, so they may create them, at least in part, so that they and the client can use the awards to advance their personal interests.)

However, there are examples of effective commercials that advance the drama of the product. If you look at a commercial like the "Apple 1984" spot (which ran only once, during the Super Bowl), you'll see a gut idea that was close to perfectly executed. I had the pleasure of working with Steve Hayden, the writer of this spot, just before he left the advertising agency where we both worked to go work on the Apple Computer account at Chiat/Day Advertising. Hayden, a real idea guy, and Lee Clow (the art director) brought together the idea of Big Brother, from George Orwell's classic book, and Apple's breakthrough Macintosh product. The TV spot brilliantly depicted a powerful woman protagonist effectively neutralizing Big Brother's rant, portraying the followers as zombielike "lemmings" standing in her way. The wrap-up was a rallying cry and challenge to the viewer to make sure that this year wouldn't be like the world in Orwell's *1984*. The tag line at the end announced, "On January 24, Apple Computer will introduce Macintosh. And you'll see why 1984 won't be like '1984.'" Almost every baby boomer watching the spot (or at least the ones who might buy a computer) had read the book, so the concept in the spot struck a resonant cord. Even though the one-minute commercial ran only once, it did everything right all at once. It was one of the first spots to really take advantage of the Super Bowl environment and, while it was certainly very well produced, the genius of this TV spot was the reference to the lone human defeating the Big Brother we all fear—the concept of basic human survival, once again evoking the struggle of David versus Goliath.

From this spot, the agency must have received many kudos and awards, which undoubtedly resulted in new business and more profits. Clow got the corner-office promotion, and Hayden went on to parlay the success of the spot into a big job at the agency that does IBM's advertising. And Apple got a perfect launch for its new product.

As they say, you only get one chance to make a good first impression. And in the ad business, nothing is more important for a new product (or a "new, improved" existing product) than a good launch. If done right, it cements in the mind of the consumer the unique position the product holds in the marketplace. In advertising-business vernacular it's called the "unique selling proposition" (USP). If a launch spot is good enough to effectively lock that USP in the mind of a consumer who may be in the market for a product like yours, then you have a reasonable chance of getting your product on their shortlist and then making a sale. It may sound easy, but it never is. Many things conspire to prevent all the elements from coming together in this way.

In my work in the advertising business, I had the pleasure of being part of a number of excellent marketing efforts where my creative contributions were integral to the success of the product. Each has its particular story that exemplifies what comes together when it's done right, or how it can fall apart so quickly when all the key elements don't crystallize.

CONTRACT WITH CONSUMER

When we did the launch advertising for LaPizzeria Frozen Pizza, we focused on saving the consumer a trip to the local pizzeria. The spot smartly conveyed the fact that the kitchen was as far as anyone had to go for a pizzeria-style pizza. This high-quality product was basically the first frozen pizza that lived up to the promise of a pizzeria pizza in your freezer. Even though we had a minimal budget for the TV spot, we had some fun with it and it scored through the roof in consumer testing. The entire marketing effort (a well-named product, excellent package design, a TV spot that communicated the proposition well, excellent magazine promotions, and a solid effort by the sales force to get shelf space in the supermarket freezer case) was a hit.

The product brand manager (our client) reportedly got a big promotion out of the deal, and everyone was happy, since sales took off. Unfortunately, the story (heard through the grapevine) goes that somebody figured out that if they changed the recipe a bit (taking out content to save costs), the relative profit would increase quite nicely. In the short term maybe this worked fine; satisfied consumers of the original product bought their second, and maybe their third. But soon they stopped buying it, because the pizza didn't seem to taste as good as they remembered it tasting.

Because freezer space in a supermarket is limited (and very expensive), products that don't fly out of the freezer case get yanked pretty fast. And once a product is yanked by the supermarket chain, it's almost impossible to get the space back for that particular product again.

In this case, we all did our job, but a "contract" with the consumer was broken when the product quality was lowered. The LaPizzeria product went away, and today freezer cases are full of high-quality frozen pizzas that reflect their pioneering USP.

STICK WITH IT

How does a small supermarket chain from Boise, Idaho, manage to stand out? When our agency got the new-business pitch assignment, David Anderson and I were assigned to work on their advertising, and a group of us went off to visit their stores. While the others in our group were getting the royal tour, David and I poked around behind the scenes in the back of the store (I knew my way around a supermarket, having worked in one during my high school days). When we asked a produce manager why he felt it was better to work for Albertsons than for one of the competitors, his response was that Albertsons had a (small) profit-sharing arrangement. Bingo!

We went back to our office to brainstorm, and developed the line "It's Joe Albertson's supermarket, but the produce department is mine." The storyboards of the TV spots showed proud bakery, meat, and produce department heads singing the line. Our talented creative director Jean Craig (today, a best-selling author) got behind the campaign and convinced the client of its merits. The theme-line ran for more than *ten years* and helped Albertsons go from the number ten supermarket chain in the country to number three.

The client once asked one of the subsequent creative directors working on the account as to when he thought Albertsons should move onto another theme for the advertising? He responded, "At least not in my lifetime"—a true compliment, since most creatives will think of any excuse to switch a theme line that isn't theirs. It's almost an art form, and it takes some genuine guts to know when to stick with something that's working. Consumers won't tire of a good idea, particularly if the ad agency is constantly finding new ways to keep it looking new and fresh. In other words, switching to something new is not necessarily better. Sometimes the smartest thing for a marketer to do is to stick with a theme-line long after the agency is starting to get bored with it and wants to do something different. Avis Rent-A-Car's "We try harder" (begun in 1963) is the perfect example of an evergreen slogan that has been constantly refreshed.

SIMPLY SIMPLIFY

As for long-running campaigns and slogans, the agency I worked for created Smokey Bear for the USDA Forest Service and the Advertising Council in 1944. Each year we would do a new forest service poster that would hang in schools, fire and ranger stations, and other locations all across America. When the agency got the assignment for the new campaign, I went through the Ad Council's research studies and realized that the Smokey Bear theme line "Only you can prevent forest fires (or 'Wildfires,' since 2001)" was one of the most recognizable ad slogans ever. I then sat down and started to strip away anything extraneous, simply because with any advertising message visual impact is primary. I got it down to "ONLY YOU" and the Smokey Bear head. I then put the Bear head over the *O* in the word *YOU*. The message had been distilled to six letters and the iconic face of the bear. Even though the line had been around for almost fifty years, I found a way to refine it and make it fresh. That poster pays homage to the immense power of simplification and to the fact that a new twist on an old idea can always be found.

PROPER POSITIONING

In 1977 Mazda was close to going out of business. It got so bad, that it was rumored that a day went by without a single Mazda sale in the United States and one car actually being returned (good old gallows humor). The dire situation was due to poor gas mileage and a reliability problem with the rotor seals in their engines. During those dark days, the designers and engineers in Hiroshima (the location of Mazda's headquarters) concocted a rescue plan using an affordable sports car as a spearhead. The clever design of the car took advantage of Mazda's unique rotary engine's inherent light weight.

The agency where I worked had handled the account for years and was suffering along with Mazda. The executive creative director, Jack Foster (a legend in the Los Angeles advertising community and best-selling author), was excited to get a new product from Mazda to work on, and he walked into everyone's office showing off a photo of the car. I jumped at the chance to work on the advertising for such a cool-looking new car. Roger Honkanen (coauthor of the book *How to Turn Your Ideas into a Million Dollars*) and I came up with an idea that every so often a great sports car comes along, and we featured this premise in the work. The obvious insinuation was that this new Mazda RX-7 was the consumer's chance to catch a shooting star. One top-level client queried whether we were sure this new product could live up to such a lofty claim. I answered, "If it can't, we'll soon be out of business, and no one will care about the cars or ads anyway." As it turned out, the 1979 Mazda RX-7 lived up to its promise, and the marketplace responded. The RX-7 product, with its campaign, was a giant hit that kicked off Mazda's rebirth.

CELEBRITY CLOUT

James Garner, an actor who has been in our homes (through the magic of TV) for more than fifty years, was our choice for spokesperson for the next-generation Mazda RX-7. Garner has one of the highest "Q" scores, a system used to evaluate the familiarity, likeability, believability, popularity, and credibility of TV personalities that also helps to determine a celebrity's appropriateness for a particular product or brand. We first met with Garner at his agent's house in the Hollywood hills. We had gone to the trouble to park a new (yet to be released) Mazda RX-7 at the top of the driveway, so he would see it and (being a car guy) be drawn to check it out on the way in to the meeting. He was impressed with the car and he liked what we had to say, and so he signed on as Mazda's spokesperson. For the next four years my creative partner, Jim Barr, and I had some fun knocking out some cool work with James Garner; his association with the Mazda product did a lot to elevate its image over the pack of other Japanese cars in the marketplace. Mazda's U.S. sales hit record highs during this time.

After a while, however, the client started to feel that the car (and not Garner) should be the star in the commercials. With this new direction, the message in the next batch of commercials became convoluted, no matter how hard we worked to strike the right balance between Garner and the car. Ultimately, because these new spots didn't work as well as the previous ones, Mazda dropped James Garner as spokesperson. I always felt we could have done something clever to make the spots work, but sometimes no amount of cleverness can fix an unfocused idea.

FIRST IMPRESSIONS LAST

The Mazda Miata's outstanding success is a prime example of the power of ideas: when a breakthrough product is promoted using a focused idea that is expressed through breakthrough advertising—and the timing is right. The Miata added a new dimension to the car business. It offered a return to the classic wind-in-your-hair sports car but in a reliable modern package—the best of the past combined with the best of today (called "newstalgic" by some magazine wags). My coworker Jim Herwitz and I created a spot with the concept "It takes you back, but it also takes you into the future," which was ultimately successful because it depicted the inherent drama of the product so well.

The Miata and its launch spot created an automobile industry trend that is still going full blast today. Almost every car company now offers a retro-style vehicle, and commercials that say, "Remember when . . . ?" still appear regularly on TV. It was smart for Mazda to capitalize on a void in the marketplace, to bring their refined manufacturing expertise to such a fun product, and to launch it with an ad campaign that appealed to both the public's yearning for simpler times and its appreciation for modern technology.

STANDING OUT

Further back in my career, I was given the assignment to help out on Hughes Airwest. According to a joke at the time, in a market of ten airlines it ranked eleventh, so the company obviously needed some help. While doing some research into the company's history, we noticed that its customers had given Hughes Airwest the nickname "the banana" because the planes were painted a bright yellow. I kept digging through all of the materials we had, and I saw that, because of the milk-run nature of their flight schedule, Hughes Airwest actually offered more flights in the western United States than any other company. Combining the two thoughts, I added some wings and the company's logo to a drawing of a banana, along with the headline "Top Banana in the West." With this advertising, Hughes Airwest's business literally took off—it soon had the top consumer awareness of any airline in the Western marketplace, which contributed to a boost in ticket sales. The only problem was that The Summa Corporation (owned by Howard Hughes) used this new higher profile to snag a buyer for the airline. In other words, we did a fantastic job, and in doing so we effectively lost the business.

GETTING THE CONSUMER OFF THE COUCH

In the theme park business, the goal is to get the average customer to visit more than once every three years or so. Like most products, theme parks depend on a core audience that uses their product often, therefore it's particularly great if you can get the casual user to come back more often, specifically every year would be fantastic.

Many people will say that they plan to visit Disneyland soon, but occasionally they put the visit off until next year. It is the job of any theme park's R&D department to come up with new attractions that will make people want to get off their sofas and come back to the park. And it's the job of marketing to get the word out, to convince people that this new attraction is a must-see, so the customer will come this year instead of next.

For Walt Disney Imagineering (WDI), Disney's attraction builder, to conceive a ride, get it approved, and then get it up and running is generally a very expensive, daunting, protracted process. Because there was a gap in WDI's new-attraction schedule for Disneyland, the people in the Entertainment Division at Disneyland, headed up by a bright guy named Bob McTyre, dreamed up a water show that could take place on the Rivers of America in *Frontierland*. It incorporated three enormous water-fountain fans that images could be projected upon at night. The water show artfully combined classic Disney movie images, practical show elements, pyrotechnics, and a state-of-the-art sound system cranking out Disney music. It's still a show you've got to see to believe.

Disneyland needed a name to somehow describe what was going on with the show, and the creative department I headed up generated over a hundred possibilities. I dragged all of the names into the office of Jack Lindquist, the then-president (and genuine idea guy), and we brainstormed. Eisner was leaning toward something along the lines of "Phantasmagoria" (defined in the Encarta World English Dictionary as "1. bizarre images: a series or group of strange or bizarre images seen as if in a dream; 2. ever-changing scene: a scene or view that encompasses many things and changes constantly"). Lindquist, after reviewing the top picks, adapted it and came up with a moniker that captured the spirit of the show and as a plus, made a nod to Mickey and *Fantasia:* "Fantasmic!"

We did a huge marketing push for Fantasmic!, and some research showed it had overall impact (helped by the great name and solid marketing) in the neighborhood of a full-blown attraction. You'd think everyone at Disney would be excited. Well, if I remember right, the people at WDI weren't jumping up and down, since their function had been upstaged by a mere light-and-water show.

From everything I've come to learn, the customer doesn't give a rodent's rear end where the ideas come from. For that reason, a successful company will let ideas percolate up from anywhere in the organization; it will also encourage an environment where people won't feel threatened if someone else comes up with a good idea.

PAYING THE PIPER

The Indiana Jones Adventure attraction at Disneyland was a great marriage of big ideas (and egos). The trouble was that quickly almost everything about it got way too expensive. For example, when my creative department was developing the commercial, we were directed, by one of the upper-management types, to develop original music so Disney could possibly circumvent using Lucasfilm Ltd.'s highly recognizable theme music (which would necessitate having to pay its licensing fee). I felt it was absolute folly to try to outdo a piece of music that had established such enormous equity in the marketplace. While I presented the spot to Eisner, he asked (paraphrasing): "What were we thinking by not using the Indiana Jones theme music?" Of course, no one in the large meeting spoke up, so I had to tell him that it was in the interest of saving money. He just scoffed and directed us to use the highly recognizable theme music. Later, I was chastised for mentioning "money" to Eisner.

The launch was still a big success because everything came together, and thankfully even the music. But sometimes you have to pay the piper, and things can get expensive, especially when you're borrowing on a powerful equity. But the take-away here is that if you're in upper-management, you can't let a creative person hang out on a limb like that, especially if the person is acting in response to your "second-guessing" directive. Such political gamesmanship kills the spirit of creativity, so the next time a boss like that really needs a great idea, he or she'll be lucky to get handed an average one.

DISCOUNTING DONE RIGHT

So what do you do when you're in the middle of a recession, tourism is down, a war is looming, and therefore your attendance is trending down? Well, you come up with a way to get the consumer closest to you off their butts and into Disneyland. We kicked around several ideas, and then we came up with a "Resident Salute—Special $20 Offer" to Southern Californians. The bean counters fought us like crazy; they hated to lose $5 with every person who came in the gate. Jack Lindquist eloquently argued that it was a whole lot better to get $20 than the zero they'd get if the consumer didn't show up at all.

In developing the advertising campaign, we pushed not only for the local-resident-only focus but also for a dedicated spot that would use a play on classic

California icons to get the word out. The spot showed vignettes of locals in stereotypical situations (e.g., the obligatory surfer dude on the beach) reacting to the amazing deal. This spot, which was very well received, had some fun and didn't lead the viewer to presume that Disneyland might be having even the smallest amount of difficulty.

The campaign kicked off, and our business took off because the local consumers felt Disney was recognizing and rewarding them. The interviews with people who took advantage of the deal showed that they actually thought that Disney was nice to do the Southern California locals a special favor. A few weeks into the promotion, the 1991 Gulf War started but our business continued to hold up, while our competitors' business nose-dived. Although discounts can diminish the perception of a product's quality, if done right and for a limited time they can sometimes enhance the product's position in the marketplace.

FINDING A PLACE IN THE HEART

So what do you do to keep Disneyland in the consciousness of those out of state? California state tourism research shows us that things like exceptional weather and clean public beaches were at the top of the list of reasons families came to visit. Of course, a visit to Disneyland park was right up there too, along with a day spent poking around Hollywood and hoping to see a star. With this knowledge, we built a spot showing kids frolicking on the beach, convertibles cruising down palmtree-lined boulevards, and people having fun at Disneyland, and we wrapped it all up using an adaptation of the 1960s rock classic "California Sun (Goin' Out West…)." It was almost unfair to run that spot back East during the middle of winter. The TV spot ran for years and helped Disneyland (the heart of the fun in the warm California sun) retain its special place in the heart of all Americans.

Yep, marketing's all about making the connection with the consumer and grabbing the heartstrings. The ad biz isn't all BS, and even though this sounds like a bunch of BS, it really isn't: good marketing can work toward establishing the inherent drama of a product/service in the psyche of the fickle consumer.

FORGOING THE HYPE AND AIMING FOR THE HEART

If you want to get a person's attention, dig deep to find a core idea based on some truth that the consumer will respond to on a human level. As we'll discuss in chapter 4, humans are programmed to search out the inherent truth in life, and they will seek and even demand *real*. Fake food won't keep you alive, and phony friends won't be there when you really need them. And marketing tricks, sequels, and such will never fill a real need. In the long run only excellence and high quality will sustain anything. Nature may abhor a vacuum, but filling the marketplace with only sequels, retreads, remakes, marketing tricks, replicas, and other non-ideas just won't do.

If you want to find a real-deal idea, you'll need to know how to recognize one. Long discussions with my sons, Mike and Dan, helped me formulate this hierarchy of ideas—a list that just might help you get some clarity about the type of idea you're wrestling with.

THE SEVEN LEVELS OF IDEAS AND INNOVATION:

1. "WHAT THE HELL WERE THEY THINKING?" IDEAS

These are the bonehead thoughts that we've all had but were (we hope) smart enough not to act on. Teenagers are absolute masters at coming up with these kinds of non-ideas, like "Let's jump off the roof and into the pool!" But dumb ideas like these aren't limited to teenagers. Many corporations get sucked into believing that unrestricted (read: sloppy) thinking somehow equates to creativity. Putting the image of Mickey Mouse on toss-away potty training pants is one of these ideas (I guess we should be thankful that they didn't put Mickey on disposable diapers, using Winnie-the-Pooh characters [oh, I get it—Pooh on diapers] instead, still under a Disney license). *The Godfather: Part III* was another stinker of an idea for a lot of reasons. Ford's Edsel automobile and the New Coca-Cola (1985) were both answers to questions no one was asking. In 1996, removing the Main Street Electrical Parade from Disneyland was another ("Glows Away Forever" was the theme—in the short term it brought people in, since they believed it indeed was going away forever, but when it returned in 2001 "due to popular demand" to Disney's California Adventure, the beloved nighttime parade's overall drawing power seemed to be diminished). These ideas aren't hard to spot: Just pretend you're the laziest, most boneheaded teenager you've ever met. If the idea makes you think, "Hey, wouldn't that be crazy if . . . ?" prepare to start running the other way.

2. NON-/POSER/CHICKENSHIT/FLUFF IDEAS

These may look like ideas, but they're actually copies of copies of copies. In certain corporations with a rich creative history, like Disney, at times the easiest thing

to do is to just stir the same old pot. "Let's put Mickey or a princess on a
_____(fill in the blank)" is now getting boring even for the most asleep of
consumers. Paraphrasing the classic duck saying, "If it don't look like an idea, if it
don't sound like an idea, then it probably ain't no frickin' idea." A lot of TV commercials fall into this category; they aren't substantial or compelling enough to
watch, and so they end up as a sort of visual wallpaper (that is, if the viewer doesn't hit the remote button a few seconds into them). Later, the viewer vaguely
remembers seeing the spot but can't recall the sponsor or very much about the
spot at all.

3. SEQUELS, RETREADS, REMAKES, MARKETING TRICKS, AND REPLICA IDEAS

A fake Rolex and a Ferrari replica are classic examples of this kind of idea. Whom
do the makers of these things think they are kidding? TV is full of these kinds of
non-ideas—rip-offs of the latest hit shows (or even TV spots) that producers air,
thinking nobody will notice. To elevate out this category, a remake or sequel must
be more than a copy of what went before.

4. "FARM-READY" IDEAS

This is the first echelon of real-deal ideas: The cowboy hat. Bailing wire. Cola
or beer in an aluminum can. A nail and hammer. The paper clip. The plastic zip
tie. A staple/stapler. The T-shirt. Plastic wrap. Aspirin. Though often taken for
granted, these are the kinds of ideas that are desperately needed and can make a
difference in people's lives. They can also make their inventor or company very
rich. The key is that they effect some change in the human condition.

5. SOLID, HARD-WORKING, KICK-SOME-BUTT IDEAS

Elvis on a postage stamp. A circular hand saw. "Grand Slam" breakfasts at Denny's.
The rotary lawnmower. Fuel injection. A $30 digital watch. The Swiss Army knife.
Arc welders. Teflon/titanium/ceramic replacement hip joints. Seat belts. Stainless
steel "silverware." The affordable chocolate bar. You've got to love these ideas, as
they are what keep everything moving incrementally forward. With these ideas
you don't see giant leaps, rather lots of evolutionary baby steps until what you
have is quite revolutionary.

6. BREAKTHROUGH, PARADIGM-CHANGING, DISRUPTIVE, PURELY INNOVATIVE IDEAS

The television. The telephone. The Internet. The American Constitution. Cheap steel. Monetary currency (and now the credit card). Wireless transmission of radio waves. Glass. The fiberglass (over rigid foam) surfboard. Computer-generated images and special effects. A "wow" factor is a big part of these kinds of ideas, since they replace the ordinary or primitive with something that is so much better.

7. LIFE-CHANGING, PRODUCT-OF-GENIUS, LET'S-SEND-A-HUMAN-TO-THE-MOON IDEAS

The wheel. Fire. The computer. Jet and rocket engines. The automobile. Playing cards. Ice cream. Nuclear fission. The guitar (or any musical instrument). The steel fish hook. The satellite (used in image and signal transmission). The light-bulb. These go beyond "wow" because they almost change the entire human condition. Once these ideas become part of life, nothing is ever exactly the same again. (You could easily argue all day long that some of these category 6 ideas should be in category 7, or vice versa. The ideas in both categories are the best of the best; it's just that ideas in the latter group are the ones that changed the world in a very big way.)

• • •

Now, do some hard thinking about your approach to generating ideas. Be honest with yourself: how much organic anarchy (more about this in chapter 6) and general craziness are you willing to put up with in your life as you search out the higher echelon of ideas? Take stock of how much truth you are finding lately. Then think about how hard you want to work in order to move up to the next level. Expect there to be tension. Don't look for the oxymoronic "safe risk," because all ideas, and even life itself, emanate from a certain elemental chaos. The process of finding ideas should be fun or, at the very least, more real.

CHAPTER 4

HOW WE'RE LOSING OUR WAY IN THE SEARCH FOR THE REAL-DEAL IDEA

Every morning when we put our two feet on the cold floor, we begin a search for things that are *real*. We want *real* friends. We want *real* relationships. We want *real* food. We want *real* moments and authentic experiences.

As a hypothetical example, let's say you call a friend at three o'clock in the morning and ask that he or she bring you $1,000 cash to a specified location, and tell your friend to do so without asking any questions. Well, you're one lucky person if you can name even one person who you think would be willing to do this for you. Such a person is a real friend.

Tomatoes simply taste better when they're grown under natural sunlight and in organically rich soil, and better yet if you grow them yourself. The ephemeral beauty and smell of a single rose is better than one hundred plastic ones and a spray scent. A genuine smile on a child's face can't be bought—it's real and priceless. There's nothing comparable to a really good belly laugh, or even the simple pleasure of a good hug.

It's easy to understand why a real-leather jacket costs more than a Pleather one—just try one on. As inspiring as an Ansel Adams photograph of Yosemite Valley is, looking at one still pales in comparison to standing there gazing at the majestic Half Dome. Automobiles designed by humans using their hands and clay usually end up more attractive and interesting than those designed using computers (which my designer friend Todd Gerstenberger calls "those aero-potato" cars). The best rock 'n' roll groups are a bunch of like-minded musicians/friends who were drawn together by their real love of music, and not those contrived "pretty boy" groups assembled by slick promoters. You end up loving the people who love you; in other words, real friendship and real love cannot be fabricated. Real is simply, in all its purity, just that: *real.*

To capture authenticity you have to accept all aspects of life: the good, the bad, the ugly, the ups, the downs, and even the stinky. It is just that today it can be quite confusing to figure out what's real and what's not. How often have you spent hours of your time doing something nice for a person, only to find he or she doesn't have the common decency to offer a word of appreciation? How often have you been sold a bill of goods? Why does the fine print only get longer with each business dealing? Does a handshake deal not mean what it used to? Is everyone just out to serve themselves so even the proverbial win-win partnership is now a thing of the past? Why would anyone think that they can buy a decent steak at the price of a hamburger? Just whom can you trust? Just when is a deal a deal? And, more important, what's the real deal?

CAVEAT EMPTOR IS STILL IN PLAY TODAY

A sign in a restaurant window reads "T-Bones 99¢." It sounds like a great deal, right? Human nature wants life to be easy, and therefore we are programmed to be on the lookout for ways to get something for nothing, or at least something of high quality for very little money or effort. Look closer: the fine print reads "with meat, add $5." A classic "gotcha." Obviously, the restaurateur was having a little fun at the public's expense, but the lesson here is that hype can easily suck us in if we don't watch out. And every day there is more and more evidence of misleading hype in the marketplace.

Caveat emptor (Latin for "Let the buyer beware") is as true today as it was two thousand years ago. But the buyer-seller problems we need to beware of today are often somewhat hidden; some of the relationships you have with a manufacturer or corporation may not be what you believe them to be. For example, you may think that a certain car is made in the United States, but some or all of its parts may be made in other countries. There's a small Chevrolet at your local dealer made in Korea. Some Hondas sold in the United States are built in Canada using only 10 percent Japanese parts—and some Toyotas built in Kentucky are assembled with 80 percent American parts. Does the average person realize that a car billed as "North American production" may have been made in Mexico (after all, Mexico *is* in North America)? The popular VW New Beetle and Chrysler's PT Cruiser are assembled in Mexico, for example. And did you know that the historically all-American Jeep brand name is now owned by a German company, DaimlerChrysler AG? (Rather ironic since the originnal Jeep was developed for use in World War II.)

Switching gears a little, looking at the snow-capped mountain peaks on the bottle's label, do you get the impression that Crystal Geyser Alpine Spring Water has a bottling plant that takes its water from an aquifer in the Mojave Desert? (OK, technically, those snow-capped peaks do contribute to filling the aquifer.) And, by the way, the natural Crystal Geyser is a rare cold-water geyser on the banks of the Green River in Utah.

Did you know that Nestlé, the world leader in coffee, is a giant food conglomerate based in Switzerland that owns brands like Carnation, Tidy Cats, Alpo, Purina, Taster's Choice coffee, PowerBar, Juicy Juice, and Stouffer's Lean Cuisine, and more than seventy brands of bottled water including Arrowhead, Calistoga, Perrier, and San Pellegrino—not to mention 75 percent of Alcon, the contact-lens-solution company, and 26 percent of cosmetic giant L'Oréal? (Just think of the clout they can use to get one of their new products onto a supermarket shelf, compared with the negligible clout of a small entrepreneur.)

What about Philip Morris (which, to confuse things even more, changed its name to Altria Group in January 2003), the largest tobacco company, which owns 84 percent of Kraft Foods, the makers of Kraft Macaroni and Cheese? In a round-about way, when you serve your kids Macaroni and Cheese you're supporting and adding to the coffers of a giant cigarette company. Beyond the obvious Marlboro, Parliament, and other cigarette brands, Philip Morris, now known as Altria Group, also owns Nabisco, Post cereals, Balance Bar Co., Altoids mints, Life Savers, Ritz crackers, and Oscar Meyer. Yep, it's weird to think that a cigarette company owns a piece of the Weinermobiles. In 2002, Altria sold the number two beer heavyweight Miller Brewing to South African Breweries, now known as SABMiller, and Altria now owns 36 percent of the newly formed company. And Red Dog beer, whose label identifies the maker as Plank Road Brewery, is in actuality brewed by SABMiller. If a cigarette company owns so much, just think what Disney, the biggest entertainment company in the world owns—but, more on this in the next chapter.

Did you know that Fujitsu offers one of the few laptop computers actually made in Japan, and that many Sony products aren't made in Japan, but produced in Taiwan, Korea, or China? Did you know that cereal giant Kellogg owns Kashi, the health cereal company based in La Jolla, California, or that Coca-Cola bought Odwalla, the natural juice company? Many companies today are purely licensing arms—for example, Body Glove is simply a brand name that gets stuck on selected items for a royalty fee (they closed their wet suit manufacturing plant years ago).

Other anomalies abound: A "pound" of coffee in a supermarket today is usually less than sixteen ounces, and sometimes only thirteen ounces (in her day, your grandmother would have objected if the general store's proprietor tried to pull a fast one like that). Due to a recent change in federal rules, initiated at the behest of the french fry industry, *frozen* french fries (even the batter-coated ones) are now defined by our U.S. Department of Agriculture as "fresh vegetables" (Granny wouldn't have bought into this mumbo-jumbo either—but I guess this is one way to get America's children to eat more *fresh* vegetables). Even as early as thirty years ago, many autographs were signed by machines. Of course, hand-scrawled personal notes are now eminently more collectible—because they're real. Diamonds aren't necessarily worth what jewelers charge for them, since DeBeers, a giant South African conglomerate, has tightly controlled their supply for close to a century in order to keep prices high. Did you know that Disney doesn't own the Oscar-winning song "When You Wish Upon a Star" (the Bourne Co. does)? Did you know that regular unleaded gasoline is pretty much all the same, and companies will often fill the underground tanks at a competitor's gas station and vice versa? (Next time you see a tanker truck, with those big hoses, filling up a station's tanks, note the corporate logo, or often lack thereof.) The point is that what you see these days isn't necessarily what you get, and as time goes by it's only getting more confusing for the consumer.

Marketing used to mean finding and establishing a place for your product in the marketplace and carefully building a cozy relationship with the consumer. But now the average person has to try to outsmart the marketing geniuses who are working around the clock to try to trip him or her up. Everywhere you look today you see spin and dazzle. So if you're starting to feel like "they" are out to get you, maybe you're right.

Take the words of Edward R. Murrow in his speech at the Radio-Television News Directors Association (RTNDA) Convention on October 15, 1958:

> Our history will be what we make it. And if there are any historians about fifty or a hundred years from now, and there should be preserved the kinescopes for one week of all three networks, they will there find recorded in black and white, or color, evidence of decadence, escapism and insulation from the realities of the world in which we live. I invite your attention to the television schedules of all networks between the hours of eight and eleven P.M., Eastern time. Here you will find only fleeting and spasmodic reference to the fact that this nation is in mortal danger. There are, it is true, occasional informative programs presented in that intellectual ghetto on Sunday afternoons. But during the daily peak viewing periods, television in the main insulates us from the realities of the world in which we live. If this state of affairs continues, we may alter an advertising slogan to read: LOOK NOW, PAY LATER.
>
> For surely we shall pay for using this most powerful instrument of communication to insulate the citizenry from the hard and demanding realities which must be faced if we are to survive. I mean the word *survive* literally.

In 2008 it will be fifty years since he spoke those prophetic words. Murrow was worried that the line between responsible journalism and entertainment would be blurred by the control of mass communication by the television studios and their sponsors and advertisers. He was afraid that the hard realities of life would be glossed over because of conflicts of interest between the news departments and the corporations' need to make a buck. Murrow's premise foresaw detached-from-reality news coverage of wars (an almost "Rambo Olympics" with no daily photos of coffins on the tarmac—rather, an overt focus on the detached bombing from high altitude; the impact of war spending never seriously addressed or even highlighted, instead quietly deferred by increasing our national debt). And he feared that the general news would become somewhat sugarcoated or twisted so the average citizen wouldn't know what was really going on. As Murrow predicted, we've come to expect the same stream of BS from our nightly news programs that we might get from a used-car salesman. How would he view the public's tendency to turn a blind eye to the use of performance-enhancing substances by overpaid athletic superstars so they can shatter old home-run records (which, let's not forget, helps boost ratings)? You don't have to be a sports junkie to understand that what went on in Babe Ruth's era just isn't the same as what's going on today—you just don't get biceps that big from eating your Wheaties and lifting weights. What would Edward R. Murrow think of today's "reality" TV? Unfortunately, he probably wouldn't be surprised at all.

Edward R. Murrow was warning us that the public airwaves could be hijacked by greed. It's worth some thoughtful consideration: how much reality (and I don't mean through reality TV shows) are we actually getting these days?

CAN YOU BELIEVE EVERYTHING YOU THINK YOU THINK?

If you're experiencing something that's real (especially if it's also ingenious), something that truly engages your senses, then that something will tug at the essence of one's humanness. Like sitting in a well-designed, high-quality leather-covered chair versus a vinyl-covered one, it will leave, dare I say, an impression on you.

Today, what is truly real is getting tremendously confused in almost all aspects of our lives. (It strikes me as weird, and sad, that I felt forced to modify the word *real* with an adjective, as if *real* wasn't *real* enough.) We strive to have real conversations, but these conversations are sliced and diced by interrupted cellular-phone connections, TV viewing, music playing, automated telephone keypad prompts, voice mail, email, and so on. How often these days are you frustrated because you can't find a real person to talk to, an actual employee of the company you're calling who could easily, after some reasonable discourse, have resolved your problem? Having a good old one-on-one conversation is getting almost impossible. And the communication world we live in conspires by becoming more and more visually oriented. Hey, even some phones have cameras in them. And, all this saturated bombardment of visual information is inundating us, creating a situation where the average person now demands life be dished up in one easy-to-understand visual package and put on his or her lap—or rather, laptop (referring to the Internet, in that we're living through a powerful visual paradigm shift where you have almost all the information of the entire world at your fingertips).

This is a good place to talk about the power of photographs and their part in the growing confusion over what's real and what isn't. "Of all of our inventions for mass communication, pictures still speak the most universally understood language," espoused our friend Walt Disney. (It's hard to know if Walt was talking more about "moving" pictures here, but the point is the same either way you read it.) When homeowners are forced to vacate a property due to an approaching flood or fire, the first things they grab (after their loved ones, of course) are the family photographs. These pieces of paper represent a person's special memories, fixed in time. A simple black-and-white photo can convey the nature of personal relationships, special events, and even socioeconomic status, beyond the obvious marker of time. We treasure our personal photographs because we know that they can unlock a memory and trigger a warm and satisfying response.

During the 1930s, 1940s, and 1950s, when a person looked at a photograph, he or she saw an objective representation of a captured moment. *LIFE* and *National Geographic* magazines set the standard for visually capturing real moments. But things changed in the decades that followed. By the 1980s, we as a culture had started to question the retouched perfection passed off as real beauty in places such as *Playboy* magazine's centerfolds. Real women had wrinkles, sags, pimples, and moles—except those in the pages of Hefner's rag. In a way, we had wanted to believe that such perfection was possible and had started to measure our daily reality against it. But soon we began to realize that the photos were merely subjective representations of what a magazine or advertiser wanted us to see.

In the mid-1980s came computer manipulation of images (computer-generated imagery, or CGI), and the visual world got weird. In the movies we saw the first big conceptual shift. By 1991, in *Terminator 2*, a morphing liquid-metal T-1000 cyborg was shown walking through prison bars, his body just flowing around them. We all knew it was the result of special effects, but it was no longer obviously fake and crude like the stilted effects in *Godzilla*. The "mercury man" played by Robert Patrick looked so damned real.

With movies like the *Harry Potter* series, *Pirates of the Caribbean: The Curse of the Black Pearl*, and the *Lord of the Rings* trilogy, it seems that we are now experiencing certain movies as more than mere escapist entertainment; they are so visually powerful, they're evolving toward being viewed as more of an altered, confused reality, similar to dreams. This CGI reality may have further contributed to a general societal anxiety about what is real. It's almost gotten to the point where we may suspect the manipulation of any image we see. We may even look at the ducks floating in the moat around Disneyland's castle and wonder whether they are real or animatronic. Kids who have grown up with this technology will most often recognize a CGI frame when they see it; they have become trained to look for vector glitches and perspective anomalies. Even though a CGI frame is often seen for what it is, we, as a culture, have come to allow for, accept, and like this altered reality, and our general perceptions may subsequently be getting warped. Partially because of the warped reality constantly being presented to us, skepticism has become a basic tenet of many young people. We're all getting more than a little tired of being fooled and manipulated, and it may be turning us all into a bunch of cynics. And as Esa Saarinen pointed out, "The opposite of creativity is cynicism."

MINING FOR IDEAS IN A WALT DISNEY KIND OF WAY

Now, let's take a look at Disney's theme parks. How do they relate to our confusion between real and not-so-real? Walt Disney focused on the wonderment of the child in all of us. He would go as far as to constantly stoop down to the eye level of a child while he was strolling through the park. He understood that many people would be bringing their children to Disneyland and would therefore experience the park more through the eyes of a child than their own. In other words, if the child was smiling, the parents (the ones with the money) were smiling too. And to keep the children and their parents smiling, he built almost everything on the "Boo! . . . Gotcha! . . . Whew. . . (Hug)" premise. What, you say? OK, let me explain how I see this play out. When a parent hides around a corner and steps out to scare a child ("Boo!"), emotions explode. The kid is at first petrified with fear, then simply startled, then somewhat relieved, and finally ecstatically happy, all within a matter of seconds. Usually, the final outcome is a big warm hug, and a request from the child to "do that again." In Disneyland this particular process plays out over and over, all in a controlled and safe environment. Walt, the genius, recognized this particular dynamic and made it accessible to anyone who arrived at the front gate with enough money in his or her pocket. He took the thrills of an amusement park and added an overlay of a story line, which, when constructed to create a scare, contributed to a stronger emotional connection. When kids leave Disneyland at the end of the day, their heads are typically nestled restfully on the shoulder of the parent, and they are exhausted and spent. After all, they could have encountered pirates, ridden a bobsled down a mountain past a red-eyed Yeti, seen ferocious dinosaurs, rocketed through space, flown over London with Peter Pan, had a head-on collision with a train, maybe even glimpsed the wicked Queen from *Snow White*. The basic human component of survival is evident in so much of the park. The craziest thing about all of this "survival" is that it's going on in a contained world where everything is fun—and the big, bad real world doesn't intrude. It's oxymoronic, but it works. It works because it's great entertainment and because it tugs mightily at the human condition and the soul.

Anyone who has visited Disneyland may be questioning my sanity here since I'm talking about real things and a Disney theme park in the same sentence. After all, isn't the Jungle Cruise ride about as phony as it gets? Isn't Mr. Lincoln merely a mechanical puppet? Isn't Mickey Mouse just some guy (often a smallish woman) dressed up in a costume? Yes, but Disneyland provides *real* entertainment. In other words, the value comes in part from the fun of being in on the gag. People go along with the lark, because, like moviegoers, they are willing participants who will suspend disbelief because they know that what they're seeing isn't being presented as real. A theme park is very much like a three-dimensional movie; it presents a fantasy, a warped reality, a time shift, or a drama played out on the stage called Disneyland. In order to advance this notion among park employees, Disney even goes to the trouble of calling its workers "cast members." As Walt himself said, "Disneyland is a show." The intent of the park, like any theatrical performance, is to offer the wonderment, spectacle, drama, and escapism of entertainment, all without triggering any skepticism. And entertainment works when it is offered up as such, and not confused with what is real.

A problem arises when the "entertainment contract" (that is, the "show") is diminished and only fluff is put in its place. As with LaPizzeria pizza, where the quality of the product was diminished by reducing the content, with a lessening of show content the contract is broken between the viewer (in this case the park guest) and the entertainment provider.

Let's suppose you're entering the gates of a Disneyland park (in Anaheim, Orlando [Magic Kingdom], Tokyo, Paris, or soon to be Hong Kong) and you pass through the tunnel under the train tracks and start by walking down Main Street, U.S.A. Walt's idea was to transport you to a different place and time, a conceptual replication of 1890s Marceline, Missouri. There were to be horse-drawn trolleys, ladies with lacework dresses and parasols, and ice cream parlors. Even the second story of the buildings and the steam locomotive were done in 5/8 scale to throw off your perception and make it appear more intimate. "For those of us who remember the carefree time it recreates, Main Street will bring back happy memories. For younger visitors, it is an adventure in turning back the calendar to the days of grandfather's youth," said Walt. (Next time you're at the original Disneyland, spend a few minutes playing checkers on the boards set up at the potbellied stove in the Market House [general] Store, if they're still there—it almost takes you back to Walt Disney's original concept.)

Today's merchandising wizards have converted more and more square footage of Main Street into space for selling Disney-licensed products, and in the process they have removed some of the cues that made visitors feel as if they'd been transported back in time. There are still some old trolleys and cars and salesclerks in costumes, but the period elements are now vastly overwhelmed by all the new merchandise being sold. The average kid today may look at Main Street, U.S.A., and see just another themed shopping mall, and that's essentially what it has become. When the contract is broken, the consumers may go along for a while, but how long will it be before they become disenfranchised and just simply not return?

A business enterprise must perceive and respond to the needs and the actual experiences of the customer. The customer only sees (more clearly than many give him or her credit for) what happens in his or her real day-to-day world. Innovative products and services are what we respond to, not boardroom shenanigans, marketing hype, and Wall Street buzz. In its communications and offerings, a corporation must supply a respectable answer to the consumer's question "What's in it for me?"

Why, exactly, has the consumer-business relationship become so warped? Is it because there isn't anything much that's actually new anymore? Is it because the spoiled consumer wants it all? Is it because everyone in the whole country has turned into a bunch of liars? Well, it's a little of all three. Let's take a closer look.

THE INVASION OF HYPE IN OUR LIVES

1. INSTEAD OF IMPROVING THEIR PRODUCTS OR CREATING NEW ONES, SOME BUSINESSES JUST RATCHET UP THE HYPE

The greed that causes businesses to focus on serving the stockholders above all, while having a detrimental effect on quashing innovation, has also led to the exaggeration of many claims and slogans. Just being good just isn't good enough these days. It's also possible that because many products and services are pretty much at parity to each other these days, no product is really that much better than the others; therefore the overpromising (read: hype) stems from the proposition that every company wants its product or service to stand out and above the rest.

Of course, it's natural that companies desperately want their product or service to be perceived by the consumer as a cut above. But how can *every company's* product be vastly superior, or entirely new, or totally revolutionary?

This particular dynamic is at work big time within ad agencies as well as companies. For instance, I've often witnessed excellent presentations where the client is bowled over by the dog-and-pony show (although all too often the advertising executive is presenting hype in place of any real idea); the client later has mentioned to me that the actual advertising work produced didn't turn out as well as he had expected. Business clients, like all of us, want to be sold the next big thing.

2. A SENSE OF ENTITLEMENT LEADS US TO WANT THE BEST OF EVERYTHING, SO WE GET SET UP AS A SUCKER FOR THE HYPE

Has the American consumer gotten so used to being spoon-fed that he or she doesn't even see it happening? How else do you explain the proposition where we seem to be willing to work a bunch of extra hours to pay for a price-engineered (if it costs more then it *must* be better) brand name? Almost *every*where we look, we see evidence that almost *every*one wants more of almost *every*thing. It reminds me of what greedy little Veruca Salt had to say in the movie *Willy Wonka and the Chocolate Factory:* "I want the world. I want the whole world. I want to lock it all up in my pocket. It's my bar of chocolate. Give it to me now." So is all this greed not only effectively blinding corporations but also starting to blind the consumer? It sure looks like it is.

Why do we feel extra special when we buy an expensive pair of athletic shoes, like the ones that some successful athlete wears? I guess we think, "If it's good enough for a celebrity basketball star, then it must be good enough for me." But if you take a few minutes to analyze how truly ludicrous this concept is, then you'll never pay more than $50 for a pair of athletic shoes. Why would the average guy need to purchase such expensive tools of the trade? Some people want to believe that an expensive camera somehow makes them a professional photographer, or a high-dollar titanium hammer gives them the skills to build a house. Tools are tools, not magic wands.

Our greed sets us up to be an easy target. Instead of eating less bread when we want to shed some pounds, we expect bakeries to make "oxymoronic" low-carbohydrate bread—and, of course, they typically charge us extra for it. And we will purchase an item far beyond our means by "paying for it" with a credit card—causing us to effectively lose the connection between effort and reward. And how does anyone reconcile the notion of "investing" in a car—especially when a majority of financed cars today aren't worth what the owner still owes on them?

Also contributing to the current market dynamic of entitlement are the baby boomers. The baby boomers (born in the years from 1946 to 1964) are probably the second most spoiled-rotten group that ever walked this planet—only eclipsed by the pre-boomers (born in the years from 1935 to 1945), who have a slightly longer list of "gotta haves." These two groups, both momentous and monumental in their nature, grew up in a world of phenomenal prosperity that created a very high standard of living. The pre-boomers also had the amazing advantage of low numbers (due to much fewer births occurring during the Great Depression and war years), in combination with the prosperity of the post–World War II years (the pre-boomer birth rate in the country was only 2.6 million births in 1940, with the peak boomer year birth rate at an enormous 4.3 million in 1961). Never has such a large group had more food to eat, larger dwellings, more disposable income, such advanced heating and cooling systems, more personal mobility, more entertainment options, and better health. It's not that the boomers aren't working long hours to keep up with it all, it's just that greed has them stuck on this strange "hamster wheel" of always wanting/needing/expecting more. These groups are always complaining when they don't get everything they want, which has contributed to their progeny becoming even more insatiable.

Such consumer greed encourages an increase in advertising hype—the marketers start figuring that hype must be what the consumers want because that's what the consumers respond to. More hype then begets even more hype, which further blinds the consumer to what's really going on in the marketplace relative to returning *real* honest value. We get to the point where we can no longer identify a product with real value and a reasonable price (tradeoff). For example, is paying extra for a pair of cotton socks with a little man on a horse embroidered on them something we should consider a reasonable tradeoff? With all of the hype we're exposed to, we can forget that what we're actually buying is just a pair of socks, not a status symbol that will change our life.

All this escalating consumer greed can only lead to the next set of greedy questions: "If the party is almost over, then why shouldn't I start grabbing all I can?" and "By the way, my card's over the limit, so who's gonna pick up the check?" We'll talk more about this in chapter 7.

3. WE ACHE FOR THE REAL DEAL, BUT WE OFTEN SETTLE FOR NOSTALGIA-INDUCING IMITATIONS

A new-millennium distorted sense of reality at least partially explains the baby boomer's affinity toward things retro. These children of a simpler, more honest time are searching for something authentic in their life. They remember having real, genuine experiences when they were young, and they now search for touchstones to that reality. They remember a time before AIDS and terrorism. They remember a Good Humor man, dressed in sparkling white duds, driving around in a white truck selling wonderful ice cream treats. They even remember hitchhiking as a reasonable form of getting around. They remember florists' roses that smelled like roses (in an effort to get roses to stay fresh longer, commercial growers have, through excessive hybridization, removed the fragrant oils from many types of roses—pretty crazy when you think about it, as a big component of a rose is how it attacks your sense of smell, the one sense most closely linked to memory).

This search for a better reality is manifested in many ways, and may explain why middle-of-the-road suburbanites are buying *real* badass Harley-Davidson motorcycles. Also, it appears that even GEN Xer's are spending money (which they don't necessarily have) in their search of something real. Bottled Evian must be better than any tap water. No? Maybe that BMW is more real than a Ford or Chevy? Maybe reality TV is actually real? Don't think so . . . reality TV shows may be currently hot, but these contrivances are hardly the viewers' (or even the participants') reality. And video games are the fastest growing segment in the entertainment business—"They're so real!" fans scream . . . as if. If you've ever driven at speed in a real race car you know there is not a car-chase video game that can come close to replicating the genuine experience.

The street rod business provides a great example of how nostalgia leads consumers to succumb to hype disguised as the real deal. The original hot-rodders were renegades who took old cars that were lying around (in the 1950s it was twenty-year-old Fords and Chevys) and through inventiveness and real effort created vehicles that went against all formula and convention. These hot-rodders, clever and industrious but typically broke, had to make things happen through hard work. They made something cool out of almost nothing. This was good old Yankee ingenuity at its best.

In present-day California it has become almost typical for hot rods to be built by custom fabrication shops for large sums of money. The owner gets to be involved in developing the concept but essentially just writes the big checks. These hot rod replicas are built according to a very tight formula and are often incredibly overdone because the owners are attempting the impossible: to rediscover their lost youth (in other words, hot rods are classic midlife-crisis mobiles). Most of these vehicles end up as "trailer queens" because they hardly get driven. Some owners actually spend thousands of dollars just detailing their rod for a particular show. Others take their vehicles from show to show in enclosed trailers, spending days at these events bragging about the minutiae of the build. If one could possibly take one of these perfectionistic rods back to 1950s California, the original hot-rodders would be aghast that their pioneering efforts had become so mutated.

There are still parts of America today where these trailer-queen hot rods aren't much appreciated. A lot of old timers will first ask whether the owner did the build-up themselves. If the owner's response is no, then these guys will scoff and say something like "If you didn't build it yourself, then it ain't shit" and walk away. And in a way they're right—it doesn't take any cleverness or ingenuity to write a bunch of fat checks.

There is a whole industry built around the replication of hot rods (street rods). The customers want to be thought of as renegades and freethinkers, but in reality they typically follow a prescribed formula as to what constitutes a hot/street rod. For instance, the vaunted National Street Rod Association has a section on its website in its membership info that defines what a street rod is: "In addition, a street rod is a means of self expression for the creator. The builder of a street rod is not confined to guidelines set down by someone else . . . he can be his own man, and the street rod can be whatever he wants it to be," but then finishes with: "*as long as the basic vehicle was manufactured prior to 1949.*"

So what they're intimating is that a teenager who takes a beat-up 1980s Chevy S-10 pickup, and then shoehorns a V-8 into it, *hasn't* built a street rod. But in fact this industrious, and typically broke, teen has done exactly what the original street rodders were doing in the 1950s.

What's really going on here is the aging street rodders' desperate desire to be thought of as the kinda guy who misspent his youth back in the 1950s. They want to be that cool renegade whom the girls were attracted to in high school: a cool, filtered through forty years of memories to be relived, all measured against the prospect of aging and dying. Trying to recapture what was always a somewhat delusional dream—especially such perfectionistic re-creations of these totems of youth—at best only produces a false hope.

Well, maybe you've figured it out, but hot rodding is just another cult protecting its own view of how things must be. Bottom line, street rodders are protecting their investment in a false premise by perpetuating that false premise.

If they all buy into the premise that what they're building are precious collector items, then maybe the rods *will* be worth the ridiculous price they paid for them—very much like a house of cards. In this way, these street rods are really no different than overpriced, heavily accessorized Harley-Davidsons, gargantuan Aspen ski chalets, Nantucket trophy homes, garish Las Vegas hotels, or even the skillfully manipulated stock market. The pre-boomers and baby boomers seem to need to perpetuate their view of the world, so as to protect their financial and *emotional* investments in this world they created. They will accept perfectionistic replicas in an attempt to recapture a previous time. In a *big* way, they're looking backward instead of looking forward. In my view, a society should study the past instead of getting mired in replicating it. Or, as Kierkegaard Soren so profoundly put it, "Backwards understood be only can but, forwards lived be must life."

What's going on in the world of street rods is quite similar to what's going on at Disney (and many other corporations) these days. It looks like the collective Disney intelligence thinks that ideas are good only if they are extensions of precepts put forth by Walt Disney in the 1950s. One problem we, as a society, are about to face is that "nostalgia is old" (meaning looking back isn't the cool thing anymore). Yes, the America of the 1950s was spectacular because we were rich in both time *and* money, and we were looking forward. World War II had been won, the industrial age was exploding, transportation was easily accessible, television was changing everything, and the fiberglass surfboard had been invented.

Let me explain. A kid traveling down the coast of California in a beat-up old station wagon in search of a perfect wave is the stuff of songs and movies. Even the Japanese and Europeans get how immensely cool that was. (I apologize for the overuse of the word *cool,* but there really isn't another word that says exactly the same thing.) There are surf wear stores all over the world, some hundreds of miles from a "surfable" wave. Visitors from all over the world who come to California are still awed by the bikini-clad coeds frolicking on Malibu's Zuma beach, or by the seventy-plus golf courses in Palm Springs, or by the vastness of the American West. The classic California lifestyle is revered the world over. Walt Disney's Disneyland capitalized on that; Michael Eisner's California Adventure is a vain attempt at replicating it. The difference between the two parks is so screamingly obvious when you measure each one against the idea of "having some family fun in the warm California sun." One provides real family fun and a shared entertainment experience; the other comes off as phony and trying way too hard to be cool.

So is Disney the only company tripping all over themselves trying to be real and packaging reality up with a bow on it? Well, not even close. Budweiser's advertising theme line is "Budweiser TRUE." Coca-Cola's line is "Coca-Cola Real." Despite the false ring to these claims, marketers are reflecting and reacting to the consumer's desperate need for something real.

Looking backward while trying to go forward is not a good idea. We've got to figure out how to stop this vicious cycle, this "merry-*greed*-go-round," and start looking and working forward, toward the future, and toward what's real.

4. REALITY IS MESSY AND TAKES HARD WORK— AND WHO REALLY WANTS TO WORK THAT HARD?

"Anyone who isn't confused really doesn't understand the situation," said Edward R. Murrow. Boy, was he ever right about that—reality is confusing. Despite this, every day we do our best to make it less so, though it's not exactly an easily achievable task. Walt Disney summed it up by saying "I always like to look on the optimistic side of life, but I am realistic enough to know that life is a complex matter." Many marketers and producers are foolishly trying to find some sure bets in this confusing, messy world. The complexity of it all requires some determined effort to unravel, and the best you can hope for is mere moments of clarity. But what the heck, that's life.

It takes work (both time and effort) to establish a friendship, start a relationship, search out a real quality product/service, or even grow a stupid tomato. Basically, work is just that—and fun it ain't, necessarily. It has gotten to the point where we want it both ways. For instance, we collectively hate the couple at the end of the street who designed/built some wild house and then painted it chartreuse. So, what do we do? We create "art committees" to establish tight guidelines to preclude such gaffs. We then end up with sanitized cult-like "gated communities" where all the houses look like they were spit out of some giant manufacturing plant and then dropped in place by helicopter. We accept pseudo-art and pseudo-communities with formulaic rules, then we wonder why life in such communities seems boring. Hey, but at least there are no crazy, bright-green houses—but then again there aren't any architectural masterpieces in such communities either.

The average American seems to be on a serious quest to avoid real thinking—you know, the hard work that may actually advance the human condition. Instead we are drawn toward easy answers with the surface dazzle. We want diversions that protect us from the brutal realities of life—gated communities, maxed-out credit cards, and adulation of entertainment and sports stars are all symptoms of the malaise. It seems we all want jobs where we are paid to play.

For instance, our culture is, in many ways, disproportionately excited about sports—which are intended as an escape from the boring and harsh realities of daily life. In ancient Rome, as is happening in our own society, the populace began to demand more and more games. The gladiatorial games, once a seasonal occurrence, became a monthly event, then weekly, and, at the time of the fall of the empire, daily. Even as early as the time of Emperor Claudius (41–54 C.E.), the Roman calendar had 159 public holidays per year. It was as if no self-respecting Roman citizen thought that work was something he or she should be doing. "Work is for fools, and let the games begin!" was the aristocrat's cry as the Roman Empire imploded.

Today we seem to be living by the same philosophy. If you asked a jogger to deliver some newspapers as he went on his daily run, he'd probably be insulted. And what if we attached electric generators to the treadmills and stationary bikes at sports clubs (just think of all the free electricity that would be generated)—but would the people working out on those treadmills and bikes now eschew this "real work," believing they were being taken advantage of?

There's a sand dune in Manhattan Beach, California, that gets eroded by the large number of people, from all over Los Angeles, who do their daily workouts by climbing it. It's rumored to cost the city over $100,000 a year to monitor the situation and constantly move the eroded sand back to the top of the hill. To save the city a bundle of money, how about handing out empty buckets and letting these climbers fill them up with sand at the bottom of the dune and carry the eroded sand back to the top? By carrying these buckets full of sand, the people would get an even better workout! But of course these people would probably take their workout elsewhere, since they wouldn't want to do all that work for no pay.

What gives? Have Americans really gotten that lazy, or is it that we've lost our moral compass, or are we just confused about what makes a genuine work task, or has it just gotten too damn complicated for us to deduce what's really real? The answer is probably a combination of all of these.

It's time we got back to some solid realness. Life's stinky, messy, illogical, and sometimes ridiculous organic process is always better because what it produces is real, like real friends. But it's not necessarily as cheap, profitable, or expedient. The biggest problem with finding realness is that it always takes extra effort. Nothing that has any staying power is easy. And the same goes for generating ideas.

WHOOOOOOOOOOOOOAH!
IT'S TIME WE ALL SLOWED DOWN AND PUT ASIDE THAT FIFTH CAFÉ LATTÉ FOR THE DAY

It's time everyone took a deep breath and got out of the gotta-have-it-all-right-now fast lane. We need to take some time to ponder the fact that, in reality (in the purest sense of the word), life is all about the search for substance, truth, and beauty. If you reestablish this quest as your mission, you will never be bored. This is the simple, but daunting, quest that all humans face. It isn't getting any easier, especially when the honest truth is getting harder to find with each passing day. And it sure doesn't help that our presidents, celebrities, priests, and sports heroes are so often being caught in a lie. A little humble honesty is the thing that's needed most in America today.

As consumers, we are going to have to get off our butts and do our home-work to dig through the hype, schemes, and spin to discover the honest, inherent value in products, services, and goods. We need to become curious, educated con-sumers and learn to ferret out the scammers so we can spread the word. Likewise, if we find something excellent we need to make the extra effort to let others know about it. We need to go out of our way to patronize and reward companies that offer high-quality products or services, and we need to be willing to pay them a fair price and feel good when we do. We also need to understand the fiduciary relationship we have with the corner hardware store and the impact to the ma-and-pa businesses if we are always buying on low price at a big box store. In other words, realize how Wal-Mart's business model can undercut the local and always helpful ma-and-pa bike/hardware/fishing/you-name-it store, helping contribute to these small enterprises not making enough money to stay in business (although according to Bill Quinn's *How Wal-Mart Is Destroying America [and the World]*, Wal-Mart's prices aren't always lower than its competitors'—especially once there is no longer a local competitor). We need to somehow grasp what's going on when we're standing at a Sears store ready to buy a combo blister-pack of *four* different pliers (made in Asia) for only a few dollars more than what you'd have to pay for *one* Craftsman pliers (made in America and guaranteed for life). Or at a 99¢ Only Store buying pretty-damn nice pliers from India . . . for only 99¢. Effectively the whole manufacturing paradigm has been shifted, and every American is going to have to work toward a solution.

If we expect our corporations to honor innovation, we consumers need to support innovation too. For instance, if you were in the market for a kayak, you should be willing to pay more for a state-of-the-art pedal-driven design made by an innovative company like Hobie than a mass-produced imitation. Because a lot of innovation emanates from the grass roots, it's also imperative that we search out and patronize small companies making a difference, such as environmentally responsible Patagonia Clothing and Ben and Jerry's Ice Cream. And even larger companies that are solidly committed to innovation, like Apple and its cool iPod. As an informed consumer driven by curiosity, you owe it to yourself to take the extra time to find the real deal.

And Mr. Eisner (and for that matter, every CEO today) needs to wrap his head around the six simple words of the guy whose name is on the company he runs: "I believe in being an innovator" (a Walt quote so good that you'll find it twice in this book). Curiously, Steve Jobs said a similar thing at the keynote speech at Apple Expo in Paris, in September of 2003: "Innovate. That's what we do."

It all about finding something real and honest. Like, when you strip the glitz and hype away, advertising and marketing are just like a neighbor's report about an excellent restaurant he's just enjoyed, only on a much broader scale. What would your neighbor gain by lying to you about it—especially if he knew that later that week he would need to borrow a cup of sugar from you? Advertising is really no different. It is built on the basis of putting your best foot forward in a compelling way and answering the classic consumer's question "What's in it for me?" The advertising business is a way for a company to convey the benefits and enhance the inherent drama of the particular product or service.

But today, it's become very tough to play it straightforward and honest with the customer, especially when everyone else seems to be lying and cheating. When you were in high school and you saw someone cheating, what did you do—tell the teacher, and then be labeled a squealer, or just ignore it and suffer along? You probably just tried to ignore it, or, worse, you started finding ways to cheat. It was hard to know what to do back then, and even harder to know what to do as an adult. As a consumer, all you can do is vote with your wallet and go out of your way to reward the companies who play it straight.

And all those marketing wizards out there had better get real, first by demystifying their own PR BS and next by making sure their company's culture hasn't produced a cult mentality—where there is evidence of the parable of the emperor's clothes. A scenario built on hype can't last, in that the contract with the consumer must have a basis in honesty. It's like a house built on a swamp: sooner or later, it will sink into the mud. CEOs must get back to putting themselves in the consumer's shoes and doing everything they can to maximize the value they bring to the situation. To facilitate this, the company must hold up the consumer, not the stockholders, as king.

A certain amount of organic anarchy is, and will always be, necessary for progress both in the marketplace and inside a corporation (see chapter 6). There's nothing wrong with companies that want to build on their assets and conventions, but if they want to grow and succeed they had better find new and innovative ways to do what they do, and, of course, do it better than their competitors. And, they'd better make sure that they do more than just craft slick words and overpromise. Remember that Walt Disney preferred to underpromise and overdeliver—look where it got him.

Here's the supposition: if people take the time to really look, they typically know a good thing when they see it.

Don't you?

CHAPTER 5

DISNOIDS EXPOSED!

DISNEY'S CLANDESTINE CULT ANNIHILATES INNOVATION!

So, you ask, where's the evidence that cult-like thinking is starting to infiltrate The Walt Disney Company? Let's start with a couple of recent Disney annual reports. Take the photos of the gray-suited minions who now populate the ranks. These men and women look like a bunch of bankers and accountants, maybe because that's exactly what they are. Or maybe it's a reflection of the image the corporation wants to project—that we should have faith in Disney and its future because of its bank-like thinking and not so much its spirit of innovation. These managers, who are at the top of the "idea chain" at Disney, sure aren't being presented as the innovators, the dreamers, the magic-makers we think of when someone says Disney.

Now let's take a look at Michael Eisner's traditionally super-long letters to shareholders that introduce the annual reports. In Disney's 2002 annual report, among his 3,204 words, Eisner uses the word *idea* only twice: once in discussing the animated movie *Treasure Planet* saying: "Either we mis-marketed it, or the *idea* wasn't appealing"; and next in reference to the independence of the board of directors: "To help make sure that The Walt Disney Company continues to serve the best interests of its shareholders, we are instituting new rules for board governance, which will reduce the number of board members and enhance the independence of the board. This should further enhance accountability and encourage the flow of fresh *ideas* at the highest levels of our company." (Strange juxtaposition there wouldn't you say, in light of the Disney Board's poor rating for its governance?) It's also telling that he only once uses the word *innovation*. The chatty letter focuses more on brand expansion, asset management, and shareholder value.

In Eisner's 3,901-word (close to three times longer than The Declaration of Independence) letter in the 2003 annual report, he starts off with a review of the financial numbers. He again uses the word *idea* just twice, and he gets around to using *innovation* in respect to Disney's history. He even utilizes the borderline oxymoronic phrase "very low risk, high-return investment profile" to describe a few minor modest-budget films.

But saddest of all is the fact that on the cover of the 2003 report, and on the following thirty-five pages, poor, beleaguered pitchman Mickey (or his ubiquitous outlines/icons) is used something approaching forty times (or over sixty, if you count every hat with ears). Of course, it was the Mick's seventy-fifth year with the company, but come on—the poor mouse could use a siesta. (One interesting thing that did stand out in the 2003 annual report was the five men in Disney Consumer Products conspicuously not wearing ties. Bravo! I wonder what their story is.)

Maybe all this "review of the numbers" is the kind of thing that Eisner thinks the shareholders want to hear, but it doesn't project the true essence of what a company like Disney should stand for. As far as I can tell, the focus is no longer explicitly toward making magic which creates value that results in profits, but instead the equation begins and ends with profits.

You may be thinking, since when is it so wrong for a business to focus on producing profits? It's only wrong when it comes at the expense of your equity. In other words, if Disney reduces Mickey Mouse (and everything he stands for) to a corporate shill or opportunity, eventually his image becomes bankrupted; consequently the company can't expect to grow in a healthy way by using his image in the future. For that reason, it's imperative that you never "deplete the soil" to make a quick buck. Of course, a company can build new equity positions with innovation and fresh ideas, but it appears that Disney is taking the easier route of overfarming its equity.

Where is that fearless pursuit of ideas that we all think is so much a part of the Disney culture? Exactly what motivates people at Disney these days?

Let's talk motivators—the things that keep us going each day. Who can argue that greed isn't the mother of all motivators? Although it may be programmed deep into our psyche to keep us alive, it can end up as an overwhelming desire to have more of something than we actually need—like gobs of money or too much food. Good old fear can also be a powerful motivator (armies have run on it from the dawn of time), but even at low levels it can stymie creativity. It's altogether possible that the Disney corporate culture has now effectively combined these two motivations, which they then use as the greatest motivator of all time: the fear of losing money. However, there's one small problem: in such a scenario, idea generation and innovation usually wind up getting decimated in the process. Fear and greed typically conspire against creativity. On top of that, they pave the way for a cult-like way of thinking to creep in and take over.

Maybe something cataclysmic happened at The Walt Disney Company when Frank Wells died. Remember Frank Wells, who, in 1984, teamed up with Eisner to help bring Disney back from the brink of an almost hostile corporate takeover? Wells was a very different kind of corporate "gray suit." When I observed him in meetings, it was obvious he had reached a high level of fearlessness, which permeated the room. He had learned something about facing fears and dealing with failure while climbing those seven mountain peaks, and he brought that keen understanding to bear when he was working to get Disney up and on its feet once again. His aura of calm confidence and fearlessness appeared to be something Eisner leaned on. They were an awesome team, a testament to which is Eisner's book, *Work in Progress,* in which he talks at length about Wells and the relationship they enjoyed.

Wells's fearlessness made him a superb leader, but this trait may have been the thing that got him killed—jumping in the helicopter to go back to the summit for the proverbial "just one more run." Most likely this message as to where fearless-ness can lead wasn't lost on Eisner. Not too long after Wells's death, Eisner had multiple bypass surgery to avoid a potential heart attack, which may have been exacerbated in part from the stress of Wells's untimely death. Plus, Eisner was now all alone at the top.

As I mentioned before, Eisner apparently took his surgery as a sign that there was a reason he was still around, and that he had some unfinished business at Disney. And, as is oftentimes the case, this particular assertive posture is hard to keep in check, especially when there isn't a steadfast confidant, friend, and moral compass like Wells to bring Eisner back to reality.

If ever there was a time when Eisner needed a wise, trusted adviser it is now, but he has seemingly done everything in his power to eliminate any true dissen-sion in the people who surround him. Even the directors on the board are consid-ered by some to be too puppet-like to be able to offer any credible checks and balances to his initiatives. Remember how much Walt relied and leaned on brother Roy for his business sense. Of course, Eisner has a very bright and sup-portive wife in Jane, as Walt had in Lillian, but that's not the same as when a business contemporary, particularly one who you trust emphatically, calls you on it (that is, when you're caught up in your own BS).

And without checks and balances in a company, the "fear-of-losing-money motivator" and its counterpart, greed, have a much greater chance of taking over.

CREEPING CULT-LIKE CHARACTERISTICS

So how is this fear of losing money playing out in how the cult-like behavior is creeping into the Disney culture? Well . . . in general, cults are characterized by a charismatic leader, a strong iconic symbol, a dogmatic belief system, a takeover mentality, and strict rules of behavior for their adherents. In subtly incremental and differing amounts, Disney seems to have all of the above these days. Let's explore this insidious "cult of the mouse" and try to determine whether it is irre-versible, or *not*.

1. CULTS HAVE A CHARISMATIC LEADER

A cult leader sets the rules of the game, and the lieutenants put them into action. True dissension isn't allowed. The general organic anarchy of the typical creative process certainly isn't accommodated; even worse, anything creative almost gets force-fit into a strict set of rules. After awhile, when the leader issues a directive, the underlings automatically twist it into some kind of absolute rule. After awhile, the only question asked is "What will the cult leader do or like?"

First, no leader is smart enough to have the right answers for everything. Second, the underlings perpetually try to anticipate what the leader will like, so any great, or even halfway good, idea has a chance of getting second-guessed out of existence. Third, and most important, the difficult search for a truly new idea suffers greatly, because the idea isn't the "holy grail" that everyone is looking for—it's the approval of the leader that becomes the quest. (One sign that you're dealing with a cult-leader-type is that he or she hates hearing the word *no*.) The true creative process demands an open dialogue where something stupid is called out for what it is; but in an environment that doesn't allow an honest search for the truth, you'll typically find that real, fresh ideas will atrophy and never flourish.

For instance, Eisner has an honest interest in architecture (and has even been recognized for his contributions, like in 2001, getting the National Building Museum's annual Honor Award, with its press release saying, "Mr. Eisner . . . widely celebrated as one of the nation's most passionate patrons of architecture"), which may explain the fact that Disney's California Adventure got a lot of architectural focus and attention as it was being conceived and built. However, the arts (whether painting, photography, architecture, music, or any other medium) are simply methods to convey ideas, *not* ideas themselves. The architecture in the park may represent Eisner's personal interest rather than express any particular idea or clear vision as to what the concept for the park was.

While I was working at Disney, Jack Lindquist would quote Walt, saying that it's not about *who's* right, but all about *what's* right, so therefore do *what's* right for Disneyland. This is exactly the kind of open atmosphere that is so important to generating new ideas. The search for the inherent "rightness" of an idea and its expression is the basic tenet of this entire book: the *what* and the *how* are *soooooooooo* much more important than the *who*. And the search for the "rightness" in ideas is all that matters if you're looking to innovate; typically the *who* can be, at best, the facilitator. Walt Disney (the *who* of all things Disney) died, but the *what*, the ideas he championed, live on. The best any facilitator can do is to create a situation where innovation can properly incubate, and then allow new ideas to percolate to the top. Lots of things conspire against this process, and cult-like thinking in paying homage to an "idea king" is, at its worst, a sure idea killer.

Eisner isn't totally to blame. He was instituted as a charismatic star CEO to repair an ailing company. To get things going, he put on the front burner things that would maximize opportunities for profit, which may have relegated to the back burner the generation of new ideas. Eisner felt he was the guy who had ridden in on a white horse to save the company, and in a way he was. But then, it seems, he began thinking he should micromanage everything, instead of creating an environment that constantly fostered innovation. One thing that may have forced him to turn to micromanagement was a general goal to increase profits by close to 20 percent each year—a tall order to fill, and a goal that has the potential to consume his career. And, in a way, because he didn't own the company, he couldn't tell the profit-driven stockholders to back off a little. In a way he was beholden to the Bass brothers, owners, at times, of a huge amount of Disney stock, who had thrown their weight around to get him appointed CEO and chairman of the board.

At the base of it all, though, Eisner isn't specifically a creative person. Because of this, it appears that he has become increasingly disconnected from the process of originating something, starting with a blank piece of paper or empty computer screen. He has an excellent nose for ideas but has seemingly suppressed this ability; in turn, he appears to have become more of a clever opportunist adept at assessing what will turn a quick profit. If Eisner were more of a pure idea guy, maybe he would have tempered his vision with an eye toward longer-term innovation and rewards. About creativity and intuition, Albert Einstein said, "The intuitive mind is a sacred gift and the rational mind is a faithful servant. We have created a society that honors the servant and has forgotten the gift."

2. CULTS HAVE STRONG ICONIC SYMBOLS AND DOGMATIC BELIEF SYSTEMS

Walt Disney is such a mythical figure in The Walt Disney Company that his birthday is still celebrated even though he's dead. The cult of the mouse is constantly traipsing his black-and-white image around, to immense effect and profit. Any day now they'll find a way to bring him to life through CGI and he'll be back among us, as weird as that sounds (Walt's heirs sold his image and likeness to the company in 1982). Of course, the same goes for poor Mickey; more than once I've heard people in Disney meetings say, as if talking about a god, "Mickey Mouse will never die—he will live forever."

The columns in the Team Disney building, where Eisner's office is located, are constructed of dwarfs, and the table in Eisner's anteroom has contrasting Mickey-shaped wood inlays. Throughout the studio complex, iconography (almost as heavy as you might find in an Egyptian pharaoh's temple) is everywhere you look, especially the Mickey icons; it has been ratcheted up to a point that it starts to almost resemble an outgrowth of some mythology, in a way, something you'd expect from a cult. Sometime you should check out www.hiddenmickeys.org.

This weird spreading of the word has led to a glut of Disney merchandise almost everywhere you look. As Eisner has assumed the role of the living Disney figurehead, he is almost obligated to believe himself to be the new "wizard of oohs and ahs." He so wants to leave his mark; and so far he has done so with a few outstanding movies, but mostly he's made his mark in the form of excellent merchandising, licensing, and franchising schemes and grand architectural statements. And with his latest moniker for the future plans for the company, "Disney's Digital Decade," it looks like he's really on to something. If you think about it, we now get our words, pictures, music, movies/video, and telephone conversations via microprocessor manipulation of 0s and 1s. The concept of digital information and its easy/fast transmission is a genuine paradigm shift that we're living through as you read this. It has changed everything for better or worse—and at a speed that's mind-boggling . . . but I digress. It remains to be seen how that piece of artful alliteration plays out as he builds his legacy.

From what I observe, it looks as though Eisner's excellent merchandising schemes have set into motion a machine that is now flat running out of control. You can hardly go anywhere today where some Disney merchandise isn't being sold. There is Disney character merchandise present—in the over 300 Disney Stores in malls all across America—that competes directly with the stores in the parks, in almost every department store, even in supermarkets, in airport stores, inside McDonald's fast-food kid's meals, and Disney stuff all over the TV in the form of entire channels, and in commercials for things as mundane as diapers . . . ad nauseam. No wonder the Disney Stores are imploding. The world absolutely does *not* need so much Disney junk, and because of this oversaturation, many people are starting to reject it. Disney merchandise just doesn't have that special appeal anymore. It's like having ice cream with every meal—after awhile it tastes kind of yucky.

One group that is not rejecting Disney merchandise is the dyed-in-the-wool "Disneyana Disnoids," who are collecting so much Disney stuff that the company has ramped up its production of collectible goods. But for something to become a collectible it must be somewhat rare or hard to come by—the demand far greater than the supply. But Disney's collectible goods production is getting to where there is no way for the demand to keep up with it; therefore plenty of this new merchandise won't even be worth its original retail price. Plus, just how valuable can something produced explicitly as a collectible ever be?

The Disney brand managers who generate all this stuff must believe they can somehow change the classic supply and demand equation. Here's an example of how it typically works: Lindquist, who worked at Disneyland for more than forty years, enjoyed recounting how, in the late 1950s and early 1960s, Walt Disney had given him the daunting side job of digging through piles of old animation cels to find some that might have sales potential at one of the stores on Main Street, U.S.A. Lindquist said that despite having picked the best of the lot they still had a hard time selling the cels—even for a few dollars each, and most just got tossed out. Such a process led to any of the surviving cels to be selectively the nicer ones, not to mention quite rare, and so today they're worth big bucks.

Of course, the oversaturation problem stems from the fact that the Disney employees who are responsible for all this runaway merchandising believe that if they *create* more stuff to sell it will keep them in their jobs. Eisner, acting as the king of the castle, has set this tone of overexposure and merchandise overkill, euphemistically called "synergy." Eisner got lucky with his early merchandising efforts at Disney, specifically because, when he signed on, Disney's merchandising was in the Dark Ages relative to the current practice. But just as the Spaniards' greed for gold in the New World got out of control, even the simplest manifestation of business greed has no boundaries—that is, until the business implodes.

All this product proliferation typically ends only when external market forces cause it to crash, especially when the stuff produced isn't inherently valuable. At one time Spain was the richest country in the world. Why it didn't become a superpower, or at least more of a world leader, is a bit of a mystery—runaway greed may explain its quick rise and collapse. Gold is the noblest of metals, and its easy workability and resistance to tarnishing has many applications, even in manufacturing; its rarity and compelling luster cause us to put a high value upon it. But the Spaniards used up all the gold they purloined from the New World through gilding, adorning, and *creating* bigger and bigger churches—and funding and building sinkable armadas. King Ferdinand and Queen Isabella were innovative enough to bankroll old Christopher Columbus, but they (and subsequent monarchies) squandered a golden opportunity to add real value to their country. (Cortez told the Aztecs that Spaniards suffered from a disease for which the only cure was gold. Clearly a quite interesting way to put it, wouldn't you say?)

The lesson here is that more fluff will always be just *more fluff* if it doesn't do something to advance the human condition. Creating a flurry of activity gives the impression that progress is being made, but activity on its own doesn't necessarily equate to the advancement of a current situation. The challenge of any corporation is to create a belief system that carefully marshals its resources toward the building of ideas, toward a goal of innovation. This belief system will foster learning, training, and experimenting, which ultimately results in true growth. Evidently, this is *not* something a closed cult-like philosophy is wont to do.

3. CULTS WANT TO CONTROL EVERYTHING

During the past fifty years, Disney's business expanded greatly by playing to pre-boomers and baby boomers—in theatres, on TV, and even with themed amusement parks. The boomers grew up with a steady diet of Disney family entertainment. They were inundated with *Mickey Mouse Clubs,* a host of animated movies like *Peter Pan* and *Sleeping Beauty, Davy Crockett* TV shows and the resulting coonskin-hat merchandising blitz, *The Wonderful World of Color* (later called *The Wonderful World of Disney*), *Old Yeller,* theatrical releases like *The Love Bug* and *Mary Poppins,* Annette Funicello movies and songs, Disneyland, Disney-World, and on and on.

The typical pre-boomer or baby boomer kid growing up in the 1950s and 1960s could, in any given week, spend much more time with Disney than in his or her family's house of worship or working on homework. It wasn't necessarily a bad thing; it's just that what Disney offered became a pervasive part of his or her cultural growth. Disney filled the lion's share of the boomer's almost insatiable need for entertainment. This acculturation became a way of life that the boomers passed on when they became parents. Mommy and daddy boomers fed their kids a steady diet of Disney, partly in an attempt to recreate their own childhoods. You were almost considered a bad parent if you didn't take your kid to meet Mickey "in person" at one of the parks. Disney videos got their sprockets worn out from repeated use as electronic babysitters. Classic Disney animated movies were on a once-yearly video release schedule, and they flew (like Dumbo) off the shelves. This Disney thing was OK until it reached saturation, when too much Disney stuff became just more fluff and when the Disney brand and characters became shills to sell other, non-Disney, non-entertainment stuff (like diapers, phew.) But Disney's corporate ambitions only continued to get bigger. Again, greed has no boundaries.

Currently, Disney is a gigantic media conglomerate that owns, or has a controlling interest in, a slew of movie studios under the following banners: Walt Disney Pictures (includes feature animation), Touchstone Pictures, Hollywood Pictures, Miramax Films, Dimension Films, the Buena Vista Motion Pictures Group (a movie/video/television distribution and marketing arm), the ABC Television and Radio Network, seventy-six television and radio stations in numerous major markets, a DVD/video-release group, a TV-production arm, twelve cable TV channels (including ESPN [of which Disney owns 80 percent; Hearst Corporation the remaining 20 percent], The Disney Channel, the ABC Family Channel, E! Entertainment [with Comcast, which is partly owned by Microsoft and Liberty Media], The History Channel and A&E Television [with Hearst and GE], and

SOAPnet), multiple music production groups and record labels, theme parks and hotels and resorts scattered all over the world (although a few are only equity positions/licensing agreements ala a "franchise"), a cruise ship line, a professional sports franchise, three book publishing companies (Walt Disney Company Book Publishing [the world's largest children's book publisher], Hyperion Books, and Miramax Books), fifteen magazine titles, video-game-licensing deals, a theatrical production company, consumer products division, more than 300 mall stores, a direct-marketing catalog, and a giant Internet presence for all of the above (and as if that isn't enough, Disney even owns Oscar.com, NFL.com, NBA.com, NASCAR.com, and an equity partnership in TiVo). *Whew!*

It's almost as if you can't get away from Disney, and I guess that's the idea. Almost like something you'd expect from a cult, it looks like Disney would like to expand their influence and control in as many ways as they can. Following the line of thinking that Edward R. Murrow was concerned about, just how much frankness can you expect from an ABC news reporter covering The Walt Disney Company's activities, when his or her paycheck is signed by Eisner? Or how much impartiality can you expect from an E! Entertainment channel reviewer doing a piece on a Disney movie? Any way you look at it, the lines have been blurred and some freedom of expression is probably being compromised. Where is the easy exchange of ideas in a free and open forum? It all comes down to the fact that any business, including Disney, doesn't want negative press. What business wouldn't want to control what people are hearing about it? Of course, Disney would probably take issue with this, but really—how can such conflicts of interest produce anything approximating reality or the truth on a consistent basis?

The Federal Communications Commission (FCC) is supposed to protect us from such monopolistic activities, but about 75 percent of what people are watching during primetime (including cable/satellite transmissions) is controlled by five entities: Disney/ABC, GE/NBC/Universal, News Corp./Fox/DirectTV, Viacom/CBS, and Time Warner. And these guys are broadcasting on public airways, which belong to you and me. How would you like it if, for instance, GM, Ford, Daimler-Chrysler, Toyota, and Honda controlled the number and types of vehicles allowed to run on our public highways during rush hour?

In another scenario, let's say you're watching the ABC network on what could very well be a Disney-owned TV station; it would be feasible to see a commercial promoting a Disney product, movie, service, or park during a break in a made-for-TV movie produced by Disney. Maybe it's a commercial for Disneyland. Well, Disneyland pays the TV station to run the spot, the TV station pays the network for the airtime, the network pays The Disney Studio for the movie, and so on, and Disney gets rich, rich, rich. The money all stays in the happy-little Disney family. Where's the free enterprise? Where's the competition? In a very roundabout way, this situation brings to mind Al Capone's penchant for schemes that would allow him to control everything—the production, the distribution, the law—and thereby force any competition, especially the little guy, out of business.

Adding to the above situation, let's say you're wearing your Mickey Mouse shirt while sitting in a Disney hotel and watching a Disney movie on Disney-owned ABC-TV station, after spending a day at a Disney park, and you've paid for it all using your Disney Visa credit card. (Additionally, if you are watching the movie via TiVo, TiVo headquarters has the capability to observe your viewing habits; for example, TiVo was able to find out how many times TiVo owners recorded and played back Janet Jackson's 2004 Super Bowl halftime performance.) It sounds perfectly Orwellian, doesn't it? Maybe Big Brother is actually sneaking into our society under the guise of a chirpy little rodent named Mickey. Were we all distracted by a bunch of smiling animal characters, while America's laissez-faire open-commerce system was being compromised?

As with anything in the human condition, what's fair is open to interpretation. The Roman soldiers used to share a loaf of bread as part of their daily ration, and the only way it could possibly work is if one soldier tore the loaf in half, while the other soldier got to choose which half. Humans haven't changed, and no one wants another's vision of fairness foisted on them.

OK, OK, OK, this cult of the mouse corporate culture thing may not have infiltrated The Walt Disney Company completely, and Disney may not be in any position to actually take over the world, but when so much power is concentrated (or conglomerated) in one area without some factors to balance it, what you've got is a gigantic recipe for greedy practices, not fresh and open thinking.

4. CULTS ENFORCE STRICT RULES OF BEHAVIOR THAT STAMP OUT INDIVIDUALITY AND DISSENT

The Japanese have an antiquated saying, "A protruding nail gets hammered flat." This sort of thinking has had, in past generations most specifically, the effect of hampering almost the entire Nipponese culture's approach to fresh idea generation. An idea, by its very nature, must stand out and is therefore an irritant. And a similar hampering happens when a cult-like frame of mind infiltrates an organization, it can make everyone afraid to stick their necks out and be noticed. And fear and creativity can't occupy the same space.

Given the current fare coming from Disney, it appears that the fear of sticking out one's neck is rampant at Disney today. Disney employees, like most employees today, are simply afraid of way too many things: afraid to lose their job in the next round of profit-enhancing cutbacks; afraid that their immediate boss won't support their ideas and have enough guts to tell "Emperor" Eisner that he's wrong; afraid that a reorganization will eliminate their department; afraid that their new idea might not be an instant sure-bet moneymaker.

You'll know when a cult mentality has begun to take hold when getting someone's approval becomes more important than searching out the right idea. The individual ego gets subordinated in favor of the almighty belief system, and everything is set up so that the system and leader can never be blamed. The emperor-has-no-clothes syndrome is unfortunately "alive and well" at the house of the mouse, even according to ex-board members Roy E. Disney and Stanley Gold. The situation that seems to play out at Disney these days is this: if a project is a success, then, of course, that's simply the Disney way, but if things go wrong, someone is singled out as the reason for failure. "Hail! Hail! The gang's all here . . . except for anyone who fails."

As with any club or group, the team is set up as most important; this in itself is not a problem, *except* when the entire team is forced to march at the speed of the slowest person. A successful team is one that has the best talent in each position; outstanding individual effort at each of these positions combines to create a better situation for all. This kind of selfless structure brings life to real-deal ideas because of its subtle architecture of an open atmosphere where talent and fresh ideas are recognized and appreciated for what they bring to the team.

When personal fearlessness is combined with a lack of any fear of failure inside a corporation, it usually results in an amazing exchange of ideas. (Scratch the surface of any successful and innovative company, and you will see this kind of fearless culture in action.) But if individual effort is discouraged, brilliance ends up mired in mediocrity. Key to a successful balance of indivdual and team effort is that there is no one head genius, but instead a collective genius paying homage to ideas. Self-effacing Walt Disney put it well: "We allow no geniuses around our Studio."

Another thing to take into account is that creative people, by their nature, aren't necessarily joiners. Creative people are renegades, pushing against the confines of convention. As Saul Steinberg said, "The life of the creative man is led, directed, and controlled by boredom. Avoiding boredom is one of our most important purposes." Creative people are usually more interested in searching for beauty and truth. They will go out of their way to not accept the status quo. Most strive, more than anything else, not to be bored.

Today, it's possible that too many of the messy, emotional, artistic types, who were once the backbone of Disney, have been, as they say, "drummed out of the corps." This attrition probably explains why a fair number of those who remain are wannabe creative-types—the guys who talk a good game but spend most of their day managing the process instead of truly stirring things up and coming up with fresh ideas. Margaret J. Wheatley had it right when she said, "The things we fear most in organizations—fluctuations, disturbances, imbalances—are the primary sources of creativity."

How creativity is dealt with inside a corporation shakes down from the top, and many CEOs today do everything they can to be insulated from the organic anarchy of the creativity process. No one, especially a CEO, wants to deal with such turmoil, and in a way, who can blame them? But Walt Disney used to go out of his way to walk the halls of his production studio; he was known to be hands on in that he was willing to get in there and wrestle with the ideas. Today The Walt Disney Company is just too damn big. It's no surprise that Eisner has become somewhat detached from the daily dealings with the artistic types. The dichotomy here is that Eisner is known to be a micromanager, but because of the cocoon he now operates from, he can only jump into the fray on a cursory level, which can sometimes contribute to a superficial quick-fix as opposed to wrestling the problem to the ground, and potentially coming up with something profoundly innovative.

As mentioned in the first chapter, when I first started at Disney, I would consistently have one-on-one meetings with Eisner. When I left six years later, more often than not, twenty-five people would attend a typical meeting with him—not what you'd call an intimate exchange of ideas. Because of the personal nature of creativity, smaller and more intimate groups have a better chance to produce innovation. From what I observed while I was there, and from reports since, Disney has become a "meeting hell" (not unlike most corporations these days) to the advantage of the schmoozer and to the detriment of the sincere work task of researching and finding new ideas. Those who benefit most in such an environment are those who can play the system. A cult mentality promulgates this kind of "group grope" behavior, causing these meetings to become a patronizing homage to the leader, a forum for grandstanding by the true believers, and a place to ostracize any outliers—thus populating the cult with like-minded people, or in the case of Disney, Disnoids.

IDEAlly, WHAT'S GOING ON?

Let's start with what people first think of when you say Disney: animation. Their new head of Walt Disney Feature Animation, David Stainton, is a guy with a Harvard MBA whose claim to fame (among others) is that he successfully brought in, on budget, very profitable animated sequels like the direct-to-video *Little Mer-*

maid II, Lady and the Tramp II, and *Cinderella II* and low-cost animated TV programs like *Kim Possible.* I have to wonder what Walt Disney would have thought
of him. Does he have enough creative moxie to walk in Walt's footsteps? He has
obviously learned how to manage his career (started at Disney in 1989 in the
Strategic Planning group), but is he the kind of person who can allow for enough
organic anarchy and then manage it well enough to create and produce greatness?
I hope so. In an April 29, 2003, *Los Angeles Times* article, he is reported to have a
"mixed record" in his dealings with the fragile egos of artists because of his blunt
style and impatience. Only time will tell, but it could be quite difficult for him to
let the creative juices flow, given how Disney is set up to grind out the bucks these
days. All in all, I wish him the best of luck—*because, boy, is he gonna need it.*

It takes a certain emotional investment to unlock a real-deal idea. Passion is
needed to pull together disparate thoughts into something new. The problem is
that the messy and uncontrollable nature of emotion is anathema to cults, whose
overriding concern is maintaining order and power. This Disney-acting-cult-like
dilemma—being in the idea business but keeping its idea people on a tight rein—
often creates a faux emotional environment as a stand-in for the organic anarchy
that can lead to true innovation.

From what I've observed at times, many corporate Disnoids play a weird
charade of creativity, as if ideas are something to pull out of the air and then run
up and down the hall shrieking about. It manifests itself as some strange, staged
production number or game played by the idea cowboys or cowgirls—as if a dog-
and-pony show is all it takes to create new ideas. Unfortunately, when a cult
mentality starts to create these rules for how ideas will now play out, it allows the
"spin and dazzle" people to take over—and those people are typically the ones
who wouldn't know a real idea if it slapped them hard in the face. I'm not saying
that there aren't any creative people left at Disney, just that the "childlike" artist
types may be getting pushed aside by the serious game players.

Soon, the average employee gets confused by all the gamesmanship and
begins to also misuse words like *idea* and *create.* In the many meetings I attended
at Disney, I saw too many instances where people used the word *create* when they
really meant *produce* and cleverly prostituted the word *idea* when they simply
meant *profit opportunity.*

Revisionist thinking and self-serving wordplay, seen in the creeping misuse of
words like *idea* and *create,* permeate most aspects of business today, just like they
would in a cult. The commonly understood language becomes stretched to mean
something else, and after awhile the exaggeration almost becomes the common
belief. It's an insidious progression: the spin-and-dazzle creeps off the pages of the
press releases and right into the day-to-day belief system of the corporation. Over-

all, mumbo-jumbo is truly one of the most insidious aspects of corporate culture (not to mention politics!), since the language becomes so inflated that it gets harder every day to understand what's really being said, if anything at all.

Check this out. In a lengthy interview in *Newsweek* in 2003, Eisner sorta let slip "Magic is about deception," which quickly elicited a panicked admonishment from his spokeswoman, who had to remind him that " 'deceive' is really a bad word" and he might want to substitute the root term "create." Eisner, ever the one to get in the last word, replied, "No, but it's creative deception."

This mumbo-jumbo and confusion of the sincere work task isn't just happening at Disney; it's happening in governmental agencies, schools, and businesses all over America. It happens when the administrator types take over and think they're actually making progress, but in reality they're spending their efforts advancing their particular agenda, taking care of "their kind," and propagating like-minded thinking. It is said that Henry Ford once walked into one of his administrative departments and asked his right-hand guy to explain what exactly was the work they did. After hearing what they did, Henry said to go ahead and get rid of half of them, as it shouldn't make much of a difference.

I've heard it said that Walt Disney didn't believe there should be offices at Disneyland. He felt that offices and a hierarchy of job titles would detach the Disney cast member from the park guest. I guess he understood that administrative enterprises typically only breed more of the same, and that workers and doers are what's needed—and that the workers needed to be in the park almost all of the time. But new-millennium America is in love with administration. For example, it's not uncommon for school administrators to lay off teachers before they lay off administrative staff—*go figure*. Advertising agencies will have meeting kings or queens who will hold their corner offices long after the worker bees are let go, later wondering why the agency is going out of business.

Effecting change and innovation has a lot to do with the sincere work task and the people you're surrounded with—either "complicators" or "simplifiers." Military strategists will tell you that American soldiers in World War II were successful because they weren't afraid to act as free agents and improvise in the field, while the Japanese soldier would wait for directives from the top. As it worked out, the analysis of the person in the trenches would ultimately win over theoretical administration of the situation from afar.

How do those administrator "complicator" types take over? Basically it's because it is hard and messy to come up with ideas, and it's much easier to *pretend* that what you're doing is actually innovative. It's especially easier to sell an idea to upper management if it's also easy to do and a money-saving or income-producing scheme. *Easy* is the operative word here. People today want, and almost expect, an easy job that appears tough and also pays a lot. In order to make this happen for themselves, many managers have figured out how to manage their jobs (and manage to keep their jobs) instead of doing the dirty work.

What Walt Disney meant when he said "do the right thing for Disneyland" was that he wanted the cast member to wade into the problem and solve it so it stayed fixed. He didn't want a bunch of yakity-yak in meetings and brown-nosing—all he basically wanted was a happy park guest. He knew that a happy customer was the basis for every successful enterprise.

For example, Walt Disney understood how seemingly unimportant things like making your ticket book look special can actually add a lot to the customer experience and was willing to put in the extra effort and expense. He knew an emotional connection was made during your visit at Disneyland and maintained when you took that ticket book home and put it aside so that you could later revisit your memories of your park visit. Each time you handled it, that ticket became a touchstone to a happy day spent with family or friends. Even the fact that you didn't use up all the tickets in the book with one visit encouraged a return visit. Proof of the value of these ticket books is that they are for sale all over eBay.

The look and feel of today's "spitter" tickets at Disneyland don't elicit an emotional connection in any way comparable to the book of tickets, and they probably get tossed instantly in the trash when you get home (or before). Of course, today's tickets are very cost effective, and in a meeting some smart-talking manager must have made the latest iteration of a Disneyland ticket seem like a no-brainer. (In actuality, somebody should have used her or his brain and at least made the spitter tickets look extra special, like a hologram of the castle, and maybe even worth something like a free ice cream cone on a return visit.)

You can easily see what happens when good ideas start getting tossed aside in favor of the easy sell. An insular cult-like thinking process begins to infiltrate the ranks and sets up a support system that enables the easy-sell ideas to come to the top. Other employees start to notice the success of the people who propose these easy-sell ideas, and how fast they get promoted—and soon like-minded administrator types proliferate. This "cultishness" breeds an incestuous dynamic that actually makes it hard for fresh, real-deal ideas, which are eminently harder to sell, to percolate to the top.

Unless any company, including Disney, learns how to neutralize the meeting schmoozer, and subsequently nurture an organic creative dynamic that gives people latitude to stick their necks out without fear, those companies will continue to produce retreads, remakes, schemes, and more of the same.

COULD DISNEY'S INSIDIOUS CULT-LIKE MENTALITY BRING DOWN THE WHOLE (MOUSE) HOUSE OF CARDS?

Cults tend to think they have the answers to everything. The leader is set up as all knowing. Their organizational precepts are deemed absolute. They limit freedom of expression (that is, unless what you're saying specifically agrees with their teachings). Above all, a cult just isn't real and that's why it will usually collapse—eventually.

The fraternity, sorority, club, or cult (or whatever you want to call it) at Disney must be dismantled if the company is to make it successfully through the next decade. Eisner must reinvent himself and the organization behind him. He needs to roll up the sleeves on his Armani suit and get to work. He needs to find and embrace real creative-types who will dig around for real ideas. He needs to remove any wannabe creative-types from his organization and reassign a large percentage of all the administrative people and bean counters. Total turmoil, you might say. And it sure isn't going to be easy; in fact, it's going to be as hard as climbing Mt. Everest. But he (or whoever is heading up Disney) needs to get down and dirty. The directive is deceptively simple (although near impossible for most CEOs today): get in touch with the people he serves—the customer, not the stockholders. Somehow the insular cult-like thinking must be rejected, and the search for fresh ideas and innovation must once again be elevated to top-of-the-mountain status. We'll just have to wait and see if Eisner's up to the task of pushing Disney to reach that particular summit again.

He, you, I, and everybody in American business must hack away at a cult mentality when we see it, foster the organic nature of the creative process, and establish an open business culture in which innovation can take root. Each of us can get things going in our particular lives by identifying and neutralizing the idea killers, fine-tuning our ability to spot idea people, and nurturing receptiveness and childlike thinking in ourselves and in the people we surround ourselves with.

So, how and where do *we* start? One place you can start is by reading the next chapters, which should provide some insight into this crazy thing called the organic anarchy of the creative process.

CHAPTER 6

LOOK FOR THE CREATIVE SPARKS—

LOOK OUT FOR THE IDEA KILLERS

The idea business has more than its share of myths and misconceptions, so you've most likely heard things like the following: "Ideas are everywhere, and it's only the lack of follow-through that keeps most ideas from succeeding." "Pure genius isn't that far away from insanity." "There are no new ideas, only evolutions or derivatives of existing ideas." "Your idea is exactly what I was thinking about." "Ideas are a dime a dozen; execution is everything." "Ideas are in the ether, and many people can have the same idea at the same time." "Ideas are only 10 percent—the rest is the hard part." "I have the best ideas in my dreams." "Certain drugs can help open up the mind to ideas." "I have a lot of great ideas, but not enough money to get them going." "I've got this great idea for a movie. I just need someone to write it up." "No one's out to steal your ideas." And so on.

So are new, fresh ideas really all that rare? Yep. *Frickin' absopositivalutely!* Otherwise there would be better movies, books, TV shows, and more breakthrough new products. As we all know, chat is cheap, but real-deal ideas are definitely not "FREE. Help yourself." A good amount of the talk in the previous paragraph is bunk perpetrated by non-idea people in order to protect their turf (in other words, maintain status quo and protect what may be a less-than-creative job). So, let's examine the trials and tribulations of advancing a real-deal idea, whether you're at Disney or anywhere else.

The first problem every person with a new idea faces is to understand that just having an idea isn't enough. An idea is the spark that ignites the process but sometimes only makes up 5 percent of the whole deal. A critical next step is to secure enough seed money to push the research and development, which can be quite prolonged and will necessitate brutal analysis and honesty in order to produce results. Third comes the implementation: financing (more money), operations, production, and distribution—the practical aspects of bringing a product or service to the marketplace. Fourth of course is marketing (even more hard cash and hard effort)—the process of getting people to notice and then actually consider buying your product or service. All products need a careful balance of all four of the above disciplines for things to work out well. In addition, the marketing costs of most products and services will probably be more than what most people think; the costs can easily be 40 percent of the total costs, and sometimes they are more than 70 percent.

A lot of people get an idea and think, "Eureka, Martha, I've got it!" and then sit on their hands and wait. Well, if there was ever a four-letter word in the English language, it's *wait*. Waiting is the worst thing to do with any idea. First of all, no one is going to knock at your door and ask if you have any ideas to sell. You have to expose your idea to the world to see if you have something—run it up the flagpole and see if anyone salutes. This is where it can get tricky. At this point you want to protect your idea from infringement. If your idea is possibly patentable, by all means initiate a patent application for it. If it's something you can trademark, then start the appropriate application process. Since 1989, the Berne copyright convention has governed copyrights, so almost everything written today is copyrighted the moment it is written. (Just be sure to include a © and the name of the person/company who owns it. Once your written work is published, it's smart to submit your work to the U.S. Library of Congress for a definitive record.)

If you are in the employ of a corporation, you have probably relinquished all intellectual property rights to any work you do while you are their employee. Most corporations today, big or small, have an ironclad release that you must sign that ensures that whatever you create while working there remains their property. Consequently, many creative people fear that their individual rights to their own personal work done during breaks and even off-hours may be compromised. Theoretically, let's say you worked for a big corporation and your hobby was song writing. If you happened to write a hit song at home on a weekend, it could be potentially misconstrued that the corporation owns rights to that song (although that is not the intention of the release, of course). The general confusion over these kinds of issues scares a lot of creative people away from corporate jobs, because most creative people are always writing scripts on the side, drafting the next great American novel, doing T-shirt designs, writing comic strips, making greeting cards, or whatever it takes to keep their juices flowing.

As I mentioned in chapter 3, I was teamed up with Lawrence Kasdan at my first agency job, and it was common knowledge that Larry was always working on his movie scripts on the side. This was the same ad agency that produced Cathy Guisewite, of *Cathy* comic strip fame (from what I remember, a couple of the art directors around the agency gave her a few tips on how to draw her now-famous character). In those days, this particular agency was known for being a hotbed of creativity, and I believe their openness to idea generation was part of it. Because of the constant flow aspect of creativity, corporations need to figure out how to deal with and encourage real-deal idea generation inside and out and at all levels, because more ideas only beget more ideas. As John Steinbeck, a contemporary of Walt's, said, "Ideas are like rabbits. You get a couple and learn how to handle them, and pretty soon you have a dozen."

In any case, any business—big or small—deals with myriad challenges when working to allow, acknowledge, and then advance the vulnerable, just-born idea. So let's talk about a few of these challenges, or idea killers, that you need to watch out for. As John "Jock" Elliott Jr., a former major in the U.S. Marine Corps, and chairman emeritus of Ogilvy and Mather Advertising, put it, "Big ideas are so hard to recognize, so fragile, so easy to kill. Don't forget that, all of you who don't have them."

SEE SPOT RUN FROM THE IDEA KILLERS

Whether you're working in the mailroom or a corner office you will be wise to be on the lookout for idea killers. Once you are familiar with the basic types, described below, you can recognize them by their modus operandi. (Note: The use of the word *guy* in the descriptions that follow is intended to mean any person, whether male or female.)

BEWARE OF THE CAREER MANAGER

Many corporations are now chock-full of people who spend a large amount of their day just managing to keep their job. Watch out for people who just manage the work instead of actually making something happen. The reason this "juggle-meister" modus operandi is so rampant is that these people are masters at avoiding risks at all cost so they can live (in their job) to see tomorrow. Because of this no-risk (and no-idea) profile, they make no particular progress, specifically because every new idea must involve some risk. They can be hard to spot, since it often looks like they're making lots of things happen. These managers should be called "manglers," because they typically make a mess of everything by just moving stuff around in an appearance of activity.

Masters of the subtle razzle-dazzle, they seldom manage to get burned, but often the people around them end up as toast. To ferret out these career managers, bosses must force them to put in writing their concepts and projections, and then at least once a quarter measure their progress against what they said they were going to do. They don't have to hit every projection, of course, but it's important that these managers provide clear answers regarding what transpired and why.

An unfortunate by-product of the numerous layoffs over the past ten years is that there is often too much work to go around, because where there were three people handling a project, now there is only one. In a way, this has benefited the slick talker, to the absolute detriment of the real work task, because it's much easier to talk about doing the work than it is to do the actual work.

BEWARE OF THE "PLAYING THE PART" CREATIVE GUY

These guys are wannabes, and lots of accessories are typically the giveaway. Real idea people are just too damn busy and preoccupied to think about stuff like Armani suits, the latest high-tech gadget (unless it's a tool they use), or even a clean and tidy office. While sailing his little sailboat, Einstein was often found completely lost, not knowing where he was in the harbor—a great example of how idea people spend time worrying about ideas, and not the mundane stuff of life. If you study the appearance of a Picasso, Einstein, Edison, or even a Walt Disney, you'll see that they have a very serviceable look, not a scarf-tossed flamboyance the pundits would like to ascribe to those "wild and crazy idea guys." You can expect a certain kookiness from creative people, but make sure it's real, and that it emanates from their core, and not a fabrication. Obviously, the biggest problem with faux creative people is that they can supplant a real-idea player in an organization.

BEWARE OF THE NOTE TAKERS
(A.K.A. "LET-ME-RESTATE-YOUR-IDEA-AS-MINE" JERKS)

These guys will listen to everyone else's ideas, remember them, and then at an opportune time regurgitate them as if the breakthrough concept was their own. They are probably the worst kind of coworker for a genuine idea person to be around, because they absolutely exterminate creativity. These guys will ultimately cause everyone to shut up, since others in the office see no reason to help these jerks look good. These opportunists do have a small, legitimate role to play in business since they can sometimes help promote an already evolved idea, but they should not be anywhere near fragile ideas needing to be mothered and explored.

BEWARE OF THE PHONY-AGENT TYPES

A real agent has a key role to play, and the good ones easily earn their money. The ones to watch out for are the phony-agent types (PATs). You can recognize PATs by their absolute selfishness and sometimes way-too-trendy persona. They often go out of their way to be a member of the hippest club, own the hottest car, have the trendiest address, wear the newest fashions, drive around in stretch limos, and so on. These guys are more aggressive than the above-mentioned note takers. Typically they have no specific talent, except a certain talent for sniffing out and then appropriating others' ideas. PATs are often paranoid because they know the world doesn't need them. The people with talent can easily replace them, but PATs can't easily replace the talent—that is, unless they are constantly finding new stuff to snag. They lie in wait, grab creative thinking when they get the opportunity, and run off with it. Since these wannabes are constantly on the prowl for things that can make them look good, they tend to leave a path of shredded ideas and talent in their wake. The worst examples of these people are those who run the scams that promise to get your idea sold, which may appeal to the gullible inventor. If your idea is actually worthwhile, it's often the case that these scammers will figure out a way to steal it, and if it isn't that good they'll jerk you around and shake you down for a bunch of fees that will lead to nothing. The book publishing business has its share of these phony-agent types. And, of course, the people who claim they can get your cute kid in commercials, on TV, or in the movies are never lacking for suckers. "Lots of smoke and very little fire" is what this work style is often called. Keep in mind that this kind of person may actually be walking the halls of your company.

PATs are manipulators, not doers. They don't passionately embrace or understand the essence of any idea, and they will not usually take the time to secure all the information necessary to advance an idea. In fact, they might not even know a real-deal idea if they saw it. Once they've made a mess of things, the creative-types are usually left to pick up the pieces and try to make something out of the shred of the original idea that still remains. This is a sad state of affairs, because the energy gets diverted away from the potential of any innovative thinking that was there, and then only enough time or energy is left to produce fluff.

It's sometimes hard to sleuth these guys out, because they create an illusion of being movers and shakers when really, all they're promoting is themselves. Once in a while these guys end up as stars in American business, even though their opportunistic approach doesn't *actually* generate something that resembles an idea—certainly not a real-deal idea that could contribute to the long-term positive growth for the company. Enron was the ultimate example of a whole company full of PATs who just manipulated things and did nothing to improve the human condition.

BEWARE OF THE COMPLICATORS

Boy, we sure see the results of complicators a lot today. These guys love to keep adding to any idea until it's overloaded and the basic tenet of the idea can't support the weight and therefore nothing gets done. Complicators can be very subtle; for instance, in our government it is standard operating procedure for legislators to load up a bill with amendments, so the meat of the bill ends up getting undermined and sometimes even destroyed. (It's been argued that before legislators are allowed to add another new law, they should have to remove an old law. Now, wouldn't that be awesome?)

Obviously, other examples of complicators are the IRS, the DMV, and most governmental agencies for that matter. Yes, American business is being forced to deal with a lot of external complication, but they are also bringing a lot of it upon themselves. Consider how complicated McDonald's menu is today compared with what it was like in the beginning, so much so that now the average consumer is confused about whether McDonald's is even a burger joint anymore; how difficult supermarket loyalty clubs and coupons make food shopping these days; the complexity of doing business with certain banks due to all their convoluted rules and hidden charges; the classic HMO hassle that requires you to see three doctors in order to get treatment for the simplest health problem; the bewildering peak/non-peak/weekend/nights/roaming/out-of-area/in-state/out-of-state/long-distance usage charges on mobile phone accounts that confuse the users so much so that they just give up and let the charges mount; and, last but not least, the classic runaround we all expect to get at most car dealers. The reason complicators like to pile excess baggage onto a good idea must have something to do with people's tendency to jump on a bandwagon.

A dead giveaway for complicators is that they are never around when the page is blank. Don't expect to see their input early in the life of a project; they'd rather hold on to even the smallest shred of information until the time when releasing it can have the most dramatic effect. *Retaining power* is the operative phrase here. A complicator will wait to drop his or her bombshell in a big meeting, so as to increase his or her feeling of importance to the project (and simply to complicate things).

BEWARE OF THE BEAN COUNTERS

This is a pretty obvious one. Even Roy O. Disney, the money guy, was constantly at odds with Walt Disney, the idea guy. Bean counters need to remember that money spent on the right idea ends up being cheap in the long run. Bankers hate risks, but there is also a risk if they sit on their funds. In *The Matchmaker,* Thornton Wilder wrote, "Money is like manure; it's not worth a thing unless it's spread around encouraging young things to grow." So a thousand gold coins sitting in a jar, buried in the backyard, might as well be a thousand copper pennies if they never get dug up and put to use. You don't want to bet everything, but you can't really expect growth if the money isn't working toward advancing an idea. As mentioned before, Disney and most companies seem to have gotten way too lazy and want the easy money that comes from sequels, merchandising, licensing, or compounded interest. These revenue streams are based on opportunities, not ideas. A vital company needs both to survive. It is a good business practice to take the easy money route when you can (as long as it isn't depleting your equity in the process), but to also work hard to ferret out (R&D) and support the new ideas that are so necessary to your future success.

BEWARE OF THE SLOPPY THINKERS

Who says creativity has to be sloppy? Sure, the painter's loft can be a complete mess, but the artwork coming out of it has to be a jewel if it is to be respected. A musician's life may be a disaster, but the music still has to be clean and powerful.

As the creative process must deconstruct the existing reality in order to construct a new one, don't be surprised if you see messy offices and messy lives when you look at creative people. Just make sure to look beyond the mess for some clear thought and honest struggle. As A. A. Milne said, "One of the advantages of being disorderly is that one is constantly making exciting discoveries."

However, be aware that often a sloppy thinker will pass off his or her mindless drivel as creativity, and in doing so, does a giant disservice to the real process of idea generation. In fact, the creative person may appear sloppy but is, in reality, using all of his or her talent and energies to bring order to the inherent chaos of wrestling with a new idea and trying to turn it into something real. (Here's a little observation relative to how, as is often the case, a fastidiousness for certain important detail will exist in the ubiquitous mess of the creative person's life: In many studios and writer's lofts I've often noticed a strange neatness for only specific things—for example, how the paint tubes are arranged, or how reference books are stacked, or how they'll walk across the room for a certain pencil, when a common No. 2 pencil is within easy reach.)

One big way business can help keep sloppy thinking from taking hold is by clearly delineating the problem that needs to be solved. Ideally, the leader must generate a clear answer to the customer's question, "What's in it for me?" This requires a certain discipline and a large degree of leadership from management. If a leader is saying things like "I'll know it when I see it" and "Now's the time to take some safe risks," then expect confusion and a lot of finger pointing when things go wrong. Sloppy thinking early on in any project typically only then leads to more sloppy thinking later on.

BEWARE OF THE NICE GUYS WHO "WOULDN'T DO THAT"

A really good thief is one who doesn't look like one. Both managers and creatives have to be wary of the idea thief who undermines the hard work of others, even if no one can believe this guy would ever do such a thing. They say things like "Let me tell the big boss," "It's my job to present," or "I think I can help you with that." What they are truly saying is "I think I can help myself to that." These guys are usually in middle management and have gotten there by riding along on other's ideas. They will often tweak the idea a bit in order to make themselves believe that it's actually theirs (and in doing so typically mess it up somewhat). Because they usually have nothing to contribute to the basic construct of innovation, they stand by, ready to grab and run. Unfortunately, they often run the idea into a dead end since they don't have any true interest in ideas and are preoccupied only with making numero uno look good.

BEWARE OF THE FEAR MONGERS

Non-idea people love to put fear into everyone around them. Real-deal ideas are scary and risky, and these guys will run around and make everything seem too hard and too risky. These people don't want anyone to rock the boat, so they try to get in the way of the advancement of anything that even resembles a real-deal idea. If anything, these guys are masters at faking change while maintaining the status quo; these professional naysayers put themselves in a position where they can't be wrong. If the idea succeeds, they can claim it was their contribution to temper the concept in the gauntlet they so skillfully put down. If the idea tanks, they of course can offer up the proverbial "I told you so." They live for this win-win, but in reality it's actually a lose-lose for everyone around them, including the corporation writing their paycheck.

BEWARE OF THE HAND WAVERS

We've all seen the great presenter who didn't later deliver on what he or she sold in a meeting. Carnivals and revivals are full of them, and so are corporations. Because of the glitz offered by these hand wavers (offering "smoke and mirrors" as they gloss over ["hand wave"] the critical details), often a real, solid idea gets put aside for something that sounds more exciting and flashy. P. T. Barnum would have a great career in corporate America if he were alive today.

Many corporations want and reward the easy way to gain a quick buck. They want to brag to the stockholders about all this wonderful activity going on. The corporate culture becomes set up to perpetuate the easy sell, to take the expected and redress it to look new, all the while projecting to the world that they're at the vanguard. This kind of quick-fix culture is hand-waver heaven.

Straight talk isn't the strength of these guys, so they are pretty easy to ferret out if you talk to them straight, especially regarding the details.

BEWARE OF THE HANGERS-ON

It is said that almost everything *of great consequence* happens at the top 1 percent. The top 1 percent rule also applies to idea generation, making real-deal ideas quite rare. I'm not saying that only 1 percent of the population can come up with a real-deal idea, but that at any given moment, only 1 percent of what people are calling ideas are actually the real deal. Because of this, a person who is in the throws of wrestling with a real-deal idea will attract a lot of hangers-on attracted to the inherent excitement of a good idea. In a way this is good, because all ideas need champions, and hangers-on can help move an idea through the system. An open atmosphere allows ideas to get disseminated and expanded. But watch out—

in an unhealthy business culture, hangers-on may have designs on appropriating the idea to promote themselves, breeding competitiveness that leads to protective, insular thinking, and overcomplication that can often suck the life out of a good idea. So don't let your hangers-on become leeches, allowed to run amuck and undermine progress toward innovation.

SEE SPOT RUN TOWARD REAL CREATIVITY

So what do you look for, and what kind of people do you need to surround yourself with if you want to jump-start innovation and establish a constant flow of ideas? It would be nice if it were just a matter of getting Tinkerbell to sprinkle some pixie dust, but it isn't going to be that easy. The following is what you'll need to look for.

LOOK FOR CHILDLIKE THINKING

What you want here is *not* childish, sloppy, or crazy, but more full of wonder and awe. As Pablo Picasso put it, "All children are artists. The problem is how to remain an artist once he grows up." Walt Disney said, "Every child is born blessed with a vivid imagination. But just as a muscle grows flabby with disuse, so the bright imagination of a child pales in later years if he ceases to exercise it."

It's said that most people are locked into what they are going to be and do by the time they're thirty-five years old. In other words, a journeyman plumber may feel that "I yam what I yam" (Popeye's famous words), so why try experimenting with anything else? He or she then stops being adventurous and puts his or her life on auto-pilot until retirement. Creative people haven't given up on adventure; they haven't completely "grown up" and become attached to a staid routine. They're always trying new things, always curious—not unlike a child. Constant interest in learning is a key characteristic of any creative person. An idea person faces the fear of the unknown because he or she knows that the only way to make progress is to embrace an inquisitive and curious approach. All in all, any truly creative person has an intrepid desire to remain adolescent in the enthusiastic pursuit of knowledge. He or she figures you can always grow up later—if at all.

LOOK FOR A "LET'S TRY IT ANOTHER WAY" ATTITUDE

The world-renowned architect and designer Eliel Saarinen reportedly said, "There must always be an end in view, and the end must not be final." The creative process has been described this way: spend about a thousand hours doing hundreds of drawings, then spend another thousand hours working the ideas out in 3-D, then spend another thousand hours refining it, so that when the average person views the completed work, the first response should be "Hey, that looks so simple. Why didn't I think of that?" Constant evolution and improvement is the mantra of any creative person. Most writers know that fourteen rewrites is about what it takes, and they usually have at least twenty rough ideas in the back of their mind that are just begging to be fleshed out. *Prolific* is a way to describe most successful songwriters, lyricists, and composers. Most painters are constantly evolving their style and looking for a more effective way to express their vision. Leonardo da Vinci was productive even after he went blind, and right up until his death. Basically, creative people figure that there could always be a more profound way to express the idea, so therefore they are seldom, if ever, completely satisfied. Disney, and most other companies today, is way too focused on ways to earn a quick buck for this attitude of persistence and flexibility to prevail and flourish. Today, it isn't hard to believe that everyone in corporate America is asking for (and wants to "lock 'n' load" on) the instant silver bullet idea, instead of having the persistence to struggle with the incremental advancements that typically produce innovation.

Ford's idea for the moving assembly line only came after years of trial and error. Hershey's chocolate success came after he had failed in business many times. Bill Gates's operating system became great only after years of constant improvement. Babe Ruth struck out more often than anyone else in his pursuit of sixty homers in a year. Simply put (and beating the baseball analogy to death), the best plan is to go for lots of singles that advance the business, so that when you do get a home run it's a grand slam.

LOOK FOR DEDICATION AND A PASSION TOWARD ADVANCING THE CORE IDEA

Creative-types will develop a vision *and try and try and try* to push it forward. They will mother it and nurture it as if it's their baby. If you're a manager, respect their vulnerability at this moment, because new life (even of an idea) is very fragile. Expect the authors of the idea to act like proud parents at this time. Let them be a little unrealistic and overprotective. If you are truly sympathetic and hang in there with them, you just might see big results. Spend some serious effort trying to truly grasp and understand their vision. If it is clear and strong, then let them run a bit; if it's unclear, send them back to the drawing board to refine it. To get the best result, make sure your directives aren't capricious, but instead careful and thoughtful (as if you're holding a two-month-old child in your hands).

This can be a difficult task for a manager, as the expectation today is to get at the quick fix, but the rewards can be outstanding if you show patience, understanding, and true support at this point of idea generation.

LOOK FOR AND EXPECT A CERTAIN ORGANIC ANARCHY

Convention and status quo don't produce real-deal ideas. Innovation comes from risky behavior and outside-the-box thinking (now a cliché, but still true). This organic process of origination can appear at times to be anarchic, or even mildly insubordinate. From what I've experienced, controlled chaos is the best you can expect from a creative department. So let the creative people jump out of the box; it's then your job to corral them back toward something resembling reasonable thinking. Don't expect to get them back into a tight box; instead, offer a loose structure that is workable and they will go along, particularly because they will want their idea to succeed.

LOOK FOR THE WAY-TOO-BUSY, TRYING-TO-DO-TOO-MUCH, DISTRACTED-ARTIST KINDS OF PEOPLE

Part of the chaos of creativity comes from the non-linear process of reconstructing dissimilar concepts into a new structure, while working toward an ideal. As Lucille Ball smartly observed, "If you want something done, ask a busy person to do it." Therefore, it's not atypical for an idea person to be juggling many unrelated activities and concepts as he or she attempts to formulate new thinking. A kind of multitasking schizophrenia may be necessary to produce greatness in idea generation, along with a certain dogged, on-task attitude that is required in order to push through all this confusion and develop a clear thought.

This is typically where upper management gets impatient with R&D. Looking at R&D people work, it's easy to see just sloppiness and distraction and get frustrated. But it is important for management to crack the code for developing and appreciating the multidimensional creative chaos where true innovation lies.

As F. Scott Fitzgerald said, "The test of a first-rate intelligence is the ability to hold two opposed ideas in the mind at the same time and still retain the ability to function." It is therefore important that successful non-linear thinking be both constrained and unconstrained at the same time. A delineated problem may need to be solved, but it must happen in a decidedly un-delineated way. A creative person looks at the equation $A + B = \_\_\_$ and sees "bananas" as the answer. Or, as Buckminster Fuller put it, "There is nothing in a caterpillar that tells you it's going to be a butterfly."

Expect and gracefully accept a certain amount of angst, since the creative person is always coming up against unfamiliar territory. Make sure this angst over this exploration of new frontiers doesn't get transformed into fear, as it so easily can. Lots of positive reinforcement is necessary when things are going well—and especially when something fails.

LOOK FOR AN EMOTIONAL RESPONSE

If the truth is to be told, this task is where most corporations fall down, because they may have marginalized the soul of the employee for the good of the collective "team." These same corporations are then surprised when they get zombie-like regurgitation instead of from-the-gut explosiveness. Truly creative people bristle when they must get in line or dance to the tune of the corporation. This is why you don't see many brilliant, creative people in cults (except possibly among the leaders).

One true sign of genius is that the person hates to have his or her talent hemmed in by untalented people. Of course, no one likes to toe the line, but idea people will resist it more than others. A lot of creative people will tend to play games here too, but if what they are offering up is from the heart as opposed to some juvenile rant, then it's possible that an idea just may be under there somewhere trying to get out.

Another key element to remember is that generally when emotion becomes suppressed, so will ideas. Many ideas come from the gut, not from analysis. In fact, too much analysis typically leads to paralysis.

Talented, hard-working, creative people hate to lose, because they know that the emotional investment they made in order to perform at their peak can also leave them exposed and vulnerable in failure. It's sad that big business is now chock-full of people protecting themselves from the pain of failure by not taking risks. Ideas are the result of wrestling organically with conflicting thoughts and feelings. Playing to not lose usually leads to a loss in the arena of idea generation as it does in other arenas.

HONOR THE INHERENT CHAOS, TENSION, AND CONFLICT IN IDEA GENERATION

The bottom line is this: if you want to foster innovation, surround yourself with people who discuss ideas. Ideas need a forum, and people must feel comfortable enough to toss them out on the table—not just in structured brainstorming sessions, but also in general day-to-day discourse. A lot of corporations pay lip service to this open-idea-exchange policy, but get confused by how complicated idea generation is, and end up creating a constipated atmosphere where only non-ideas (level 2 "fluff," see chapter 3) can be advanced.

It all comes down to creating a culture where people who have ideas and talent will thrive and be recognized. It's not unlike a winning basketball team: The guards bring the ball in and initiate the process. The forwards must advance the ball and keep things moving toward the goal. The center must be the big "go-to" guy. No one person on the team can do it all, and talent at each position makes things happen. If you have a weak link at any position, you will probably lose. Also, for the team to succeed, the dynamic must remain responsive, fluid, yet focused—and the job of maintaining this dynamic will fall to the coach.

Taking this five-discipline analogy a little further, look at the five fingers on your hand. You carry with you a constant reminder of this creative dynamic, a *cheat sheet* of the creative process. Your thumb and pinky are the guards that initiate things ("thumbs up" means you must remain positive; the pinky reminds you to not overlook the small details). The index finger and ring finger are the forwards that press the initiative (your index finger points the way toward a new frontier, while the ring finger is your commitment and established base that you must draw upon). The middle finger is the "go-to" guy (and also the one that says "screw you" to convention, habit, and the status quo). And you are the coach who carefully marshals and maximizes the forces behind each position. A coordinated hand, with an opposable thumb, is one of the main things that separate humans from other mammals—a trait second only to thinking and the generation of ideas.

Americans understand and praise talent when they watch a football game, but then tend to underappreciate or even abuse talent when they show up for work. It's as if they believe that creating an environment where talent succeeds is not necessary in the business world. Managers expect to find a formulaic sure thing in the competitive business world, even though they know full well that formulas don't work for long in the sports world. Even as early as high school, you'll see parents getting all excited and bragging about their sports-star children, but then get confused when someone mentions that their particular kid got all A's on his or her report card. The smart-thinking kid who got all A's has the potential, and maybe even the talent, to make the world a better place, and the kid who's a football player, for instance, has an almost one-in-a-million chance of even making a living in professional sports—and if he's amazingly good and lucky enough to get a pro contract, the best he's offering to the world is entertainment. (He can also expect his career to be over in less time than it takes to get a college degree, as the average career in the NFL is only 3.5 years.) These same people who are confused about academic talent are often the managers who are more than willing to bitch and moan that their people never bring them anything innovative. What should they expect, especially when they're not willing to praise talent and foster an environment that grows ideas? "Garbage in = garbage out" is as true in business as it is in computer programming.

SOME PITFALLS ALONG
THE PATH TOWARD INNOVATION

Here's another cheat sheet to help you recognize when you're hindering, instead of helping, the process along the path toward innovation. For convenience, the pitfalls are grouped according to those experienced by "manager-types" and "creative-types," but you may find both categories of information useful, since roles can—and should—be completely fluid at any point along the way. In fact, you'll probably notice some purposeful redundancies.

PITFALLS OF MANAGER-TYPES

If you ever hear yourself saying (or even thinking) any of the following statements, take a beat, and then try to reassess your approach toward fostering innovation.

1. "*They* never bring me any new ideas."
   First of all, remove the word *they* from your lexicon, because it detaches you from the process, and the advancement of any idea requires the involvement of the collective intelligence. To encourage the growth of new ideas, you can offer clear problem delineation, provide an infusion of R&D dollars, and provide myriad support opportunities. In other words, don't act like a rocking-chair manager (one who just sits in one spot and creates a lot of back-and-forth motion but never gets off the porch to effect actual progress and change). These types of managers are the bane of innovation. If you have such a person working for you, plan on addressing the problem soon.

2. "I'll know it when I see *it*."
   This statement also detaches you from the process, because it only sets up a gauntlet of perplexity, which will contribute to the burning of resources (time, money, *and* people). A leader needs to eschew obfuscation. To get to the real-deal ideas, you first need to really think through the problem that needs to be solved, identifying the genuine obstacles to finding the solution and admitting your personal biases. Then, working in small groups (less than ten), throw the problem on the table and set a one-hour time limit for everyone to freely toss out as many wild and crazy ideas as they can (the more stupid the ideas the better, with no judgmental comments allowed). Have someone take notes and put

together a list of ideas generated in that one-hour session. Spend the next hour with these same people paring down the list to less than seven ideas that will need focused evolution. At this point you just may begin to see the "it." (And these two hours could very well turn out to be the best couple of "meeting hours" you've spent in some time.)

3. **"We already tried that, and it didn't work."**
Talk about a wet blanket thrown on the creative process. First, maybe what you did before was actually a good idea that was poorly executed, or was improperly funded, or was rushed into service, or failed for reasons that had nothing to do with the idea itself. Second, it's entirely possible that the corporate or market situation has changed so that now the idea can prosper. It's best if you only refer to past experiences for what can be learned from them.

4. **"Sorry, but there's just no budget for that."**
This is the oldest excuse in the world. If the idea is powerful enough, and it has the potential to generate revenue, then there must be at least the tiniest glimmer of a chance that some seed money could be found for it.

5. **"My people . . . "**
Yuck. Say, "my department," maybe, but never "my people" or "my group." Such a "my" statement typically doesn't acknowledge the wider contribution. Saying things like "my people" makes you look like you're putting yourself first as opposed to honoring the group. It's a good move to remove *my* and *me* from your lexicon too. By the way, certain "I" statements like "the way I see it" or "I think" don't necessarily present an exclusionary platform, but typically show some commitment and accountability—which is good, because people usually appreciate commitment from a leader or expert.

6. **"They'll never buy it."**
Second-guessing is inherently unfair and likely to be inaccurate. Would you like it if someone went around telling other people just how smart they were because they knew exactly how *you* would respond in a certain situation? On top of that, saying "They'll never buy it" doesn't allow for change, and change is what idea generation (and life) is all about.

7. **"I'm not the creative person."**

   What a frickin' cop-out. In order to survive each business day, any manager will have to tap into her or his creative energy somewhere along the line. If you're uncomfortable with the concept of creativity, just think of it as juggling a bunch of disparate thoughts until you have collected enough data to arrive at a clean solution. You wouldn't be a manager if you couldn't perform such juggling acts on a continuing basis.

PITFALLS OF CREATIVE-TYPES

If you ever hear yourself saying (or even thinking) any of the following statements, take a beat, and then try to reassess your approach toward fostering innovation.

1. **"It's my baby."**

   Ah, the classic selfish and overprotective motto of the creative person. As every mother and father have learned (typically the hard way, as is the case with most lessons), the art of parenting is giving your children "wings" so they can fly on their own in the world. Ideas also have a life of their own and will need to grow and evolve. You won't shortchange the idea if you can stop yourself from going over the line from *mother* to *smother*.

2. **"I love this idea so much; there really can't be anything better."**

   Don't fall in love at first sight, in fact be ready to "kill your babies" (or if you prefer, as William Faulkner put it, "Kill your darlings.") and search out some constructive criticism. Once you have one good idea in your pocket, look around to see if you can find an even better one. Then try bouncing what you have off some people you respect. Believe deep down that if your idea is the real deal, and really any good, it will have "legs"— so always be open to finding ways to grow it, evolve it. Often, this growing process is where you do your best creative work—and potentially elevate your idea above the morass of mediocre ideas.

3. **"I really hate to look stupid."**

   It's best to stay out of the idea business if you're afraid to raise a stupid question or make a stupid suggestion. If you aren't willing to go out on a limb and be laughed at a bit, then you'll never get where you need to go. By definition, challenging the status quo with new ideas involves some risk because new ideas don't lie inside convention. And sometimes one absurd idea will lead you to another idea that's completely new and fresh, and maybe more doable. So write that memo or raise your hand during the next meeting—you may discover that that "stupid" thought is not so stupid after all. At the *very* least you may encourage others to follow suit, which is no small feat.

4. **"*They* never want anything new."**
Remove the *they* word from your lexicon, because it detaches you from the process and polarizes everyone involved. The advancement of any idea will require the involvement of the collective intelligence. If you think the management-types don't want anything new because they're so used to seeing rehashed remakes, and don't know what *new* is, then it's your job to work toward changing that. With your creativity you can offer a spark that initiates fresh thinking and ideas, add a certain tenacity in mothering the ideas' growth, and experience myriad evolutionary tweaks along the path toward achieving greatness.

5. **"Wait, wait, it just needs one more tweak."**
There comes a time in the life of any idea when it is necessary to "shoot the writer/designer/and so on." In other words, the real constraints of time, money, and quality will come to bear on the process eventually. You have to know when to move on before the idea starts to die from being overworked.

6. **"There's no way they're gonna buy that."**
Second-guessing is very likely to give you inaccurate results, and its resultant negative energy and cynicism will typically nuke creativity. By capriciously doubting the outcome of an idea you're not allowing for change, and change is what idea generation (and life) is all about. Plus, the only way you can be sure no one will buy it *is if you don't try to sell it.*

7. **"Hey, I'm the creative person here."**
What a crock. Granted, your opinion should carry some weight if you have training and specific expertise. But creating a persona that allows you to hide inside the cocoon of your creativity will most likely be counterproductive. If you want to make something innovative happen, you'll need to venture out and wrestle with the chaos of it all while you're out there. "Exclusionary comfort zones" typically only create mush. By the way, certain "I" statements like "the way I see it" or "I think" don't necessarily present an exclusionary platform, but typically show some

commitment and accountability—which is good, because people usually appreciate commitment from a leader or expert. (Kudos to those of you who noticed that this sentence is the same admonition as number 5 under "Pitfalls of Manager-Types.")

SO LET'S LOOK TO DO THE RIGHT THING

In the history of the United States, ideas (like freedom of expression) are what made us great. It all started with the Declaration of Independence (all of 1,317 words), Constitution, and Bill of Rights. Since their inception, these simple, brilliant ideas have been the victims of idea killers' attempts to undermine them. Runaway greed is probably the biggest culprit here, especially of late, as it seems to be accelerating out of control. This is happening in the big business and political arenas because of an all-too-cozy relationship between the two. Special-interest groups currying favor with politicos tend to produce a greed-driven outcome, instead of what is right for the whole of society. In basketball, the players on winning teams share the ball instead of hog it. It's exactly this kind of sharing that has made America great.

It's every American's daily duty to fight the good fight to protect and nurture ideas. Our parents, and our parents' parents, somehow understood this. Our children's children's world will be the better for it if we help restore this amazing breeding ground for innovation called America. The next generations deserve their chance to live the American dream as much as we do.

CHAPTER 7

SO, IS THE (GREAT AMERICAN) PARTY OVER?

We've talked a lot about Disney, a company known (for over three generations) for its imagination and big ideas but that just isn't cranking them out like it used to—so much so that their bank of ideas is getting horribly overworked and somewhat trivialized. We've investigated what real ideas are and how they must capture the imagination—and, at their most basic level, contribute to change in the human experience. We've reviewed how solid ideas, when used properly, connect with an audience. We've explored how non-ideas (like copies, replicas, and remakes) don't leave a lasting impression or necessarily have the desired societal impact. And we've reviewed some of the forces at work in the corporate world that quash individuality and innovation.

All of this investigation raises some critical questions: Is the whole *idea* of idea generation in American business doomed? How long will it be before American corporations (like Disney) reach into their bag of ideas and find it empty? Is our culture going to shuffle along in rehash hell and be sequeled to death? Is the idea (intellectual property) world going to be reduced to a roving gang of thieves who devour anything fresh and new? Is the modus operandi in business going to be covering one's behind instead of actually trying to make something of importance happen? Is America going to relinquish its lead in the world of ideas and innovation? As Steve Forbes, the CEO of *Forbes* magazine, said, "Inventions don't come out of Europe anymore." How soon will it be before similar things are said about us in the United States?

The global first-world market is currently dominated pretty much along these lines:

Idea Generation/Innovation—America
Engineering/Design—Europe
Engineering/Production—Asia
Consumption—America

How much longer can America's role as innovator continue? Are Americans just going to end up a bunch of debt-heavy (and overweight) super-consumers who take, take, take without adding anything more to the world at large?

Why has America had the corner on idea generation in the past? Let's take a few minutes to review America's role in the world. Why have we enjoyed such a rich history and reputation for coming up with innovations and real-deal ideas? Why can the Japanese sell you some hardware like a DVD player and make a small profit, while most every disk you slide into it comes from America—and at a much-higher profit margin? (Think about it: you've probably made Steven Spielberg more money by renting or buying video tapes or DVDs of his movies than you have the guys who produced and sold you the machine that plays those video/DVDs.) Why have the Europeans ended up with a running-in-place economy? Why do some of the countries of Central and South America continue to go bankrupt by spending money they don't have? Where is China (with over one-fifth of the world's population) in all of this? Why does the third world now want to be called the developing world?

HOW THE HECK DID AMERICA CORNER THE MARKET ON INNOVATION?

ELBOW ROOM

Idea people need "elbow room" to strut their stuff. Elbow room in America is what has made a rich field for growing ideas. *Elbow room* was the exact phrase Daniel Boone used to describe what he was looking for (and to justify what he was doing) each of the four times he picked up and moved farther west to start up a new homestead. Our vast resources (which we basically appropriated from the natives) helped America grow fast, and this growth allowed for ideas and positive, expansive thinking. Amazingly, the United States of America has 17.8 percent of the world's arable land (close to one billion acres of farmland) and less than 5 percent of the world's population. Cool beans, wouldn't you say? Simply put, we don't spend much of our day worrying about feeding ourselves, unlike much of the world. This allows Americans the luxury of thinking about other things, beyond a growling stomach.

Abraham H. Maslow's Holistic Dynamic Needs Hierarchy explains how it works. The levels are as follows: (1) physiological needs, (2) safety and security, (3) love and belonging, (4) esteem or ego, (5) self-actualization, (6) knowledge and understanding, and (7) aesthetic achievement. In general, when it comes to needs, the lower levels supersede higher levels when the organism's "degree of satisfaction" at the lower level is "threatened." As a society, Americans don't need to worry about the basic needs, because our general prosperity allows us to go all the way up the hierarchy and enjoy the luxury of thinking about ideas.

Sometimes it takes a common societal ingenuity to take care of the needs on the lower level so that the average person can ascend the hierarchy and tackle the higher needs—which can then contribute to opening whole streams of innovation. Having traveled to Japan something like twenty times, I can tell you that the Japanese definitely lack elbow room. They don't have enough land to grow the necessary food for their populace, so they must rely on foodstuffs from other countries. They basically live on a barely habitable rock with very few natural resources. Tokyo is at the top of the list of the world's most expensive cities, and Osaka is fourth (New York City doesn't even make it into the top ten). In round numbers, their country has about half of the population of the United States, and even though the island is roughly the size of California, it has a concentrated habitable landmass around Tokyo only about the size of our smallest state, Rhode Island. This precarious situation has forced them to adopt a generally reactive mode. Japanese must take what raw and scrap materials they can buy from other countries and then convert these materials into products that they can sell back to the world. They are then able to use the profits from these transactions to buy, from the food-producing countries, something to eat. If Americans (or any other country for that matter) tell the Japanese that they can keep their TVs, DVD players, cars, and so on, then Japan is basically out of luck. It's a tough life, from what I've observed, but because they are willing to work so diligently, modern Japan is progressing at rocket speed toward a situation akin to what we've enjoyed for the past 50 years.

In America we are so fortunate to have so much of almost everything. This amazing abundance produces a vast and open frontier, and expansive horizon, which allows us to sit around and ponder the imponderables.

EASE OF COMMERCE

Why does the European economy seem to flounder? Europeans make some exquisite premium cars, a lot of superb designer goods, and even excellent chocolates and wines, but what about the *new* stuff? Well, until recently Europeans were still stuck in a provincial mentality. Only one hundred and fifty years ago, Europe was a bunch of small feudal city-states that were only loosely unified by allegiances formed through constant warring. During the past three hundred years England, Germany, France, and Italy have always been fighting somebody, including various combinations of each other, and war sure redirects creative energy. Plus, doing business with these small states (or loosely unified republics) required constantly changing money from one currency to another (and paying tolls, duties, and dockage). The Rothschilds managed to take advantage of the need to change currencies and became extremely rich as moneychangers (for a time, they were also sneaky enough to file off a little gold from each coin they touched—that's why coins now have a serrated edge that would show evidence of such tampering).

Beginning in feudal times, the common folk paid allegiance to the local ruler, city-state, or republic who would offer protection and a secure marketplace to do business in. All this provincialism kept markets small and insular, discouraging big investments and making synergistic collaboration and cross utilization of resources difficult. But this is changing dramatically with the establishment of the

European Union (EU) and the acceptance of the Eurodollar. Soon, Europeans will realize the advantage of not having to exchange currency or pay tolls, duties, or fees when doing business with other states, just as we have all along.

DIVERSITY

Because our American society is specifically *not* homogeneous, we have been almost forced to recognize differences in each other and work things out. As a result, societal rules are established according to what does business, not some doctrine that is subject to some bureaucrat's or religious leader's interpretation. The majority of us are basically good, solid citizens, and we respect and honor the process of negotiating in good faith. This has led to good business practices in which both sides can and must prosper for the system to work. The agenda is that simple. If business gets any more complicated than that (whether through rip-offs, scams, dirty dealings, or favoring special interests), it sure doesn't work well for very long. These principles are so basic that just about any twelve year old knows what it means when you say "Hey, a deal's a deal."

SECULAR GOVERNMENT AND BUSINESS

Our forefathers were smart enough to purposefully keep religion out of government and, coincidentally, out of business. In the history of mankind you can find way too many examples where misapplied religious doctrine only messed up governmental policies and business enterprise. Just look at how sixteenth-century Spain got overzealous about gilding churches when the Roman Catholic Church ran the show, as mentioned a few chapters back. Think about the fact that the underlying reason for most religious wars is greed to acquire more land and more power. And consider how Henry VIII started his own religion so he could control all aspects of the English life and rewrite doctrine to fit his particular needs. There are many countries today that suffer from the intertwining of disciplines. When money and religion mix, watch out. I guess we can thank God that our forefathers understood this.

LET'S NOT SQUANDER OUR JACKPOT

The past century was an amazing environment for idea generation. The context and infrastructure were in place to make ideas flow more abundantly than at any other time in the history of mankind. In the eight profound words of Michael Porter of the Harvard Business School, "Innovation is the central issue in economic prosperity."

Let's go back a few generations in the United States and look at how prosperity and advancing technology have changed consumer expectations, using an expensive product like the automobile as an example. In the early 1900s, Ford's assembly-line workers couldn't afford to own the cars they were building—that is, until Henry got smart and doubled their pay to $5 a day so they could afford to save up for a Ford. After the ravages of the Great Depression, the survivors *hoped* to someday get back on their feet and have a nice sedan for transporting their family. The generation who fought in World War II *believed* that they'd probably someday have a good transportation car and maybe even be lucky enough to have something nicer. (Up to the 1950s, most cars were purchased with cash—until Ford offered a '57 Ford for $57 a month.) Their children, the pre-boomers and baby boomers, *demanded* a car as part of their life; now some even collect and over-restore old cars just for the fun of it (or spend huge amounts on expensive motorcycles that they rarely drive). The "Gen-Yers" now feel that they are *entitled* to have a car, and a nice one with all the bells and whistles at that (often spending far beyond their means). It's interesting how something as expensive as a car would start out as something the average person would only hope to have and evolve to something that everyone expects to have (and a premium one at that). And this all happened over the course of four generations.

As I mentioned, this abundance we enjoy is unrivaled in the history of mankind. The past sixty years in America have been one gigantic and fantastic party. The San Joaquin Valley in California could easily feed the entire United States. We have so much food that obesity has become an epidemic here. The average person can travel from coast to coast in only four or five hours and probably won't have to pay more than a week's salary to do so. Plenty of people keep an extra car that they only drive for pleasure, while most Chinese people still get around on bicycles. We have so much extra stuff that we need to rent storage units to house it all. We enjoy music everywhere we go. Damn near every household has a computer, not to mention multiple TVs, radios, and phones, while even in successful Japan it's unusual for a family to own more than one car or large TV.

SO FAR, SO GOOD—SO WHO'S COMPLAINING?

We buy big, car-like trucks outfitted with power windows, locks, and everything else—monster vehicles that guzzle gas, contribute to pollution, and fearfully exacerbate global warming—and we get upset if gasoline prices go above a price that's half of what most of the world pays. As I've mentioned before, modern Americans eschew hard labor but love high-dollar health clubs, where we fight to get a parking spot near the front door (no one wants to be seen breaking a sweat in a parking lot). We spend lavishly on express delivery because we can't be bothered to plan ahead (or wait) for a few days. We raise salmon in farms in order to lower the price but are baffled by the health and environmental consequences of such practices. There's even a guy in Beverly Hills who makes over $100,000 a year plucking eyebrows (Madonna has flown in from Scotland to have him pluck hers). Americans build huge cities in the middle of the desert because we can control interior temperatures with air-conditioning even on a 100-degree day. We build gigantic cities far away from any major rivers and move water from hundreds of miles away.

You get the idea: we're partying our brains out. But as with any good party, it must maintain a good balance. If the room is too big or too small, then it feels wrong. If the food arrives too late, or there's not enough of it, then it doesn't work. If the guests aren't the right mix, the party may fizzle. If the guests don't mingle, then the party becomes a bunch of cliques. If the wrong music is played, everyone starts to get uncomfortable. We've all been to parties that were excellent, and also ones that were just disasters waiting to happen.

One has to wonder: Is the excellent American party over? Is our greed a manifestation of a fear of being left behind, so the guests at the bash are all hurriedly grabbing up what's left? Are ideas going to stop flowing, like a tapped-out keg? Well, if the great-American partygoers ramp it up so that the greed gets further out of control, to the point where the populace eschews and cynically demeans the real work that needs to be done, then we have, as a country, a serious problem on our hands.

LOOK OUT YANK, HERE COME THE PARTY CRASHERS (AND WHO CAN BLAME THEM?)

If you put together a party of one hundred people who represented the world, roughly fifty-seven people would be Asian, twenty-one European, eight African, nine from the Western Hemisphere outside of the United States, and only five Americans. As the world is set up now, those five fortunate Americans would consume something like one-third of the buffet while the ninety-five other people would have to fight it out for the remaining two-thirds. For instance, the average American consumes *eleven* times the resources of someone living in Asia or Africa.

Well, my fellow Americans, the world is awakening to this imbalance.

The people in the rest of the world have come to understand the power of ideas, and they are now carefully nurturing idea generation in their own countries. In 1989, when the Sony Corporation (the first Japanese company to be listed on the New York Stock Exchange [1961; ticker symbol: SNE]) bought Columbia Pictures Studios for $3.4 billion, the pundits in Hollywood howled about how much they overpaid for it. Before the purchase, the Columbia studio lot was run-down and sleepy, but under Sony management the whole complex is now a-rockin' and a-rollin.' Sony is getting the last laugh, since they now crank out hit movies like the *Spider-Man* (1, 2, etc.), TV fare like *Joan of Arcadia* (CBS), the top two rated network U.S. daytime serials—*The Young and the Restless* (CBS) and *Days of Our Lives* (NBC)—the top two rated U.S. syndicated game shows—*Wheel of Fortune* and *Jeopardy!*— not to mention their syndication library that includes *Seinfeld, The Nanny, Married . . . with Children, I Dream of Jeannie, Bewitched, All in the Family, Charlie's Angels, Fantasy Island, The Jeffersons, The Dating Game, The Newlywed Game,* and *The Three Stooges* (yep, Larry, Moe, and Curly are the property of a Japanese corporation)—and that's just a small portion of what they own. And because of their current relationship with Michael Jackson, Sony Music may someday end up with the Beatles catalog (which Jacko now owns in partnership with them, known as Sony/ATV). On top of all that, Sony Music is planning a merger with Bertelsmann Music Group (BMG, owners of the Elvis Presley catalog), which would produce the second-largest music company in the world.

As a country, the Japanese have awakened to the elemental need for ideas, just as we Americans are nodding off. As a culture, they are throwing a lot of money and effort at idea generation, and they're getting some excellent results. Also, the Japanese apparently understand the importance of, and are willing to stick to, a long-term strategy. Hey, America, that Asian-produced alarm clock is beeping, so it's time to wake up and smell the cappuccino.

As I mentioned earlier, the European Union (EU) is also changing the world game. The Eurodollar (euro), which is the U.S. dollar on deposit at European banks, is becoming firmly established throughout Europe. Once the "open-border" Euro Zone is complete, the European economy will be very close in size to that of the United States. Europe will then enjoy the same multiregional synergy between businesses that we in America have been able to capitalize on for centuries. For instance, the logging industry in Sweden can now more easily work with the furniture industry in Italy. The wheat farmers in Italy can spend less on shipping grain to the United Kingdom, and so on. You can thank our early American leaders for establishing our own very open federal system for the moving of goods from coast to coast, or anywhere in between. And now Europe will enjoy that same advantage.

It may be time to wake up and smell the double espresso regarding developing nations. Their motivation for change is pretty apparent when you consider the following. Nobel Laureate and U.N. Secretary-General Kofi Annan has referenced the United Nations' "Human Development Report 1998: Consumption for Human Development," stating that the 20 percent of the people who live in the developed nations consume 86 percent of the world's goods and services—and produce 53 percent of all carbon dioxide emissions. For example, the richest fifth consumes 45 percent of all meat and fish; uses 58 percent of all energy and 84 percent of all paper; has 74 percent of all telephone lines; and owns 87 percent of all vehicles.

Of course the giant of all developing nations is China. This country is gigantic in so many ways (1.29 billion people, 22 percent of the world's population). Of the fifty most-populated cities in the world, nine are in China. To understand what large-scale issues they are dealing with, the people of Shanghai are trying to figure out how to recycle 80 percent of their water. And unlike Americans who spend less than 12 percent of their income on food, the average Chinese consumer spends 48 percent.

As a wake-up call to the Western world, the Chinese are starting to branch out into our world of capitalism—and they're doing so right in our backyard. For example, the state-owned China Ocean Shipping Co. of the People's Republic of China (COSCO) has a gigantic state-of-the-art, containerized-freight port facility in Long Beach, California (in combination with twin Port Los Angeles, it's America's largest West Coast port, and the third largest seaport complex in the world) that operates around the clock. The Chinese have also established gigantic port facilities on either side of the Panama Canal. These actions are hardnosed (and also very smart) business moves intended to position the Chinese perfectly in the Western Hemisphere to do business here. Plus, they're building a fleet of gigantic container ships (configured to carry more than four thousand standard-sized containers; previously just over two thousand was the maximum a container ship could carry) that can travel from China to the United States in twelve days. These ships return to China loaded up with raw materials—and lots of our old scrap paper and scrap metal to supply their burgeoning industry.

We'll have to carefully watch these "*goods* guys" because they're really *not good* guys when it comes to idea protection. China's general lack of respect for other countries' designs, patents, and copyrights make it almost impossible to do business with them while still protecting our intellectual properties (IPs). As our American software companies began to deal directly with the Chinese software market, it was reported that up to 98 percent of American software products already being sold there were pirated copies. An article in *US News and World Report* reveals that their general strategy is to grow their fledgling auto industry by taking advantage of China's lax intellectual property laws. At a recent Beijing Auto Show, look-alikes were displayed throughout the show including virtual clones of the Chevy Spark called the Chery QQ being sold for only $6,000. (Because the Chery QQ undercuts the Chevy price by about $1,500, it is outselling Chevy's version by nearly six to one—and even the gigantic General Motors, Chevy's parent company, can't seem to get the Chinese government to address this particular problem.) There were cars from newcomer BYD with an emblem looking suspiciously like BMW's (although BYD studiously stayed away from replicating BMW's signature kidney-shaped grille), and oak-leaf crests appeared on Shanghai Wanfeng Auto's lineup, which offered vehicles borrowed from what you might see at a Cadillac dealer. On top of all that, on street corners in China you can buy DVDs of blockbuster films like *Spider-Man 2* and *Shrek 2* for less than $5—even before their official release in U.S. theaters.

Somehow we're going to have to figure out some reasonable way to conduct business with the Chinese, because they are growing into too big a market to ignore. For example, the market for light vehicles grew at an annual rate of 80 percent in 2003, where there were over 4.4 million sold (up from only 1 million ten years ago, and now surpassing Germany to become the third largest car market in the world). It is expected that by 2007, the Chinese auto industry will have sufficient capacity to start to export their cars in sizeable numbers. And because they will want to export, they will need to develop a reciprocal business model that honors what is meant when Western businesses offer to negotiate in good faith, where the protection of every country's intellectual property rights is necessary. The Chinese government promises to address the thorny issue of IP rights as it expands its status in trade relations and in the World Trade Organization. *Stay tuned, because somehow doing "good business" with the Chinese has gotta happen.*

Don't forget about India. It has a population nearly as big as China's. And, these people are hungry for work, as the average Indian consumer spends close to half of his or her income on food. Plus, thanks to years of British rule, over 5 percent of their population of just over one billion people (which equates to 50 million!) are fluent in English. Because of the advent of globalization, English will remain the preferred language in elite education there. Expect India's smartest and brightest to continue to make their mark on the world stage.

Like the Chinese, Americans also have a history of being hardnosed (but usually fair) business people, but we may be getting soft (hmm, it's interesting that "soft" ware is our strength these days). Americans have an advantage today due to our long history of innovation, and hopefully we can continue showing enough Yankee ingenuity so our prosperity can continue. Because, basically, the rest of the people in the world are tired of getting the scraps, and they're trying to figure out ways to grab a bigger share in almost any way they can.

Overall, people in much of the world think we Americans are arrogant, fat, lazy, and spoiled rotten. Well, at least they hope that we are. Of course, we need to prove them wrong. We must find innovative ways to embrace the changing world market and assure our value in it.

HAS AMERICA UNKNOWINGLY PUT THE BRAKES ON INNOVATION?

It usually takes some loose money to create an environment where ideas flourish. Recreation—a little "head scratching" time—also helps lead to creation. And a little humility and artful collaboration—instead of an attitude of entitlement and greedy competition—are essential for ideas to take root and grow. As Michael J. Mandel, *BusinessWeek's* chief economist, offers in his book *Rational Exuberance: Silencing the Enemies of Growth and Why the Future Is Better Than You Think,* "What might be called the Silicon Valley mentality—favoring experimentation, innovation, and change—faces a hostile climate today." So, let's go over how America *isn't* living up to the requirements for innovation.

TAXATION

Americans do business because we're allowed to do business. "What?" you say. Well, for starters our forefathers got tired of the heavy taxation by Britain. After about one hundred and fifty years of British colonization and governance, the average New England colonist felt he could never get ahead. If, for instance, he had an idea for making a better wagon wheel, then worked hard to produce and sell it, and started to make some money—the next thing he knew he had lost a good chunk of his profits to taxes. The resistance blossomed over the requirement to get an official "by order of the king" stamp (which, of course, cost a "royal" fee, or royalty) every time you wrote a contract or any important paper. The colonists bristled at this Stamp Act, and King George was forced to capitulate and rescind it. But to teach these "ungrateful upstarts" a lesson the king added taxes on basic stuff like tea. You know the story—the colonists rebelled. The amazing thing is that their total tax burden was less than 10 percent, and they felt that even single-digit taxes were too much to put up with, especially when the monies went back to England without proper representation. It does stand to reason that if you don't stand a chance to make an extra buck, then you have two options: give up and not go through all the extra effort, or make a stand.

Today, it's not hard to see that taxes have gotten out of hand in America, and that partly because of these taxes the average person has trouble getting ahead. If you look at what the average John and Suzie are paying in taxes today (federal income taxes, state income taxes, property taxes, sales taxes, plus special taxes on luxury items, gasoline, alcoholic drinks, and tobacco products; DMV fees; rental car fees; airport taxes; hotel taxes; not to mention all the taxes hidden in the price of everything you buy), you'll find that the average two-earner household in the United States today is shelling out close to 40 percent of every dollar earned—and in 1958 it was only about 18 percent.

Generally, if taxes are in the 10 to 20 percent range, the average citizen will complain but be willing to ante up for the general good of society. As the tax burden gets nearer to 30 percent, people start to search out creative ways to protect some of their hard-earned money. When taxes get close to 40 to 50 percent, people will start looking for ways to cheat. At first it starts in small ways, like buying things for cash at swap meets, on the black market, or by bartering. In countries like Italy, where the combined taxes are approaching 60 percent, tax cheating or avoidance has become a high-art form—effectively wasting valuable creative energy.

Practical idea generation, pursuing ideas that add value, becomes a giant luxury when there is just barely enough money to "feed the bulldog." If the tax burden is too great, whether for a private individual or a corporation, the first thing that is often put on hold is R&D. The money guys promise that when things "loosen up a bit," the company will restart those programs—but (surprise, surprise) any money that breaks loose only seems to get tighter scrutiny.

If ideas are to flow they absolutely need some cash flow. The Wright brothers had a very successful bicycle business that helped bankroll their flying experiments and gave them the luxury to experiment. They managed to have the wherewithal to be in North Carolina in the middle of December, when less successful and ambitious people would have been back in Ohio minding the store. It stands to reason that when money is tight, ideas also become tight.

While working at Disney, I kept hearing "cut, cut, cut," and I started to see less and less room for the luxury of experimentation. The bean counter at Disney who said that they just wanted to pay for good ideas, and outsourcing was the way to go, didn't care to comprehend that in order to get one good idea you need to generate a critical mass of one hundred, or more. It would be like saying to a dairy farmer, "Can't you get your cows to produce just cream?" Or to a baseball player, "Only swing at pitches that you can hit for a home run." Or to a songwriter, "Don't waste your time writing anything that isn't going to be a hit song."

America is headed for trouble if we don't open up the purse strings by reducing the tax burden of John and Suzie Public—and do so in a way that encourages commerce. The extra cash poured into the economy of late, which came from refinancing homes and increasing credit-card debt, won't help in the long term. We need to find a way to back off on the taxes in a meaningful way (without increasing the national debt, which would only put the burden on the next generation's shoulders—with compounded interest, of course) and enhance the infrastructures that encourage commerce and idea generation. Someone's got to do it somehow. Maybe you, in the position you're in, can do even a small part to reverse the trend. I really don't think JFK was talking about taxes when he said, "Ask not what your country can do for you, but what you can do for your country."

LESS AND LESS R&R

Let's talk a little about the dichotomy of recreation: sometimes wasting time isn't a waste of time after all.

For many years, Foote, Cone, and Belding, the Los Angeles ad agency I worked for, had a policy that allowed us to take every other Friday off during the summer months. That extra day allowed for weekend trips to places one wouldn't normally go during a regular weekend—like Yosemite National Park, or trips to the San Francisco Bay Area. Today such a policy sounds almost quaint.

Most businesses, including ad agencies, have executed massive cutbacks and layoffs, so most everyone I talk to today complains that they can't get all of their work done in a *sixty*-hour week. (I've heard that Walt once did a study showing that there were diminishing returns when anyone worked more than fifty-seven hours a week.) A July 2003 *Washington Post* article stated, "We're now logging more hours on the job than we have since the 1920s. Almost 40 percent of us work more than fifty hours a week." And from that same article comes evidence that it's only getting worse: "Americans manage to live with the stingiest vacation allotment in the industrialized world—8.1 days after a year on the job, 10.2 days after three years, according to the Bureau of Labor Statistics." From www.hazards.org comes this revelation: "Vacations can cure even the worst form of stress—burnout—by re-gathering crashed emotional resources, say researchers. But it takes two weeks for this process to occur, says one study, which is why long weekends aren't vacations. An annual vacation can also cut the risk of heart attack by 30 percent in men and 50 percent in women."

One big reason for the increased workload today is that the remaining workers have had to assume the work of the laid-off personnel due to cutbacks. Hey, the work didn't go away, just some workers did. Of course, a lot of companies have shown sharp increases in productivity as the economy returns to health (more work to do), and the current reduced staffs are somehow stepping up to handle the extra load. The net effect of an increased workload is that workers have less time for dreaming and experimenting. This may be fine for the short term, when everyone will somehow just dig deeper and find a way to get the work done, but such practice will as a rule undermine the future projects of any company. Any "fuzzy-return" projects get relegated to the back-back-back burner, along with the office games, picnics, and other recreational activities that help keep everyone fresh and enthused.

For instance, the artists at the Walt Disney Studios concocted a game in which they stuck a pushpin in a wad of clay, balanced a ruler on the point, and came up with different designs to see how many revolutions they could make their particular ruler contraption do. The artists, wishing to appear productive, used to hide this little toy whenever Walt was around. But one day, when he picked up on what they were doing, Walt asked all about what was effective and what wasn't, and he even contributed a few ideas of his own. The artists were flabbergasted that they weren't in trouble, but Walt Disney well understood that the mind is still working and the wheels are still turning while it is "re-creating" itself.

Thinking of recreation as "re-creating" is key here. Recreation can be amazingly helpful to idea generation, if it is indeed a method of reenergizing and refreshing one's soul. But it's no longer helpful when recreational activities become an end unto themselves. If you have to also work hard at a hobby or avocation it too will cause you to burn out. Some of us have forgotten how to recreate with simple joy, laughter, and relaxation. We want our kids to play on organized teams that win city championships. We buy $400 golf drivers in the hopes of improving our friendly weekend golf game. We have people who actually make a nice living by winning fishing or poker tournaments.

From everything I can see, the whole hobby world has gotten way too serious. Hey, wasn't the whole idea behind hobbies and recreation to have some fun? Many a boomer wrestles with this very truth as he or she lies in bed on a Sunday night, incapacitated by aches and pains after a weekend spent trying to act like an eighteen year old again. Recreation has its place, and can contribute immensely to the human spirit, but it shouldn't be work—it should be play.

Early one Saturday morning, when I was waiting in line at a local bagel store, the guy behind me was stressing out about running late. It turned out he was running late for his group-meditation stress-management class. I teasingly pointed out to him the irony of his situation, and at first he was taken aback, but then he realized what I was saying and thanked me with a chuckle, saying, "You know, you're right"—but he was also happy when I let him cut ahead of me.

THE GOD OF GREED

Everyone wants to be a "big wheel." Everyone wants preferential VIP treatment— to be chauffeured in a limousine, to get backstage passes, to eat jumbo shrimp, to drive a luxury car, to fly first class, and to watch a game from a skybox. Well, this attitude of entitlement has actually made it extremely difficult for simple ideas to grow. If everyone got special treatment, it therefore wouldn't be very special; it could only be average at best. In other words, the more-more-more scenario can only contribute to ratcheting up the excesses.

Greed sets us up to expect to get everything. We want a new car with all the goodies, so dealers then lease us one that is far beyond our means. We want a job that's relatively easy and on top of that also pays a lot—but then we still want to complain that it's hard. We refuse to delay any gratification, so we dig ourselves a deep hole with credit card debt at double-digit rates of compounding interest. We actually think we have a chance to win the lottery (sometimes jokingly referred to as a "tax on the stupid") or hit the jackpot in Vegas (just how does anyone think those casinos pay for all those marble-festooned edifices?). We want big SUVs, and we then bitch and moan about the lousy gas mileage. We want low-risk stocks that grow at double-digit annualized rates. *Never-ending greed . . . again, no boundaries.*

Think about the following couple of scenarios:

> 1. Imagine that you're at a fancy party waiting in line at the shrimp bowl, and the guy just in front of you takes five of the last ten shrimp that are left. Human nature kicks in and makes you want to take five also, but maybe you feel a twinge of guilt because you'll have then taken all that's left. Also, you wouldn't want to appear greedy to anyone who might be watching. You take three shrimp, and find yourself resenting the guy in front of you and making a silent promise to yourself to take more shrimp next time you're in his position. Even if you initially wanted only three shrimp, the competitive nature of human existence makes you want more.

> 2. Put a five-dollar bill on the ground just outside of your cubicle or office, in a common area where a passing person wouldn't necessarily think the money was in your space. For just 25 bucks, you'll find out more about human greed than you'd ever want to know. Some people will just pick it up, some will kick it along and then pick it up, and some will even make an announcement that they must have dropped the money on an earlier pass by. It will be the rare person who will pick it up and hand it to you. (A friend, David Farrow, told me about this test, and I only played it once. And, if you play it, you'll also find that once is enough.)

It's funny how this greed thing can really take over. For instance, in the 1990s companies competed to have a "star CEO." The high-flying stock market at the time demanded high-profile players. Soon every corporation wanted its CEO to be paid in the top 25 percent. Well, such thinking led to incredible salary inflation among CEOs, because it's utterly impossible for 100 percent of CEOs to get into the top 25 percent. The average big-cheese CEO in 2002 was getting compensated at 282 times what the average worker received (up from 1982, when it was already a ridiculous 42 times the average worker's wages), and it's only gotten worse since then. Unsurprisingly, Michael Eisner is above average, and pretty much at the top of all this craziness as he's earned over a billion dollars (think of it, that's 1,000 millions) in the past 20 years—and, of late, when his unexercised DIS stock options were upside-down, he convinced the board to grant him a $6.25 million yearly bonus. Some 65 percent of the $1,046,741,701 that he earned in those 20 years was in stock options exercised since October 1997, and he holds exercisable options for 21 million more shares. If we were to look honestly at this, no CEO, sports player, or race car driver should be worth more than ten to twenty times an average worker's salary.

The money taken out of the company to pay these ridiculously high CEO salaries has helped contribute to massive layoffs and also large cutbacks in R&D. On top of that, when layoffs loom, workers start to fear for their jobs, and fear and creativity don't necessarily work well together. Disney, for one, seems to be suffering from the ripple effects of this belt-tightening for profits (possibly in order to help it afford its high-dollar CEO). As stated before, greed will willingly consume everything in its path.

All you have to do is look at the history of South America to see where greed can get you. Brazil has enormous natural resources, but historically the average person isn't doing very well (reportedly more than one out of five of its population are living below the poverty level). There are pretty much the elite rich and the struggling poor, but few well-to-do middle-classers. Brazil's rich have, for years, squandered vast sums of money on palatial estates, boats, cars, jets, and helicopters—even their own private armies—and they love sponsoring race-car drivers, soccer (football) players and teams, and beach volleyball players. Venezuela, Argentina, Colombia, and other countries are often in the same boat. It seems as if there's always a country in South America that is on the verge of bankruptcy and requiring the loan-restructuring assistance of the World Bank. I've been to oil-rich Venezuela, and I pray that the United States isn't on a path toward becoming more like them, where the filthy rich get richer and the poor get even poorer . . . and even filthier. Idea generation needs hope, and without hope the best the average guy can do is to drown his or her sorrow in booze and revelry, just as the throngs do during Carnival. But, Brazil, Venezuela, and most of South America are getting their acts together and starting to act much more fiscally responsible, so we Americans best watch out for them, too.

Now, Walt Disney was kind of a greedy guy too, but in his own way. He desperately wanted the money for his next project. He made millions from his wild projects, but he would take whatever money he made and pour it into an even wilder project. It was almost as if people wanted to give him money just to see what crazy thing he'd do next. Obviously, because his name was on the door he had a lot of freedom to do what he wanted to do. But he was dedicated to using his (and the corporation's) money to further the search for ideas, instead of acquiring a trophy chalet on the slopes in Aspen, a palatial beach cottage on Nantucket, a giant yacht, or even fanciful office buildings.

Greed is a damn good motivator, but how can we possibly get back to where there's a decent balance between money, creativity, and common sense? For instance, if a person buys a tiny, gas-sipping economy car, people may look at the person as if he or she isn't successful, instead of admiring the person's environmental awareness and concern for the world we're handing our children. What's happened to the American ideal of doing the right thing for the common good? Can any CEO making over $5 million a year (forty-eight CEOs in California alone make at least this much on a yearly basis) ever truly understand what it's like for a family to live on an average household income of around $50,000? In the United States, the rich *are* getting richer and the poor *are* getting poorer. Over the past twenty years or so, the gap between the wealthiest and the poorest families has expanded from 11 times to 19 times.

David Friedman, a senior fellow at the New America Foundation, said, "Societies with skewed distributions of wealth tend to be less dynamic. Wealthier classes naturally want to preserve the status quo, and they have the financial and political wherewithal to do it." Take the big pharmaceutical companies, which have diverted R&D resources away from new antibiotic development because antibiotics, due to their short use cycles, may not be as profitable as some other extended-use drugs. The Centers for Disease Control has cited antibiotic resistance as a looming problem, and new antibiotics are desperately needed. We can only hope that the impending need will drive the innovation and that someone somewhere will come up with a fresh idea for the next new antibiotic, *or every single one of us is in serious trouble.*

On top of all this, the dutiful pre-boomer and baby boomer parents desperately want their precious "boomlet" kids to have the stuff of their dreams. Even though most of their parents' dreams remain unfulfilled (as is the case with most dreams, or they wouldn't be dreams), their kids show tendencies to be insatiable in their entitlement. The boomer parents keep spending and spending until they reach their resource and/or credit limit. It starts off benignly, since almost anyone can find a way to buy that first pair of $100 sneakers for their little precious one. But soon it's a $125-per-month cell-phone bill for a fourteen year old. Next it's a $2,500 soccer camp. After that it might be a BMW convertible for your fifteen-year-old daughter, when you mistakenly thought it was her sixteenth birthday. (Reportedly, this actually happened—and, boy, was the teenager embarrassed and devastated that her dad was so detached.)

I recently had the pleasure of sitting across the lunch table from many times millionaire Meshulam Riklis (he's the guy who is quoted as saying "The big will get bigger; the small will get wiped out") as he described how he had given many millions of dollars to each of his kids when they turned eighteen. He offered that they were enjoying an amazing "Great Gatsby" lifestyle. "Rik" (whom my dad befriended in their college days when Meshulam had a wealth of big dreams in his head, and literally hardly a nickel in his pocket) was obviously quite proud, as any parent would be, of the money he had entrusted to his kids. I have to admit that I felt a little jealous when I then told him that my kids know they can have any car they want, as long as they plunk down half—which obviously means a beat-up old car. I found it somewhat ironic that Rik told me he appreciated the essence of the deal I had worked out with my kids.

This conversation made me think: Maybe the best thing I can hand my kids isn't a rock star's existence, because if the country is a mess all around them, then what good would such an existence do them (or the larger society)? Our American forefathers handed both Rik and me (and any American reading this book) such a great place to live and prosper. I wondered whether our generation is doing as good a job of passing along a better place to the next generation. Shouldn't our legacy be our contributions to making a better world? In no way is it my intention, or place, to question Rik's approach to providing for his kids, nor am I commenting on his particular philanthropic endeavors, of which I understand there are many. But our conversation led me to reflect on how poorly today's parents (including myself) are performing relative to our forefathers' altruism—which made a better life for all Americans.

Maybe you're thinking about tossing this book in the round file right about now. After all, we all want our particular stock portfolio to double every seven years. It's got to be OK to want the nicest car and house you can get your hands on, right? And what the hell is so wrong with giving nice things to our kids? What's wrong with wanting more than your share of the jumbo shrimp? It's only that right now the balance is out of whack, and therefore almost everywhere you look greed is speeding ahead like a runaway freight train. If we don't do something to arrest it soon, it will most likely tear right through the station, like in that scene from the movie *Silver Streak*.

We each need to do our part to rein in the greed and get back to playing fair on a grander scale (like our American forefathers did for the common good), so all our kids will have a decent country and world in which to live and prosper. It may look like a tall order, but if we keep praying to the god of greed we'll never make any progress—especially toward innovation.

(NOT) MADE IN AMERICA

Of late, American businesses have learned to manipulate the fast-track/high-quality/low-cost conundrum by moving jobs out of the country. An American-based company will develop and engineer a product on its computers, establish tight parameters for production, and send the digital files off to Asia, and bingo: fast, cheap, high-quality production. In the past it's been typically impossible to get all three in any business situation. Most big companies, especially ones like Nike and Disney, have mastered this scenario. If you walk through a Wal-Mart and study the labels, you won't be surprised to find that most of the merchandise is not American made. The Waltons are a bunch of billionaires (five children of Sam Walton appear on the list of the ten richest people in the world!) because a majority of the stuff for sale in a Wal-Mart is sourced overseas. We Americans love the big-box stores because of the great deals they offer, but the reason they are such great deals is because our jobless neighbor didn't manufacture the stuff. You can hardly blame a company for getting its products from the cheapest source, and you can't blame yourself, the consumer, for wanting the best deal, but we must recognize the high price that we are actually paying. With this shift of jobs to Asia and other countries overseas, America's continued prosperity is being seriously threatened. It will take America's best minds to figure out how to make the best of it. Hopefully, all those millions of people laid off from manufacturing and other industries will be able to refocus their energies into growing other business opportunities.

UNRESTRAINED LITIGATION

Many ideas these days are stillborn because a corporation must go with products and services that come with fewer inherent liability issues. Take something as simple as a stepladder—if you read all the stickers on a ladder today, you'll soon realize that the manufacturer doesn't want you to use it as it was intended. Of course, it's a bunch of small print written by a lawyer in order to protect the ladder manufacturer from the lawyer you might hire if you fell off the ladder and hurt yourself. Even theme and amusement parks have closed, or had to modify rides, due to the growing list of liability concerns, such as the worry that an extremely obese person (4.7 percent of our population in 2000, and growing) might sue the park owners if he or she couldn't fit on a ride.

Because insurance protecting against such litigation is costly and almost prohibitive, companies, almost by necessity, are working to eliminate any risk of liability. Companies may switch their focus to products or services with limited liability exposure like T-shirts, instead of more practical, needed products. More lawsuits are filed in the United States than in the rest of the world combined. One reason for this is that litigation on commission is illegal virtually everywhere in the world except in the United States. However you look at it, the sticky-wicket problem of frivolous lawsuits is very counterproductive, and the sooner we get a handle on it, the better.

DISRESPECT FOR INTELLECTUAL PROPERTY RIGHTS

Innovation would benefit greatly if we could contain the mounting disrespect for intellectual property rights. Innovators, whether in music, medicine, or the movies, need ownership protection. Without it, we can count on less progress toward innovative solutions being made in the future. When someone else can so easily steal their efforts, fewer people will be willing to work their butts off to come up with something new. Like stress, a little greed is okay and necessary for sustaining life, it's just that too much greed (pirating, stealing, or whatever it's called) can kill innovation in its tracks. Music theft on the Internet is just one area where disrespect for intellectual property rights is raging out of control, to the detriment of innovation. You would be angry if a fellow employee got paid for work you did. It's only human to want to be rewarded for effort expended.

A case in point is the dune buggy. Bruce Meyers created the first fiberglass dune buggy in the 1960s. It was a breakthrough idea, a work of art, and the dune buggy's look is still fresh today. But, even though it was a giant hit, he never got very rich off his idea. Right away, twenty or so other companies started making copy molds (pulling "splashes" in the fiberglass business jargon) from his proprietary parts and selling copies of his dune buggy design for much less than he could. How could they do this? First, these pirates didn't have any R&D to speak of (and therefore amortize), so what they received for their buggies was almost all profit. Second, Meyers had to ship his parts from the West Coast, so a pirate in the East could save an East Coast customer the shipping charges. As a result, Meyers spent almost all the money he made fighting these guys in court. When he would finally get a cease-and-desist judgment against one, another pirate would pop up. He ultimately built about 5,000 Meyers Manx buggies, but there are now something like 150,000 look-alikes out there.

Meyers is still trying to shake the mantle of the starving artist. He's a little wiser for sure, and ever the visionary (with a twinkle in his eye—I've had the pleasure of his company several times, and it's always a joy), so we can only hope that his latest Manxter 2+2 dune buggy will do some business. Unfortunately, Bruce Meyers' dune buggy experience is a classic case where an innovative idea got used and abused.

The U.S. Patent and Trademark office is having a hard time keeping up with the amazing number of requests for property-rights protection it receives (in spring of 2004, there was a backlog of 475,000 applications). From what I've heard, cheaters have even found a way to take advantage of this backlog. The premise is that they watch for new patent applications and drawings (an application, after all, is a public record), and then, using an offshore corporation, they start a business to market the products. Yes, these people are violating infringement laws, but as long as the patent is still pending no suit can be filed. Once the patent is issued, it then takes years in the courts to hash out who got burned. Even if these expensive proceedings go in favor of the patent holder, he or she then faces the impossible task of collecting from an offshore corporation in Jamaica, Tuvalu, or some other place. Big corporations don't find it easy to thwart these unscrupulous practices, but the small guys have an even harder time dealing with this kind of piracy. More often than not all of their money has been used up just getting the prototype built and a patent application filed, and the exorbitant attorney fees necessary to put up a fight will only drain their precious business start-up funds.

There has to be a way to figure this all out. For instance, the health care industry is experiencing amazing growth, and some medical device companies have been smart enough to partner with private-practice doctors to facilitate R&D. The lawyers on both sides have worked it out so both sides win. In this process, the doctors are encouraged to develop better devices and procedures; medical-device companies will work with them to produce, distribute, and market their idea; and the doctor ends up with a piece of the action. It's really no different than how a publisher handles an author's work.

Many companies, like Disney, are too petrified to look at any unsolicited ideas, since in the past companies have been seriously burned by reviewing an idea from the outside. For Disney, this has led to many an acrimonious lawsuit over movie scripts, Disneyland signs, sports complexes, and so on. This is unfortunate for two reasons: it leads to insular thinking, and it limits ideas to those generated only by the company's employees or specific outsourced personnel.

As we explored in chapter 5, Disney understandably wants to control all that it can. For instance, the company often bases its movies on stories in the public domain, and it then fights to extend the copyrights of the properties it does own in order to keep them out of the public domain. (President Clinton signed the Sonny Bono Copyright Term Extension Act in 1998 to extend copyrights by an additional 20 years—*Steamboat Willie's* copyright was set to expire on September 18, 2003. Note that Mickey Mouse is a corporate *trademark*—which never expires as long as it is in use.) Anyhow, this general hypocrisy only helps perpetuate confusion and some fear among any outside people who think they can propose an idea to someone in a big corporation like Disney.

Obviously, an unambiguous medical device and copyrighted manuscript are less nebulous an idea than a park ride or movie concept, so I don't know exactly how this idea partnering is going to happen practically. I've heard of a few companies trying to build a business model around " . . . brings together creative inventors and innovation-driven companies," and I wish them the best of luck. As a society, we simply have to figure out how to better protect the rights of innovators. It's a bit naive to believe people will just stop stealing, whether they're misleading and stealing from customers at the corporate level or downloading pirated music, but at least we need to make the practice more discouraged and more difficult to get away with. To solve this infringement problem, maybe big business will have to get together with the U.S. Patent Office (although it sure sounds like they're too busy) to form a bonded clearinghouse for idea exchange. New problem-solving ideas are needed, since the whole area of worldwide intellectual property rights needs some propping up if innovation is to blossom—particularly if broad-based innovation is to fuel a big corporation like Disney again.

SO HOW DO WE STOP THE "GREEDY GRAB?"

Americans have had the amazing luxury to dream about what and who we can be, and then pursue it. This elbow room (known as R&D) is running out as maximization of shareholder equity squeezes it out of business, and taxation removes the luxury of experimentation from the average person's grasp. The golden rule has been changed to "He who has the gold, rules." If the profit taking and tax burden get much more out of control, R&D money will just dry up. And if we continue to waste all our time bragging about our personal property, our local teams, and our precious little offspring—or trying to untangle litigation issues— not much is going to improve either.

We all have to stop thinking that the party's almost over and grabbing for what's left. We need to think more about all the great things around the next corner. If we continue with this greedy attitude and pursuit, it will eventually kill all the naive wonderment that leads to great ideas.

All of humankind reaps the rewards from the Thomas Edisons of the world, who love ideas first and foremost. Even good old President Franklin D. Roosevelt had it figured out: "Happiness is not in the mere possession of money; it lies in the joy of achievement, in the thrill of creative effort."

So what can any of us do to reinvigorate America's search (and research) for innovation? First, don't be afraid to sweat a little. Ideas need sweat equity to grow. Second, look around the place where you work to see whether ideas are flowing or getting abused (see chapter 6 for tips on how to do this). If it's the latter, do something about it or plan an escape. Third, support companies that support ideas; for example, buy stock in companies like eBay and Google, which are constantly coming up with new and better ways to do business. Vote with your pocketbook and take action to protect the environment, like buying a small car that gets over thirty miles per gallon, or even an innovative hybrid car. Don't purchase copies or knockoffs of anything. Finally, try to learn the skill of balancing two disparate thoughts at the same time.

Let's all, well at least everyone reading this book, take a stance that the great American party isn't close to being over. We can all start by thinking, eating, observing, consuming, embracing, and loving anything that has to do with ideas. You'll be in good company, among the likes of Albert Einstein, Benjamin Franklin, Eleanor Roosevelt, Thomas Edison, and Walter Disney. Overall, it's most important that you stop being passive and set out on a quest for ideas, even if at first it's as simple as taking a different route home from work each day for the next two weeks so you can observe the interesting sights and people along each route (I know creative people who have done this exercise for years). At the next baseball game you go to, instead of posturing to get into a skybox, try sitting in the bleachers. For viewing entertainment, people watching beats TV watching any day. Even Walt Disney observed, "There's nothing funnier than the human animal." Make an effort to wear only clothes you truly like as opposed to what's in current fashion, or even try shopping at a thrift store—you'll find it will take some guts and also some thoughtful consideration.

The best each of us can do is try taking on the mantle of a contrarian, and force yourself to look at life from an atypical perspective—yours.

So be ready to get to work dreaming up ideas. Plan to persevere, and you'll start to find out that ideas come from ideas that come from ideas that come from ideas that come from ideas that come from ideas that come from ideas that come from ideas that come from ideas that come from ideas that come from ideas that come from ideas that come from ideas . . . *you get the idea.*

Don't ever stop, the party ain't close to being over. Now get to reading the final chapter.

CHAPTER 8

HOW THE "I GENERATION" CAN REFOCUS ON "IDEA GENERATION"

The idea of self-expression has gotten confused with self-indulgence. It's as if people (including CEOs) have come to believe that a position of greedy self-aggrandizement can actually lead to greatness; that raw selfishness can be a catalyst for innovation. It would be hard to believe that a non-slick Bob Dylan, coming-up-the-hard-way Bruce Springsteen, or grungy Kurt Cobain would have any chance to break through if they were starting out in today's over-hyped music world. Sure, the proverbial artistic temperament is inherently a self-absorbed and selfish one, but the art and the ideas behind the art need to be selfless. Dylan, Springsteen, and Cobain were focused more on the expression of their art than on their self-promotion.

In an interview of Michael Eisner conducted by Charlie Rose in 1997, Eisner referred to Frank Wells as "completely selfless." He also mentioned in this same interview that Wells "was very good creatively." Well, this is no surprise—ideas will flourish if ideas are the ideal you serve, rather than the self.

The *selfish pursuit of a selfless ideal* is the conundrum at the heart of all creativity. How can such a seemingly unstable equation exist, let alone survive the forces working against it?

THE DYNAMIC NURTURING OF THE CREATIVE DYNAMIC

The pursuit of ideas will best work if we all strive to honor what British poet Arthur O'Shaughnessy had to say back in the nineteenth century: "We are the music makers, We are the dreamers of dreams." When O'Shaughnessy says "we," he means every one of us, all together, searching for what only humankind can bring to the world—not just money, not just goods, not just more enormous casinos and hotels and condos, but new, fresh real-deal ideas that can make things better for us all, and make the human spirit soar.

So if you're sitting in some cubicle on the twenty-ninth floor, in a noisy college dorm, or in your bathrobe with your cat on your lap, use the advice on the following pages as a lesson on how to get the idea ball rolling in your life. It's never wrong to reawaken that insatiable curiosity you had when you were a kid. Take note of what Marci Segal stated in *Fast Company* magazine: "Creativity is inherent in each of us. What varies is the way in which we express that energy. It's not how creative you *are*, it's *how* you are creative."

So, with this selfless pursuit in mind, now is the perfect time to encapsulate this whole crazy, convoluted creative process and begin to work to make it a deeply seated part of your life.

BEGIN WITH CHILDLIKE WONDERMENT

It is said that scientists are grown-ups attempting to answer the questions we asked about as a child: "How old is water?" or "Why did Grandma get old?" or "What makes people want to kill each other?" Children ask these kinds of questions all the time in an attempt to "frame up" an understanding of their emerging world. Adults feel stupid asking these kinds of naive questions, and they consequently suppress this innate desire to question all things. It is during adolescence that this fear of looking stupid is magnified, and, as a result, the teenage years are typically the period in life when one's childlike curiosity gets buried deep in the recesses of the mind. However, certain arty types (such as Steven Spielberg or Tom Hanks) will not take on the analytical, critical, cynical persona that is expected of adults and will somehow retain the pure inquisitiveness of youth. But buried or not, these questions are still inside all of us, even though adults most often make every effort to deny them. It is to your benefit to try to find ways to listen to the little voice inside. You must allow a romantic notion to percolate up from the subconscious. Take some baby steps at first to re-learn what it feels like to tap into your natural curiosity, and in doing so you may be surprised at how these questions will somehow emanate from your core. This may appear to be a selfish activity, since you're looking inward, but it is actually outwardly focused, because you're opening yourself up to the world—you are framing up your life as a continuous Q&A without actually expecting to find all the A's.

Adults are fond of Disney parks because they speak to their inner child. Adults act silly at the parks in ways they never would in the real world. But you can learn to converse from this childlike perspective every day of your life and in the real world. Life in its raw state is actually more interesting than just about anything else. Just take a small child to a local playground or city park and observe how the child is fascinated by a twig, enthralled with chasing pigeons, or captivated by tossing pebbles into a pond.

OBSERVE CLOSELY: SEE CLEARLY AND LISTEN CAREFULLY

Erich Fromm held that "Before we create, one must first develop the ability to see, so that one can then respond." The hard part here is to strip away the filters placed in front of you by society and adulthood in order to study the true essence of what you're seeing and experiencing. Corporate America typically wants to stop at the surface and get on to the quick fix, which by definition shortchanges the potential of many an idea. Without careful observation and evolution, an idea's potential is often compromised. Disney these days is known for recognizing an opportunity and then jumping on it, but then forcing it to fit into a quick-fix past formula for success, where the outcome may be effectively trivialized and reduced to a homogenized mush, as opposed to something all-new and exciting.

Keen observation requires a certain amount of time, dedication, and contemplative thought. It's also important that you step out of your comfort zone to discover the real circumstances of life as they present themselves. Successful actors rely heavily on observation of real people as a tool to help them learn the nuances of their craft, and celebrities often bemoan their lack of anonymity, since it gets in the way of their ability to see the authentic aspects of life. It's important for you to take the time and effort to ascertain what makes sense, as opposed to what is the obvious and easy fix. So, my friend, slow down and smell the roses (a cliché, but a good one)—enjoy the day-to-day adventure that is your life.

ENDEAVOR TO HOLD DISPARATE THOUGHTS

New thoughts typically arise from the friction between dissimilar ways of thinking. If your thinking is all right-brain (creative), your thoughts may lack basic substance or clear direction. If your thinking is all left-brain (logical), your thoughts will probably lack the emotional component that would make them innovative and interesting. Conquering this "dual-think schizophrenia" underlies most all creative endeavors and innovation.

Take for instance the Caesar salad. In 1924, it was born out of necessity when an Italian chef named Caesar (Cesar) Cardini ran out of salad dressing at his restaurant in Tijuana, Mexico. He used some coddled eggs, freshly-squeezed lemon juice, anchovies, Parmesan cheese, and some seasonings that he had on hand, and a classic salad was born. Caesar was forced to think outside the realm of what constituted a salad dressing, but he still created a masterpiece within the confines and contents of his kitchen. What he did is take the concept of salad dressing and put it into an entirely new construct. If he had had the ingredients to simply evolve an existing recipe, then nothing special would have happened.

How about Nikola Tesla? You may never have heard of him, but his findings and inventions have dramatically changed the human condition. He developed the polyphase system for alternating current (AC) used in dynamos, transformers, and electric motors. Without getting into all the technical aspects, AC is one of those things that shouldn't work but somehow does, offering proof that where you end up *is* more important than how you got there. Tesla's story is a classic case of how an unconventional thought process ("Who said electrical current had to flow in a understandable path?") can allow for an almost illogical solution. He also invented the Tesla coil transformer, wireless communication, fluorescent lights, a telephone repeater, and held seven hundred other patents.

In his pursuit of ideas, he searched all over the United States to find a really dry place to do his electrical experiments. (You know what it's like when the air in the house dries out, and just the friction of walking on the carpet creates enough electricity to give you a small electric shock when you ground your hand on a doorknob.) He ended up in the mountains of Colorado, in an area that was known for its dryness—and the resulting and amazing lightning storms.

Tesla eventually locked horns with the great Thomas Edison and won. Edison was a strong proponent of direct current (DC), since its direct paths for the electrical current were easier to understand—although it turned out that DC was difficult to transmit over any distance greater than a few miles. Edison almost torpedoed his reputation by hanging onto his DC transmission position when the industry was getting behind what Tesla had to offer. George Westinghouse tried DC but ended up licensing Tesla's patent, and Westinghouse got very rich building many citywide AC transmission grids.

Next time you use a small electric motor (AC induction motor), talk on a cell phone (wireless transmission), or watch TV (Tesla coil), take a moment to think about the wild and crazy Tesla doing electric experiments high in the Rockies (and also wonder about the "free energy" ideas he was working on—which the reclusive Tesla took to his grave).

Both Cardini and Tesla understood that at times life isn't as simple as 1 + 2 = 3, and that the creative process almost never is.

BE WILLING TO GO OUT ON A LIMB

So what's next? In a word: *leadership*. In war it is easy to spot leadership, since the results are so obvious. At the height of the Civil War, Abraham Lincoln was approached by influential politicians who informed him of General Ulysses S. Grant's drinking problem. He responded (with the faintest suspicion of a twinkle in his eye), "Well, you needn't waste your time getting proof; you just find out, to oblige me, what brand of whiskey Grant drinks, because I want to send a barrel of it to each one of my generals." Lincoln understood that U.S. Grant produced results, and that his appreciation for Kentucky bourbon was somewhat incidental.

Leadership demands commitment, plus a willingness to experiment and accept risks. Whether you're a fifty-something CEO or a homeless teenager, if you're not willing to go out on a limb, then failure is pretty much guaranteed. Basically, you can't win by playing to not lose. Only if you go out on a limb (which usually means you're out there alone) will life's special survival mechanism kick in to help you achieve greatness. If you want your legacy to be the safe bet, then don't expect people to erect any statues of you in the town square after you're gone.

EMBRACE THE ORGANIC ANARCHY OF THE CREATIVE PROCESS

If you want your creativity all pretty and nicely wrapped up with a perfect little bow on it, then expect to be disappointed. Ideas percolate up from the "swirl of the primordial ooze," so to speak. In other words, they come from the gut. So it is your job to create an environment (in business, as well as in your life) where ideas can come to the forefront. It's a delicate balance to manage this chaos, but the vicissitudes of intense interaction are the real fun and the challenge of life's meaningful quests. By the way, this is the same stuff that makes roller coasters fun.

WELCOME PASSION AND ALLOW FOR A CERTAIN LEVEL OF RESISTANCE AND CONFLICT

Emotions drive creative activity. Risk and challenge are part of the human condition and are a very necessary component to creativity. Don't be like the Yale University management professor, who wrote in response to Fred Smith's paper proposing reliable overnight delivery service, "The concept is interesting and well-formed, but in order to earn better than a 'C,' the idea must be feasible." (Despite this negative feedback, Smith still had enough passion about his idea to go on to found the Federal Express Corporation.) Don't be afraid to fly in the face of convention, which naturally leads to some form of resistance and conflict.

STOP PLAYING GAMES WITH THE TIME-MONEY-QUALITY CONUNDRUM

It's almost as if people expect all three of the above to be optimized in every transaction, but, in reality, and at any given time, you have to give up one of these in order to have the other two. If you want a high-quality new idea, then throw a lot of time at it. To get that same idea faster, throw a lot of money at it. If you want it fast and cheap, then you must typically put aside the notion of quality. It's just not possible to combine all three elements of time, money, and quality in one experience. For a while we may be able to get away with it, but not consistently. In all areas of life, short-term gain is shortsighted, and a price for greatness must be paid. From what I've observed, even a free lunch usually requires you to "sing for your supper."

STRIVE FOR CLASS, GRACE, AND GRATITUDE

It is necessary to appreciate and support people, places, and things of class—not the "neuvo rich" or even "old money" kind of class, but the "look me in the eyes and honor my humanness" kind of class. If you can figure out how to show class and cool, maintain grace under pressure, and show gratitude for life's abundant gifts, you'll be amazed at the frontiers of thinking and opportunities that open up. It is fascinating how scammers are themselves always getting scammed, but people of real class and good taste seem to attract good luck—it's almost as if good searches them out. Is it karma? Maybe. Or it may be that their positive viewpoint and approach opens them up to more opportunities. For example, we've all seen the wildly successful small movie that wasn't supposed to be a hit but was made just because the independent producer knew it was the right thing to do. And we've all seen the over-hyped major movie that was a purely opportunistic venture and turned out to be a flop.

Creative people are sometimes all wrapped up in their angst, but underneath it all most love and are grateful for life's simple pleasures. They typically go out of their way to search out the good things in life. For example, artists were attracted early on to certain affordable places like Greenwich Village or SoHo in New York, or Santa Fe, New Mexico, because these had at their core a certain appreciation for the *joie de vie* (French for "joy of life")—then, of course, the "trendoids" discovered these artist communities and prices skyrocketed.

It is to your benefit to look hard for the inherent class in people, places, and things, but it's even more important to show gratitude when you actually find it.

STICK TO IT. DON'T EXPECT THE CREATIVE PROCESS TO BE EASY

An account executive once asked a writer friend of mine to help him with a memo. The writer returned a day later and handed the AE the memo. After reading the well-crafted piece, the AE gushed, "This is awesome! Jeez, it would have taken me two hours to write a memo like this. By the way, how long did it take you?" The writer responded, "Two hours."

We all want to believe that a rock star's life is as easy or exciting as it is portrayed in the media. We'd love conflict resolution to be as easy as it is on thirty minute sitcoms. But in real life, nothing is easy—the only thing that's truly easy is doing nothing. So forget about the easy ride, because there are enormous odds against you winning the lottery. Embrace the general chaos of idea generation and enjoy the wild ride. Expect that there will be ups and downs. Face the fact that to construct you must first deconstruct. Don't be afraid to dig in and get your hands dirty. Acknowledge that the path of least resistance isn't necessarily the most fruit-ful one. Enjoy the creative chaos and approach life with a go-for-the-win attitude. Negotiate with a willing-to-walk-away attitude. Shorten your "stuff I want" list, and lengthen your "experiences I want" list. If you truly want ideas in your life, get back to being more adventurous and enjoy the process of life as a human being, and less as a human doing.

GETTING AMERICA BACK INTO
THE IDEA BUSINESS

Disney, and our country as a whole, has got to stop running from one quick fix to the next. It's like business today has attention deficit disorder (ADD). Take for instance the personal electric scooter. America's transportation network desper-ately needs a short-errand vehicle that could help reduce our dependence on fossil-fuel energy. It seems far too wasteful to use a behemoth SUV to pick up a carton of milk. And college students could use such a small vehicle to get around campus quickly without significantly adding to traffic/parking problems and pol-lution. Manufacturers have only begun addressing this need. At the high end is the American-made, technically advanced Segway personal transport that sells for about $4,000. This high-tech vehicle has four slick little gyros that do a balancing act so all you have to do is stand on it and lean forward to go. At the bottom end are cheap (under $500), little opportunistic vehicles that are barely usable as much more than toys and usually end up dead in a corner of the garage. So why isn't there a real, usable, compact transportation device for a reasonable price, like $1,000 to $2,000?

The problem comes down to infrastructure support. For these *e-vehicles* to be more than merely technical gadgets or toys, America would have to develop road-ways (*e-ways?*) or enact policies so they could run on bike paths. Doing so would alleviate the problematic interface of using these one hundred pound, bike-like vehicles on public roads because they, and the rider, are at the disadvantage when "tonnage prevails." We would need to install solar-charging parking stations all over the place to encourage their use. We would need standardized battery or fuel-cell packs that can be easily swapped out at convenient stations when they run low. We would need to establish design protocol to make these vehicles adaptable worldwide, so you could carry one on an airplane as baggage.

This kind of change is not impossible. During the last century, we put in mas-sive AC power grids, coast-to-coast freeway systems, enormous airports, and many other improvements all over America, which contributed enormously to helping enterprise thrive. We need to think that big today so our culture can take the next important steps. Americans will have to cure their general ADD and apply some serious attention to solving the real problems of foreign-sourced-energy dependency, global warming, and smog-induced health issues. Once we focus on a problem, Americans will always find a way to solve it in a big way.

For instance, look how Steve Jobs invested nine long years (of pouring buckets of cash at it) to get Pixar Animation Studios rockin' and a rollin' (Jobs purchased Lucasfilm Ltd.'s computer graphics division for $10 million in 1986 and christened it Pixar, and their first big hit was *Toy Story* in 1995). So finding solutions to our transportation problems should be exciting; just think about how cool it would be to see all these little non-smog-producing vehicles zipping to and fro.

When it comes to ideas, we each can contribute something—and the ideas needn't be all that earth-shattering—but if collectively we put some effort behind generating innovation, it should be interesting what dynamic changes would take place. For instance, let me toss out a small idea that could help reduce plastic trash. The reusable fabric shopping bag is out there in the marketplace but not widely used, but with some marketing it could really take off. So how about Disney honoring Jim Henson, and printing Kermit the Frog and his famous line "It isn't easy being green" on the sides of these shopping bags? This simple action could do a great deal to encourage the use of these bags and benefit the environment. Hey, it's just an idea!

One thing we can't afford to do is sit back in our skyboxes and wait for something to happen. A classic example of not chasing an idea to the proper conclusion is the steam engine. A Greek guy named Herron invented it way back in 50 C.E., and Emperor Nero (who reigned from 54 to 68 C.E.) subsequently had both the invention and the inventor brought to Rome. But no one in Rome got busy making something more useful out of this cool (hot?) invention, and it never amounted to much more than an amusing parlor toy. One thing Nero did get busy at was burning down three-quarters of Rome (64 C.E.) and blaming it on the Christians—leading to one of Nero's other claims to fame, being the first emperor to persecute Christians for the amusement of the Roman citizenry. Because of a few other things that got in the way, like countless wars and the Dark Ages, seventeen hundred years passed before the steam engine found practical use, becoming the initial workhorse for the Industrial Revolution in the form of steam shovels, steamrollers, steam ships, steam electric generators, and steam locomotives. Talk about a missed opportunity!

Up to now, America has been lucky enough to be populated with a bunch of pioneers who had a long-term vision. The previous generations' altruistic ideals have led to the fabulous lifestyle we've become accustomed to. This amazing experiment called America is really all about the pursuit of ideas. And if we expect to restore to American business an environment that grows ideas, every single American has to believe we're part of the process. We need to reduce our greedy tendency to do only what seems right for the short term and do what's right for America over the long haul. Big business (especially the megacorporations) needs to pay more than lip service when it reorganizes to promote creative excellence, and it must then accept the general anarchy of it all.

For the past two hundred and fifty years, the ultimate luxury in our society has been the pursuit of creativity through free speech in a laissez-faire market-place. We also haven't had to worry about eating or being eaten. We have been able to reproduce and multiply in a land of amazing abundance. But a successful life really isn't about Aspen condos, oversized SUVs, and gold Rolexes. The momentous baby boomer generation needs to resolve what its legacy will be. We can only hope that its contribution won't be greedy and selfish thinking, but instead a better world based on selfless and innovative thinking.

In the words of one of the smartest men who ever lived (and also one of the least known philosophers), eighteenth-century Neapolitan Giambattista Vico, "Men first feel necessity, then look for utility, next attend to comfort, still later amuse themselves with pleasure, thence grow dissolute in luxury, and finally go mad and waste their substance." One has to wonder where we Americans are on this continuum. In order to delay and/or counter what Vico offers as an inevitable progression, each one of us must think of ourselves foremost as being in the idea business. And, we mustn't allow ourselves to forget that ideas are the most pre-cious things we give to each other, and more important, pass on to our children.

WHERE DO YOU START?

So what are you, the reader, doing in your daily search for the truth, for any real-ness, for ideas? Do you search out real-deal ideas, or typically settle for copies? Do you stick your neck out and do the homework and research necessary to support your ideas? If you discover a weak link, are you willing to fight to find a way to fix it? Do you have the faith and courage to lead instead of just following the crowd? Where should you start in your quest for innovation?

To get things going, let's once more quickly review some encapsulations of what I hold as the seven tenets of creative pursuit and real-deal idea generation:

1. REKINDLE YOUR INNATE CURIOSITY AND REGAIN APPRECIATION FOR THE ROMANTIC NOTION

If you're over thirty-five years old, you may be well settled in your adult life and not terribly excited about new things. Try to overcome this loss of enthusiasm. First, relearn how to trust your gut. Start with some baby steps to help you get your bearings and balance. Ask lots of dumb questions (knowing full well that there are no dumb questions). If you're under thirty-five, make plans now to challenge boring, old conformity. As Alfred North Whitehead put it, "The 'silly' question is the first intimation of some totally new development." Or maybe genius Al Einstein put it better: "If at first the idea is not absurd, there is no hope for it."

2. LOOK FOR THE "SHIFTS AND TWISTS" IN YOUR SEARCH FOR INNOVATION

Don't settle for a rehash, but instead push for a fresh hook that grabs the soul. Remember, no one wants to hear the same old joke, and the same old song can get boring too if you hear it too often. In 1941, Walt Disney attempted to sum up his philosophy of animation after he got mixed reviews for his wildest experiment: "No doubt, some unimaginative critics will predict that in *Fantasia* the animated medium and my artists have reached their ultimate. The truth is to the contrary. *Fantasia* merely makes our other pictures look immature, and suggests for the first time what the future of the medium may well turn out to be. What I see way off there is too nebulous to describe. But it looks big and glittering. That's what I like about this business, the certainty that there is always something bigger and more exciting just around the bend; and the uncertainty of everything else."

3. NEUTRALIZE THE IDEA KILLERS

This is not an easy task, because these guys are everywhere you look. They're the unimaginative bean counters and lawyers, the naysayers, critics, prima donnas, and mooches. So stand tall and have faith, courage, and the tenacity to find ways around, through, over, or under them. Follow Doris Lessing's advice: "Think wrongly if you please, but in all cases think for yourself."

4. ESTABLISH IDEA ZONES, NOT JUST COMFORT ZONES

"While we have the gift of life, it seems to me the only tragedy is to allow part of us to die whether it is our spirit, our creativity, or our glorious uniqueness," said Gilda Radner. Earmark a small chunk (at least 10 to 20 percent) of your life and/or workplace for freshness and out-of-the-box thinking. Don't just pay lip service to it, but actually tend it, defend it, and grow it. You find that it begins to add a dynamic dimension to the adventure that is your life.

5. LEARN TO FIND THE JOY IN THE HARD WORK IN THE HUNT FOR INNOVATION

Idea generation needs an almost-constant positive energy infusion. The best way to succeed at this is to "eat the elephant one bite at a time"; then the process won't become so overwhelming. Push toward a goal, but don't let the goal become more important than the process. If you're in management, think of idea generation as a clock that needs repair, where you're the hand pointing at twelve and the worker is the other hand pointing at six, and you both must come to the middle (you stepping down off your corporate perch, and the worker stretching up from the normal day-to-day). Once a positive atmosphere is established and ideas are flowing, you'll experience a constantly changing dynamic where no one hand is at the top or bottom for long. All this requires a positive energy stream that's especially necessary if what you want is to make progress toward something as complicated as a new idea. Remember what Buckminster Fuller had to say: "There is no such thing as a failed experiment, only experiments with unexpected outcomes."

6. RELISH AND ALSO POSSESS IMMENSE PATIENCE FOR THE CHAOS, TENSION, AND ORGANIC ANARCHY INHERENT IN THE PROCESS OF INNOVATION

Creative chaos is a big part of the idea game. If you're going to make something happen, you'll have to learn to live with it, and work with it, and somehow maximize it. Respect what the tension can bring to the situation. Accept that there will be a certain mayhem to the process. The search for innovation will sometimes be a quagmire, but with careful understanding and immense patience you just might evolve your crazy idea into a craze. As Albert Einstein said, "I am enough of an artist to draw freely upon my imagination. Imagination is more important than knowledge. Knowledge is limited. Imagination encircles the world."

7. ACCEPT THAT THERE ARE NO SAFE RISKS

Establish a pattern of first doing your homework, then taking the intelligent risk. Here's a mini exercise that will help you develop some skills at this. Try participating in a fantasy stock portfolio contest with a family member or friend. Determine a dollar amount for each of you to "invest" in three portfolios each. Study the market and watch the stock-market TV shows for tips. Then pick your stocks and write down what they're worth on that day. Place a side bet with your opponent (which will inspire you to put some focus into your efforts, as bragging rights alone will motivate everyone involved to do their homework). After six months, check to see whose portfolio choice was the smarter one. More often than not, the higher-risk portfolio, the one that seemed the least certain to get ahead, will be the more successful one—as is the case with most things in life.

Risk taking can be a lot of fun, and it can help focus your energies (as long as it's not totally blind). "Creativity requires the courage to let go of certainties," according to Erich Fromm.

LET'S ROCK 'N' ROLL!

Now is the perfect time to jumpstart the creative process called your daily life. Take out a stack of white copy paper, which you will fill with ideas (keep reading for suggestions). This is a challenge to befriend ideas in all aspects of your life, to *not* accept good enough as good enough, and to always look around the next corner and beyond the obvious.

Now, confront the proverbial blank page, and start by writing (or collecting) at least ten childlike questions. Then write a haiku (a form of Japanese poetry in three unrhymed lines of five, seven, and five syllables, often describing nature or a season). Put that one aside, and then write fourteen more (you'll be surprised at how ordinary the first one looks after you've done fourteen others). List eight dream lives or occupations—and then select one or two enjoyable elements of these lives you might want to try out. Sketch a quick self-portrait—with your eyes closed. Write a free-verse (beatnik-prose style) poem about the best feeling you've ever experienced. Construct three slightly different paper airplanes and see which one flies farthest. Try your hand at a limerick (a five-line humorous poem with regular meter and rhyme patterns, often dealing with a risqué subject and typically opening with a line such as "There was a young lady named Sue"). Try drafting a rough, one-page story treatment for a movie, TV show, or book (don't be surprised if you find this one daunting and put it off for a while). Using only paper, staples, and tape, build a contraption whose purpose is to protect a raw egg (hard-boiled doesn't count) from the impact of being dropped off a one-story balcony. Once you make a successful drop, weigh the device (sans egg); now attempt to build another, even lighter contraption.

Write four lines of a song about flying with the birds or about a broken heart. Write a letter to an imaginary perfect confidant about something that makes you happy. Now write a letter about something that makes you cry. Pre-write your obituary. Using only one page, name and describe a new line of food products, and outline how you would market them. Sketch out a design for a better golf putter, and then draw a logo for it that would look cool on a shirt. Draw, sketch, or chicken-scratch a picture of your favorite thing in your life.

Well, you're on your way. The real challenge before you is to reorient your thinking so you will fill your life with ideas, which will then lead you to find innovative ways of dealing with everything around you. You're now on the path toward becoming selfish in the pursuit of a selfless ideal.

"The way to get started is to quit talking and begin doing," opined our old pal Walt Disney. So don't be intimidated by the blank pieces of paper (computer screens, canvases, lumps of clay, and so on) in life. The best advice you'll ever get in your pursuit of ideas is to *never stare at a blank piece of paper,* but to take out a pencil and violate it. Don't wait; do it now.

Here's as good a place as any to start:

BIBLIOGRAPHY

GENERAL

General reference for quotes, timelines, and information about Walter Elias Disney, Disney Brothers Studio, Walt Disney Studio, Walt Disney Productions, and The Walt Disney Company:

Aldridge, Brad. "Biography." JustDisney.com. www.justdisney.com/walt_disney/biography/long_bio.html.

Aldridge, Brad. "History." JustDisney.com. www.justdisney.com/disneyland/history.html.

BrainyMedia.com. "Walt Disney Quotes." BrainyQuote. www.brainyquote.com/quotes/authors/w/walt_disney.html.

Cutroni, Joe. "The Dream Years." WaltDisneyLife.com. www.waltdisneylife.com/dreamyrs.htm.

Disney, Roy E. "The *Save* Disney Timeline." SaveDisney.com. www.savedisney.com/news/features/fe051404.1.asp.

Disney, Roy E. SaveDisney.com. www.savedisney.com.

Frearson, Steve. "100 Years of Magic Walt Disney Quotes." WDWMagic.com. www.wdwmagic.com/100years_waltquotes.htm.

Grover, Ronald. "The Great Innovators: He Built a Better Mouse." *BusinessWeek,* May 17, 2004, 20.

Polsson, Ken. "Chronology of the Walt Disney Company." IslandNet.com. www.islandnet.com/~kpolsson/disnehis.

Schickel, Richard. "Walt Disney: The First Multimedia Empire was Built on Animation; Its Happy Toons Masked the Founder's Darker Soul." Special issue, *Time,* 1998. www.time.com/time/time100/builder/profile/disney.html.

Schochet, Stephen. "The Lessons Walt Disney Learned Still Apply Today." HollywoodStories.com. www.hollywoodstories.com/a2.htm.

Solomon, Charles. "The Man Who Was Never a Mouse." SaveDisney.com. www.savedisney.com/news/essays/cs011404.1.asp.

Thomas, Bob. *Walt Disney: An American Original.* New York: Pocket Books, 1976.

Wales, Jimmy, and Larry Sanger. "The Walt Disney Company." Wikipedia. http://en.wikipedia.org/wiki/The_Walt_Disney_Company.

Wales, Jimmy, and Larry Sanger. "Walt Disney." Wikipedia. http://en.wikipedia.org/wiki/Walt_Disney.

CHAPTER ONE

Ackman, Dan. "Magic Kingdom Dissidents Make Their Case." *Forbes.com,* December 2, 2003. www.forbes.com/2003/12/02/cx_da_1202topnews.html.

August, Melissa, Harriet Barovick, Elizabeth L. Bland, Sean Gregory, Janice M. Horowitz, and Sora Song. "Numbers." *Time,* September 30, 2002, 28.

Badenhausen, Kurt. "Beyond The Balance Sheet - The Most Innovative Brands." *Forbes.com,* April 2, 2004. www.forbes.com/business/innovators/2004/04/01/cz_kb_ 0401innovation_bbsbrands.html.

Baumohl, Bernard and John Greenwald. "That's my cheese!" *Time,* April 22, 1996, 72.

Bennis, Warren, and David Heenan. Co-Leaders: The Power of Great Partnerships. Hoboken, NJ: John Wiley & Sons, 1999.

CNN/Money. "Pixar Dumps Disney: Studio Headed by Steve Jobs Says It Will Seek Other Distributors for Its Films Starting in 2006." CNN/Money, January 30, 2004. http://money.cnn.com/2004/01/29/news/companies/pixar_disney.

Deen, Mark. "Walt Disney, Banks Agree to Rescue Euro Disney for Second Time." Bloomberg.com, June 9, 2004. http://quote.bloomberg.com/apps/news?pid= 10000087&sid=a0W5d4LYYh14&refer=top_world_news.

Douglas, Jim. "Hong Kong . . . Phooey! Current Plans Show China Park Looking Like the Latest On-the-Cheap Disappointment." SaveDisney.com. www.savedisney.com/news/essays/jd042204.1.asp.

Eisner, Michael. "Leaders with David Faber: A candid talk with Michael Eisner." Interview by David Faber, CNBC, November 2, 2001.

Fonda, Daren. "M-I-C . . . See Ya Real Soon? A Cable Guy Covets the Magic Kingdom: But Don't Expect Disney's Powerful CEO to Go Without a Fight." *Time,* February 23, 2004, 30–35.

Forbes.com. "Forbes Executive Pay 2004." *Forbes.com,* www.forbes.com/finance/lists/12/2004/LIR.jhtml?passListId=12&passYear=2004&pass ListType=Person&uniqueId=C3YW&datatype=Person.

Gates, Bill. "Content is King." Microsoft, January 3, 1996. www.microsoft.com/billgates/columns/1996essay/essay960103.asp.

Gentile, Gary. "Disney Ponders Life after Pixar." *Associated Press,* January 30, 2004. www.sfgate.com/cgibin/article.cgi?f=/news/archive/2004/01/30/ financial1656EST0107.DTL.

Gregory, Sean. "Sports Television: Why ESPN Is the Crown Jewel." *Time,* February 23, 2004, 35.

Gunther, Marc. "Mouse Hunt." *Fortune,* January 12, 2004. www.fortune.com/ fortune/investing/articles/0,15114,566319,00.html.

Harrington, Ann. "America's Most-Admired Companies." *Fortune,* March 8, 2004, 80–120.

Henderson, Peter, and Bob Tourtellotte. "Pixar, Disney Trade Barbs Over Failed Partner- ship." *Reuters,* February 5, 2004. www.washingtonpost.com/wp-dyn/ articles/ A14224-2004Feb4.html.

Herubin, Danielle. "It's a Small State After All - Chunks of California Spring Up in the Postcard-like Theme Park in Disneyland's Back Yard." *Orange County Register,* Febru- ary 2001. www.myoc.com/entertainment/amusements/stories/ 022001/dca/intro.shtml.

James, Meg, and Sally Hofmeister. "This Family Was Really Messed Up." *Los Angeles Times,* June 15, 2004, sec. A.

Jeffrey Katzenberg v. Walt Disney Company, BC 147 864 (Superior Court for the State of California for the County of Los Angeles, April 1996).

Kadlec, Daniel. "A.P. Giannini: Consumer Banking Owes a Big Debt to a Produce Seller Who Refused to Say No." Special issue, *Time,* 1998. www.time.com/time/time100/profile/giannini.html.

Kafka, Peter, with Brett Pulley, "Out Front: Collateral Damage." *Forbes.com,* March 15, 2004. www.forbes.com/home/free_forbes/2004/0315/052sidebar.html.

Levering, Robert and Milton Moskowitz, "2004 Special Report: The 100 Best Companies to Work For." *Fortune,* February 16, 2004, 58–80.

Lewis, Jone Johnson, ed. "Creativity Quotes: Linus Pauling." Wisdom Quotes. www.wisdomquotes.com/cat_creativity.html.

Lubove, Seth. "Disney's Sinergy." *Forbes.com,* March 15, 2004. www.forbes.com/home/free_forbes/2004/0315/052.html.

Masters, Kim. *Keys to the Kingdom: The Rise of Michael Eisner and the Fall of Everybody Else.* New York: HarperBusiness, 2001.

Meyer, Teri. "Disney's Brother Bear Surpasses $200 Million Worldwide." Press release, Disney Corporate Press, March 22, 2004. http://psc.disney.go.com/corporate/communications/releases/2004/2004_0322_Bear.html.

Mucha, Zenia. "The Walt Disney Company Statement following Meeting with Public Pension Funds." Press release, Disney Corporate Press, May 21, 2004. http://psc.disney.go.com/corporate/communications/releases/2004/2004_0521_Pension.html.

Nielsen Media Research, Inc., Zap2it.com/Tribune Media Services, Inc. www.zap2it.com/television/news/ratings.

Palmer, Jay. "Chrysler's Make-Or-Break Year." *Barron's Weekly,* February 2, 2004, 20–23.

Pixar Animation Studios. "History: 2004." Pixar Animation Studios. www.pixar.com/companyinfo/history/2004.html.

Redstone, Sumner M. "Entertaining A New Century: The Foundations of Success." Viacom, January 12, 2000. www.viacom.com/speech_townhallla.tin.

Roberts, Johnnie L., and David J. Jefferson. "Target: Disney." *Newsweek,* February 23, 2004, 40–45.

Schiffman, Betsy. "Michael Eisner: Mouse in a Gilded Mansion." *Forbes.com,* April 26, 2001. www.forbes.com/2001/04/26/eisner.html.

Verrier, Richard. "Children's Place in Talks with Disney." *Los Angeles Times,* June 4, 2004, sec. C.

Verrier, Richard. "Disney Cruise Line to Set Sail for the West Coast." *Los Angeles Times,* July 6, 2004, sec. C.

Verrier, Richard. "Disney's TV Cartoons Enter the Spotlight." *Los Angeles Times,* November 10, 2003, sec. C.

Verrier, Richard. "Slumping Parks Try New Lures." *Los Angeles Times,* October 7, 2003, sec. C.

Viacom International Inc. "Nick to Top Total Day in Second Quarter 2003." Press release, Viacom International Inc., June 24, 2003. www.nick.com/all_nick/everything_nick/press_nickQ2.jhtml.

Vincent-Phoenix, Adrienne. "The Happiest Celebration on Earth: Disney Unveils Plans for Disneyland's 50th Anniversary Celebration." MousePlanet.com, May 6, 2004, www.mouseplanet.com/more/mm040506avp.htm.

The Walt Disney Company. *The Walt Disney Company 2003 Annual Report,* 2003.

Wilborn, Paul. "Sports, Synergy a Losing Game; Disney, Fox, AOL Put Pro Teams on Market." *Seattle Times,* May 16, 2003, sec. C.

Wolff, Michael. "Michael Eisner's Mouse Trap." *Vanity Fair,* May 2004, 246–281.

Yahoo! Inc. "Euro Disney S.C.A./EDLP.PA." Yahoo! Finance. http://finance.yahoo.com/q/bc?s=EDLP.PA and http://finance.yahoo.com/q/hp?s=EDLP.PA&a=00&b=1&c=1992&d=05&e=30&f=2004&g=m.

CHAPTER TWO

Abbey Road Studios. "History: 1960s." AbbeyRoad Studios. www.abbeyroad.co.uk/history/60s/index.php.

Adams, Douglas. "Douglas Adams on Microsoft: New! Improved! Almost as Good as a Mac!" *The Guardian,* September 1, 1995. www.gksoft.com/a/fun/dna-on-microsoft.html.

Bellis, Mary. "Charles Kettering (1876–1958): Charles Kettering Was the Inventor of the First Electrical Ignition System." About.com. http://inventors.about.com/library/inventors/blignition.htm.

Bellis, Mary. "Frozen Foods: Clarence Birdseye." About.com. http://inventors.about.com/library/inventors/blfrfood.htm.

Bellis, Mary. "The Inventions of Thomas Edison." About.com. http://inventors.about.com/library/inventors/bledison.htm.

Bellis, Mary. "Inventors of the Modern Computer: Intel 4004—The World's First Single Chip Microprocessor." About.com. http://inventors.about.com/library/weekly/aa092998.htm.

Bellis, Mary. "Inventors of the Modern Computer: The History of the MS-DOS Operating Systems, Microsoft, Tim Paterson, and Gary Kildall." About.com. http://inventors.about.com/library/weekly/aa033099.htm.

Bellis, Mary. "The History of Breakfast Cereal." About.com. http://inventors.about.com/library/inventors/blcereal.htm.

Benson, Tom. "Re-Living the Wright Way." National Aeronautics and Space Administration. http://wright.nasa.gov.

Birds Eye Foods. "Birds Eye History." Birds Eye Foods. www.birdseyefoods.com/birdseye/about_us/history.asp.

British Broadcasting Corporation. "Galileo Galilei (1564–1642)." British Broadcasting Corporation. www.bbc.co.uk/history/historic_figures/galilei_galileo.shtml.

Cleary, Marci, and Katie Koppenhoefer. "History of the Ice Cream Cone." International Dairy Foods Association. www.idfa.org/facts/icmonth/page8.cfm.

Columbia University Press. "Charles Martel." *The Columbia Encyclopedia,* 6th ed. www.bartleby.com/65/ch/CharlesMar.html.

Cool Quiz! "Did Thomas Edison Really Invent the Light Bulb?" Cool Quiz! www.coolquiz.com/trivia/explain/docs/edison.asp.

Dell, Kristina. "It Flies!" *Time,* December 8, 2003, 72–73.

Dove, Rita. "Rosa Parks: Her Simple Act of Protest Galvanized America's Civil Rights Revolution." *Time,* June 14, 1999. www.time.com/time/time100/heroes/profile/parks01.html.

Drye, Willie. "First Flight: How Wright Brothers Changed World." NationalGeographic.com, December 17, 2003. http://news.nationalgeographic.com/news/2003/12/1217_031217_firstflight.html.

East, Omega G. "Wright Brothers National Memorial." National Parks Service Historical Handbook Series, no. 34. Washington: Government Printing Office, 1961. http://statelibrary.dcr.state.nc.us/nc/ncsites/wright2.htm.

Emdee, Warner. "William H. (Bill) Gates III." Nova Online. http://novaonline.nvcc.edu/eli/evans/his135/events/gates00/gates.html.

Evers, Chia. "John Harvey Kellogg Serves Corn Flakes at the San (March 7, 1897)." News of the Odd. www.newsoftheodd.com/article1016.html.

Gelernter, David. "Bill Gates: He Controls Something the World's PCs Can't Live Without. But He's Neither as Good nor Bad as the Hype." *Time,* December 7, 1998. www.time.com/time/time100/builder/profile/gates.html.

Goodwin, Doris Kearns. "Eleanor Roosevelt - America's Most Influential First Lady Blazed Paths for Women and Led the Battle for Social Justice Everywhere." Time.com April 13, 1998. www.time.com/time/time100/leaders/profile/eleanor.html.

The Great Idea Finder. "George Eastman: Fascinating Facts about George Eastman Inventor of the First Film in Roll Form in 1884 and the Kodak Camera in 1888." IdeaFinder.com (November 7, 2002). www.ideafinder.com/history/inventors/eastman.htm.

The Great Idea Finder. "Robert Norton Noyce: Fascinating Facts about Robert Noyce Inventor of the Integrated Circuit in 1959." The Great Idea Finder. www.ideafinder.com/history/inventors/noyce.htm.

The Great Idea Finder. "Steve Jobs: Fascinating Facts about Steve Jobs Inventor of the Apple Personal Computer in 1976." The Great Idea Finder. www.ideafinder.com/history/inventors/jobs.htm.

The Great Idea Finder. "Thomas Alva Edison." The Great Idea Finder. www.ideafinder.com/history/inventors/edison.htm.

Green, Joey. "Kingsford Charcoal Briquets." Wacky Uses. www.wackyuses.com/wf_kingsford.html.

Guinness World Records. "Most Prolific Painter: Pablo Picasso." Guinness World Records. www.guinnessworldrecords.com/index.asp?id=50936.

Halsall, Paul. "The Crime of Galileo: Indictment and Abjuration of 1633." Internet Modern History Sourcebook. www.fordham.edu/halsall/mod/1630galileo.html.

Hershey Archives. "Milton S. Hershey." HersheyArchives.com. www.hersheyarchives.org/part1/milton/milton.html.

Heseltine, Simon. "Roger Bannister Biography." Page Wise. http://nh.essortment.com/rogerbannister_rzqk.htm.

Ho, Dr. David. "Alexander Fleming: A Spore that Drifted into His Lab and Took Root on a Culture Dish Started a Chain of Events that Altered Forever the Treatment of Bacterial Infections." *Time,* March 29, 1999. www.time.com/time/time100/scientist/profile/fleming.html.

Holidays on the Net. "Rosa Parks and the Montgomery Bus Boycott." Holidays on the Net. www.holidays.net/mlk/rosa.htm.

Holidays on the Net. "The Text of Dr. Martin Luther King, Jr.'s 'I Have a Dream' Speech." Holidays on the Net. www.holidays.net/mlk/speech.htm.

Hughes, Robert. American Visions: The Epic History of Art in America. New York: Knopf, 1999. Quoted in "Thomas Moran (1837–1926). The Artchive. www.artchive.com/artchive/M/moran.html.

Intel Corporation. "How Microprocessors Work." Intel Corporation. www.intel.com/education/mpworks.

Intel Corporation. "Intel Microprocessor Quick Reference Guide." Intel Corporation. www.intel.com/pressroom/kits/quickrefyr.htm.

Iskenderian Racing Camshafts. "About Us." Isky Racing Cams. www.iskycams.com/about_index.html.

Jager, W., Prof. Dr. "A Brief History of Steel." Center for Microanalysis, University Kiel, Germany. www.tf.uni-kiel.de/matwis/amat/def_en/kap_5/advanced/t5_1_4.html.

Kellogg Company. "Company History." Kellogg Company. www.kelloggs.ca/whoweare/company_history.htm.

The Kingsford Products Company. "About Us." The Kingsford Products Company. www.kingsford.com/about/index.htm.

Kirsner, Scott. "Auditing Applesoft 101." *Wired News,* August 8, 1997. www.wired.com/news/business/0,1367,5928,00.html.

Lukas, Paul. "The Great American Company: Kellogg, Champion of Breakfast." *Fortune.com.* www.fortune.com/fortune/smallbusiness/articles/ 0,15114,433756,00.html.

Massachusetts Institute of Technology. "Clarence Birdseye (1886–1956): Retail Frozen Foods." Invention Dimension Inventor of the Week series, December 1997, Lemelson-MIT Program. web.mit.edu/invent/iow/birdseye.html.

Milloy, Steven. "Smithsonian Wrongs Wrights...Again." Cato Institute, December 17, 2003. www.cato.org/dailys/12-17-03-2.html.

Mitchell, Esther. "A Brief History of Damascus Steel: A Look at One of the World's Most Highly Prized Steels and its History." PageWise. http://or.essortment.com/ historydamascus_rhcy.htm.

Morin, Cari. "The Evolution of the Beatles' Recording Technology." Northwestern University School of Music. http://music.northwestern.edu/classes/beatles/html/record.htm.

National Park Service. "The Shakers." National Register of Historic Places, National Park Service. www.cr.nps.gov/nr/travel/shaker/shakers.htm.

National Park Service. "Thomas Moran: Painter of Yellowstone NP." American Visionaries feature. Museum Management Program, National Park Service. www.cr.nps.gov/museum/exhibits/moran/yellow.htm.

Paterson, Tim. "The Dross of the DOS." *Forbes.com,* December 1, 1997.
www.forbes.com/asap/1997/1201/070.html.

Paterson, Tim. "Origins of MS-DOS." Paterson Technology. www.patersontech.com/Dos.

PBS Online/WGBH. "People and Events: Charles F. Kettering, 1876–1958."
American Experience Online, www.pbs.org/wgbh/amex/streamliners/peopleevents/
p_kettering.html.

Roosevelt, Eleanor. *Today's Health,* October 2, 1966. Quoted in Creative Quotations,
www.creativequotations.com/one/13.htm.

Rutgers, The State University of New Jersey. "The Thomas A. Edison Papers." Rutgers, The
State University of New Jersey. http://edison.rutgers.edu/taep.htm.

Sahlman, Rachel. "Thomas Alva Edison." *Spectrum Home & School Magazine.*
www.incwell.com/Biographies/Edison.html.

Sahr, Robert C. "Inflation Conversion Factors for Years 1700 to Estimated 2012." Columbia
Journalism Review. www.cjr.org/tools/inflation/inflater.pdf.

Sanford, Glen. "Graphical User Interface (GUI)." Apple-History.com.
www.apple-history.com/frames/body.php?page=gallery&model=gui.

Smith, Richard S. "A Short History of Rickenbacker Guitars." Rickenbacker International
Corporation. www.rickenbacker.com/us/ehistory.htm.

Stimson, Dr. Richard. "Wright Brothers Stories." WrightStories.com.
www.wrightstories.com/kittyhawk.html.

Stoller, Debbie. "The Secret History of French Fries." *Stim.*
www.stim.com/Stim-x/9.2/fries/fries-09.2.html.

SuperShadow. "The History of Star Wars." SuperShadow.com.
www.supershadow.com/starwars/history.html.

Sutton, Caroline. *How Did They Do That?* New York: Quill/Hilltown Books, 1984.

U.S. Centennial of Flight Commission. "Glenn Curtiss and the Wright Patent Battles."
CentennialofFlight.com.
www.centennialofflight.gov/essay/Wright_Bros/Patent_Battles/WR12.htm.

Virtualology. "Thomas Alva Edison 1847-1931." Virtualology.
www.virtualology.com/virtualsciencecenter.com/hallofscientists/
THOMASALVAEDISON.ORG.

Wales, Jimmy, and Larry Sanger. "Apple Computer." Wikipedia.
http://en.wikipedia.org/wiki/Apple_Computer.

Wales, Jimmy, and Larry Sanger. "George Lucas." Wikipedia.
http://en.wikipedia.org/wiki/George_Lucas.

Wales, Jimmy, and Larry Sanger. "Henry Bessemer." Wikipedia.
http://en.wikipedia.org/wiki/Henry_Bessemer.

Wales, Jimmy, and Larry Sanger. "Microsoft Corporation." Wikipedia.
http://en.wikipedia.org/wiki/Microsoft_Corporation.

Wales, Jimmy, and Larry Sanger. "Roger Bannister." Wikipedia.
http://en.wikipedia.org/wiki/Roger_Bannister.

Wales, Jimmy, and Larry Sanger. "Star Wars Episode IV: A New Hope." Wikipedia. http://en.wikipedia.org/wiki/Star_Wars_Episode_IV:_A_New_Hope.

Wales, Jimmy, and Larry Sanger. "Steel." Wikipedia. http://en.wikipedia.org/wiki/Steel.

Wales, Jimmy, and Larry Sanger. "Thomas Edison." Fact-Index. www.fact-index.com/t/th/thomas_edison.html.

The White House. "Biography of Eleanor Roosevelt." The White House. www.whitehouse.gov/history/firstladies/ar32.html.

White, Jack E. "Martin Luther King." *Time*, April 13, 1998. www.time.com/time/time100/leaders/profile/king.html.

White, Stephen. "A Brief History of Computing: Microprocessors." Stephen White's Homepage. www.ox.compsoc.net/~swhite/history/timeline-CPU.html.

Whitney, Mary. "Invented Here: The Circular Saw" Freedom's Way Heritage Association. www.freedomsway.org/Invented%20Here.htm.

Women's International Center. "Eleanor Roosevelt: Tribute to Greatness." Women's International Center. www.wic.org/bio/roosevel.htm.

CHAPTER THREE

Berkowitz, Ben. "Disney's Eisner Finds Something to Laugh About." *Reuters,* February 12, 2004. www.forbes.com/home_europe/newswire/2004/02/12/rtr1259615.html.

BrainyMedia.com. "David Ogilvy Quotes and Quotations." BrainyQuote. www.brainyquote.com/quotes/authors/d/davidogilv126478.html.

Henderson, Peter, and Bob Tourtellotte. "Talk about Some Animated Finger Pointing." *Reuters,* February 5, 2004. www.washingtonpost.com/wp-dyn/articles/A14224-2004Feb4.html.

Internet Movie Database. "Memorable Quotes from Field of Dreams (1989)." Internet Movie Database. www.imdb.com/title/tt0097351/quotes.

Kytasaari, Dennis. "Seinfeld." TV Tome. www.tvtome.com/Seinfeld.

Mallas, Steven. "Our Take: Disney Mousy About Movies." The Motley Fool, June 28, 2004. www.fool.com/News/mft/2004/mft04062816.htm?logvisit=y&source=est-marhln001999&npu=y.

Masters, Kim. *Keys to the Kingdom: The Rise of Michael Eisner and the Fall of Everybody Else.* New York: HarperBusiness, 2001.

Michaelson, Judith. "Divining the New Lear: Norman Lear Reinvented the Sitcom in the '70s, But Is CBS or the TV Audience Ready for a Comedy Series with a Spiritual Side?" *Los Angeles Times,* December 2, 1990, calendar sec.

Microsoft Corporation. "*Moxie* definition." Encarta World English Dictionary. http://encarta.msn.com/dictionary_/moxie/html.

Microsoft Corporation. "*Phantasmagoria* definition." Encarta World English Dictionary. http://encarta.msn.com/dictionary_Phantasmagoria.html.

Motion Picture Association of America. *NATO Encyclopedia of Exhibition, 2003–2004.* Los Angeles: National Association of Theatre Owners, 2004.

Pack, Todd. "The (FL)." *Orlando Sentinel,* January 13, 2004, sec. N/A.

Pixar Animation Studios. "History: 1995." Pixar Animation Studios.
http://nephila.pixar.com/companyinfo/history/1995.html.

TV Land. "I Love Lucy." TVLand. www.tvland.com/shows/lucy/index.jhtml.

Verrier, Richard, "Fast-Food Chain Has Beef with Disney." *Los Angeles Times,*
June 14, 2004, sec. C.

Waxman, Sharon. "Bitter Parting Words From a Disney." *New York Times,* December 2,
2003, sec. C.

CHAPTER FOUR

Baby Boomer HeadQuarters. "The Boomer Stats." Baby Boomer HeadQuarters.
www.bbhq.com/bomrstat.htm.

BottledWaterWeb. "Bottlers—Crystal Geyser." Best Cellar LLC.
www.bottledwaterweb.com/bott/bt_100crsgey.html.

BrainyMedia.com. "Edward R. Murrow Quotes." BrainyQuote.
www.brainyquote.com/quotes/authors/e/edward_r_murrow.html.

The Coca-Cola Company. "The Coca-Cola Company Brands." The Coca-Cola Company.
www2.coca-cola.com/brands/brandlist.html.

Flammang, James M. "Is Your New Car Really an Import?: Perception Versus Reality:"
Valvoline. www.valvoline.com/carcare/articleviewer.asp?pg=dsm20020501id.

Gelt, Joe. "Consumers Increasingly Use Bottled Water, Home Water Treatment Systems to
Avoid Direct Tap Water." *Arroyo,* March 1996, vol. 9, no. 1.
http://ag.arizona.edu/AZWATER/arroyo/081botle.html.

Glennon, J. Alan. "CO2-Driven, Cold Water Geysers." Department of Geography,
University of California Santa Barbara, June 17, 2004.
www.uweb.ucsb.edu/~glennon/crystalgeyser.

Hawn, Carleen. "If He's So Smart . . . Steve Jobs, Apple, and the Limits of Innovation."
Fast Company, January, 2004, 68–74.

Helliker, Kevin. "Corporate Giants Steadily Moving into Organic Sector."
Wall Street Journal, June 7, 2004. Quoted in Organic Consumer Association.
www.organicconsumers.org/Organic/corporate061002.cfm.

Illustrated History of the Roman Empire. "Roman Society/Roman Life:
Holidays and the Games." Illustrated History of the Roman Empire.
www.roman-empire.net/society/society.html.

Internet Movie Database. "Memorable Quotes from Willy Wonka and the Chocolate Factory." Internet Movie Database. www.imdb.com/title/tt0067992/quotes.

Martin, Andrew. "USDA: Frozen Fries Are Fresh Veggies." *Los Angeles Times,*
June 15, 2004, sec. A.

Murray, Barbara. "Nestlé S.A." Hoover's Online.
www.hoovers.com/nestl%E9/--ID__41815--/free-co-factsheet.xhtml.

Murrow, Edward R. "Radio-Television News Directors Association Convention speech." RTNDF.org (October 15, 1958). www.rtndf.org/resources/speeches/murrow.shtml.

Mycoted Ltd. "Creativity and Innovation in Science and Technology." Mycoted Ltd. www.mycoted.com.

Mycoted Ltd. "Creativity Quotes: Kierkegaard Soren." Mycoted Ltd. www.mycoted.com/creativity/quotes.php.

National Street Rod Association. "What is a Street Rod." National Street Rod Association. www.nsra-usa.com/members.htm.

Nestlé S.A. Nestle. www.nestle.com.

Perliski, Greg. "Altria Group, Inc." Hoover's Online. www.hoovers.com/altria/--ID__11179--/free-co-factsheet.xhtml.

Perliski, Greg. "Miller Brewing Company." Hoover's Online. www.hoovers.com/miller-brewing/--ID__55826--/free-co-factsheet.xhtml.

CHAPTER FIVE

Columbia Journalism Review staff. "Who Owns What: The Walt Disney Company." *Columbia Journalism Review,* March 16, 2004. www.cjr.org/tools/owners/disney.asp.

Disney Corporate Press. "David Stainton: President, Walt Disney Feature Animation." Disney Online. http://psc.disney.go.com/corporate/communications/bios/Stainton.html.

Dixon, Jill, Shelagh Cole, and Andrea Schwan. "Michael Eisner and The Walt Disney Company to Be Honored for Visionary Architectural Patronage." Press release, National Building Museum, February 13, 2001. www.nbm.org/Events/news/2001/Honor_Award_Eisner.html.

Eisner, Michael D., and Tony Schwartz. *Work in Progress.* New York: Random House, 1998.

Eller, Claudia, and Richard Verrier. "New Animation Chief Redraws Rules at Disney." *Los Angeles Times,* April 29, 2004, sec. A.

Fisher, Marc. "Sounds Familiar For a Reason." *Washington Post,* May 18, 2003, sec. B.

Jefferson, David J., and Johnnie L. Roberts. "The Magic Is Gone: Why Are Investors So Furious with Michael Eisner? It's Not Just the Stock Price. The Faithful Think His Singular Focus on Marketing Has Cost the Company Its Soul." *Newsweek,* March 15, 2004. http://msnbc.msn.com/id/4468640/site/newsweek.

Lewis, Jone Johnson, ed. "Creativity Quotes: Albert Einstein." Wisdom Quotes. www.wisdomquotes.com/cat_creativity.html.

Lewis, Jone Johnson, ed. "Creativity Quotes: Margaret J. Wheatley." Wisdom Quotes. www.wisdomquotes.com/cat_creativity.html.

Lewis, Jone Johnson, ed. "Creativity Quotes: Saul Steinberg." Wisdom Quotes. www.wisdomquotes.com/cat_creativity.html.

Roberts, Johnnie L., and David J. Jefferson. "Target Disney." *Newsweek,* February 23, 2004, 40–45.

TiVo. "Partners." TiVo. www.tivo.com/5.4.asp.

Verrier, Richard, "Children's Place in Talks with Disney." *Los Angeles Times,* June 4, 2004, sec. C.

The Walt Disney Company. *The Walt Disney Company 2002 Annual Report,* 2002.

The Walt Disney Company. *The Walt Disney Company 2003 Annual Report,* 2003.

Wingfield, Nick and Jennifer Saranow. "TiVo Tunes In to Its Users' Viewing Habits." *Wall Street Journal,* February 9, 2004, sec. B.

CHAPTER SIX

Badenhausen, Kurt. "Beyond the Balance Sheet: The Most Innovative Brands." *Forbes.com,* April 2, 2004. www.forbes.com/business/innovators/2004/04/01/cz_kb_0401innovation_bbsbrands.html.

BrainyMedia.com. "F. Scott Fitzgerald Quotes." BrainyQuote. www.brainyquote.com/quotes/authors/f/f_scott_fitzgerald.html.

BrainyMedia.com. "John Steinbeck Quotes." BrainyQuote. www.brainyquote.com/quotes/authors/j/john_steinbeck.html.

BrainyMedia.com. "Lucille Ball Quotes." BrainyQuote. www.brainyquote.com/quotes/authors/l/lucille_ball.html.

Jacobs, Jane. *The Death and Life of American Cities.* New York: Random House, 1993.

Jefferson, Thomas. "The Declaration of Independence." Archiving Early America. http://earlyamerica.com/earlyamerica/freedom/doi/text.html.

*Jim*World. "Writers on Writing: William Faulkner Quote." *Jim*World. http://jimworld.com/articles/writers-on-writing.

Lewis, Jone Johnson, ed. "Creativity Quotes: A. A. Milne." Wisdom Quotes. www.wisdomquotes.com/cat_creativity.html.

Lewis, Jone Johnson, ed. "Creativity Quotes: Buckminster Fuller." Wisdom Quotes. www.wisdomquotes.com/cat_creativity.html.

Lewis, Jone Johnson, ed. "Creativity Quotes: Pablo Picasso." Wisdom Quotes. www.wisdomquotes.com/cat_creativity.html.

Lewis, Jone Johnson, ed. "Money Quotes: Thornton Wilder from *The Matchmaker.*" Wisdom Quotes. www.wisdomquotes.com/cat_money.html.

Schultz, Chris. "NFL: The Running Backs." TSN.ca, October 24, 2002. www.tsn.ca/columnists/chris_schultz.asp?id=9720.

Spanoudis, Stephen L., ed. John Elliott, Jr. quote. The Quotations Home Page. www.theotherpages.org/quote-02a.html.

CHAPTER SEVEN

Agence France-Presse. "EU Set to Approve Sony-Bertelsmann Music Tie-Up." EUBusiness, July 18, 2004. www.eubusiness.com/afp/040719113255.m3ip4mup.

Ahern, Bill. "New Study Profiles Total Tax Burden of Median American Family." Tax Foundation, March 9, 2000. www.taxfoundation.org/prmediafamily.html.

AsianInfo.org. "The Languages of India." AsianInfo.org.
www.asianinfo.org/asianinfo/india/pro-languages.htm.

Bernstein, Jared. "The Hierarchy: Income Inequality in the United States." *Multinational Monitor,* May 2003. http://multinationalmonitor.org/mm2003/03may/
may03interviewsbernstein.html.

Big Idea Group. "Big Idea Group (BIG) Brings Together Creative Inventors and Innovation-Driven Companies." Big Idea Group. www.bigideagroup.net.

Boyle, Matthew. "When Will They Stop?" *Fortune,* May 3, 2004, 123–128.

Central Intellegence Agency. "The World Factbook." Central Intellegence Agency.
www.cia.gov/cia/publications/factbook.

Central Intellegence Agency. "The World Factbook: Brazil." Central Intellegence Agency.
www.cia.gov/cia/publications/factbook/geos/br.html.

Central Intellegence Agency. "The World Factbook: China." Central Intellegence Agency.
www.cia.gov/cia/publications/factbook/geos/ch.html.

Central Intellegence Agency. "The World Factbook: India." Central Intellegence Agency.
www.cia.gov/cia/publications/factbook/geos/in.html.

China Today. "People and Society." China Today. www.chinatoday.com/people/people.htm.

City Mayors website, www.citymayors.com.

Community Based Approaches. "Community-Based Environmental Protection News Online." January 19, 2000. U.S. Environmental Protection Agency.
www.epa.gov/ecocommunity/news/cno6-1.htm.

Conniff, Tamara. "Sony, BMG to Lay Off 2,000 Staffers." *Reuters,* July 18, 2004.
www.reuters.com/newsArticle.jhtml?type=musicNews&storyID=5699352.

Crossette, Barbara "Kofi Annan's Astonishing Facts!" *New York Times,*
September 27, 1998, Sec. 4.

Cyber-Nation. "Quotation Center: Meshulam Riklis." Cyber-Nation.
www.cyber-nation.com.

Eisenstein, Paul A. "China Goes Car Crazy: A Nation Takes to the Road, but Who Is Writing the Rules?" The Car Connection, June14, 2004.
www.thecarconnection.com/index.asp?article=7231.

Fogoros, Richard N. "Fat R Us: Americans Continue to Get Fatter." About.com.
http://heartdisease.about.com/cs/riskfactors/a/fatrus.htm.

Forbes, Steve. "CNBC Squawk Box with Steve Forbes." CNBC, March 25, 2004.

Friedman, David. "White Collar Blues." *Los Angeles Times,* August 3, 2003, sec. M.

International Food Information Council Foundation. "Agriculture and Food Production."
International Food Information Council Foundation, May 2004.
www.ific.org/food/agriculture/index.cfm.

Japan-101. "Akio Morita: Japanese Cofounder of Sony Corporation." Japan-101.
www.japan-101.com/business/akio_morita_sony.htm.

Kennedy, John F. "Patriotism Quotes: John F. Kennedy Inaugural Address." QuoteDB,
www.quotedb.com/quotes/1408.

Krim, Jonathan. "Bush Budget Would Let Patent Office Keep Fees; More Examiners Could Reduce Backlog." *Washington Post,* February 3, 2004, sec. E.

Kristof, Kathy M. "It's Still a Golden State. Compensation Growth Eased in 2003, but Experts Don't See Any Big Pullback." *Los Angeles Times,* June 6, 2003, sec. C.

Kroll, Luisa, and Lea Goldman. "The Rich Get Richer." *Forbes.com,* February 26, 2004. www.forbes.com/maserati/billionaires2004/cz_lk_0226mainintrobill04.html.

Leeds, Jeff. "Jackson Due to Reap $3.5-Million Advance From Sony." *Los Angeles Times,* April 30, 2004, sec. C.

Lewis, Jone Johnson, ed. "Money Quotes: Franklin D. Roosevelt." Wisdom Quotes www.wisdomquotes.com/cat_money.html.

Lubove, Seth. "Disney's Sinergy." *Forbes.com,* March 15, 2004. www.forbes.com/home/free_forbes/2004/0315/052.html.

Lynch, David J. "As Economy Grows, Chinese Hit the Gas." *USA Today,* June 15, 2004. www.usatoday.com/money/autos/2004-06-15-china-autos_x.htm.

Mandel, Michael J. Excerpt from *Rational Exuberance: Silencing the Enemies of Growth and Why the Future is Better Than You Think.* New York: HarperBusiness, 2004. Quoted in *BusinessWeek,* May 17, 2004, 76–80.

Maslow, Abraham H. "A Theory of Human Motivation." Chap 4 in *Motivation and Personality.* New York: Harper and Row, 1970. Quoted in www.xenodochy.org/ex/lists/maslow.html.

Mercer Human Resource Consulting. "List of the World's Most Expensive Cities." *Associated Press* June 13, 2004. http://biz.yahoo.com/ap/040613/expensive_cities_list_1.html.

Meyers Manx, Inc. "History of Bruce Meyers and the Meyers Manx." Meyers Manx, Inc. www.meyersmanx.com/history.htm.

Morton, Robert. "Who Needs the Panama Canal?" *World Tribune.com.* www.worldtribune.com/worldtribune/m-5.html.

Mycoted Ltd. "Creativity Quotes: Michael Porter." Mycoted Ltd. www.mycoted.com/creativity/quotes.php.

National Corn Growers Association. "The World of Corn 2004: Growing a Global Commodity." National Corn Growers Association. www.ncga.com/WorldOfCorn/main/history.htm.

Nelson, Roxanne. "Tougher Bugs, Few New Drugs; Dearth of New Antibiotics Threatens Public Health." *Washington Post,* March 30, 2004, sec. F.

Nevada and Offshore Business Formation, Inc. "Why Nevada?" Nevada and Offshore Business Formation, Inc. http://nevadaincorporation.org/nevada-corporations/nevada-why.htm.

Newman, Richard J. "Nation and World: Motorcars for the Masses." *U.S. News and World Report,* June 21, 2004, 70. www.usnews.com/usnews/issue/040621/biztech/21china.htm.

PBS/KCTS Seattle. "Escape from Affluenza: Affluenza… Diagnosis." PBS Online, July 2, 1998. www.pbs.org/kcts/affluenza/diag/what.html.

People's Daily. "Chinese Cities Fighting Water Shortage." *People's Daily,* April 15, 2001. http://english1.peopledaily.com.cn:80/200104/15/eng20010415_67745.html.

Port of Long Beach. "Tie Lines." Port of Long Beach, January 2002.
www.polb.com/html/1_about/tielinesCurrent/tielinesJanuary02.htm.

Robinson, Joe. "Ahh, Free at La-- Oops! Time's Up." *Washington Post*, July 27, 2003, sec. B.

Sony Corporation of America. "Outline of Principal Operations." Sony Corporation of
America, July 2004. www.sony.com/SCA/outline/pictures.shtml.

Spierer, Jonathan C. "Intellectual Property in China: Prospectus for New Market Entrants."
Harvard Asia Quarterly, Summer 1999.
www.fas.harvard.edu/~asiactr/haq/199903/9903a010.htm.

Svan, Jennifer H., Hana Kusumoto, and Seth Robson. "Buyers of Bootleg CDs, DVDs Rob
Companies of Billions." *Stars and Stripes*, June 13, 2004.
www.estripes.com/article.asp?section=104&article=22742.

U.S. Census Bureau. "USA Statistics in Brief." U.S. Census Bureau, March 16, 2004.
www.census.gov/statab/www/part3.html.

United Nations. "Human Development Report 1998: Consumption for Human
Development," (1998) http://hdr.undp.org/reports/global/1998/en/, excerpts found
at Globalpolicy.org (2004), www.globalpolicy.org/finance/docs/fin99-3.htm.

White, Ronald D. "New Containerships in It for the Big Haul."
Los Angeles Times, June 1, 2004, sec. C.

Worldwatch Institute. "*State of the World* Trends and Facts." Worldwatch Institute.
http://www.worldwatch.org/features/consumption/sow/trendsfacts/2004/02/04.

CHAPTER EIGHT

Bellis, Mary. "Nikola Tesla." About.com.
http://inventors.about.com/library/inventors/bltesla.htm.

Eisner, Michael. Interview by Charlie Rose. *The Charlie Rose Show*, PBS,
September 24, 1997.

Famous Quotes and Famous Sayings Network. "Art Quotes: Albert Einstein." Famous
Quotes and Famous Sayings Network. http://home.att.net/~quotations/art.html.

Famous Quotes and Famous Sayings Network. "Creativity Quotes: Gilda Radner."
Famous Quotes and Famous Sayings Network. http://home.att.net/
~quotesabout/creativity.html.

Lewis, Jone Johnson, ed. "Creativity Quotes: Erich Fromm." Wisdom Quotes.
http://www.wisdomquotes.com/cat_creativity.html.

McClure, Col. Alexander K., ed. *Abe: Lincoln's Yarns and Stories*. Chicago: Henry Neil Publishing, 1901.

Mycoted Ltd. "Creativity Quote: Fred Smith." Mycoted Ltd. http://www.mycoted.com/
creativity/quotes.php.

Mycoted Ltd. "Creativity Quotes: Albert Einstein." Mycoted Ltd. www.mycoted.com/
creativity/quotes.php.

Mycoted Ltd. "Creativity Quotes: Alfred North Whitehead." Mycoted Ltd.
http://www.mycoted.com/creativity/quotes.php.

Mycoted Ltd. "Creativity Quotes: Buckminster Fuller." Mycoted Ltd.
http://www.mycoted.com/creativity/quotes.php.

Mycoted Ltd. "Creativity Quotes: Doris Lessing." Mycoted Ltd.
http://www.mycoted.com/creativity/quotes.php.

O'Shaughnessy, Arthur. "Ode." Bartleby.com. http://www.bartleby.com/103/6.html.

Pixar Animation Studios. "History: 1986." Pixar Animation Studios.
http://nephila.pixar.com/companyinfo/history/1986.html.

Segal, Marci. "What is Your Creativity Type?" *Fast Company,* April 2004, excerpted in
Fast Company, June 2004, 16.

Wales, Jimmy, and Larry Sanger. "Alternating Current." Fact-Index.
http://www.fact-index.com/a/al/alternating_current.html.

INDEX